Understanding Migrant Decisions

'This volume creates a deeper understanding of the root causes and the reasons for migration contributing to the current refugee crisis. It is a must read for all who want to learn more about one of the biggest challenges humanity faces as a result of deteriorating living conditions for so many'.
Henning Melber, Dag Hammarskjöld Foundation, Sweden

Examining how changing conditions in the Mediterranean Region have affected the decisions of those considering migrating from Sub-Saharan Africa to or through the Region, this book represents an important and overdue contribution to international policy-making and academic discourse. In current discussions relating to this migration phenomenon, the complexity of individual decision-making is often left unacknowledged, so that subsequent policy responses draw upon simplified models. In this volume, individual decision-making takes central stage by bringing together chapters that demonstrate very different types of decision-making frameworks. In this project, it is highlighted that people move for a variety of reasons such as being affected by conflict and insecurity, by economic pressures, and by desire for other forms of enrichment. Throughout, the book's contributors find that events in the Mediterranean cannot be considered alone in understanding migration decision-making from Sub-Saharan Africa, but as part of an increasingly complicated global system not encompassed by one simplified theory or by looking at one regional context in isolation. Knowing why individual people are moving and how they decide upon which routes to take can help to ensure policy that promotes safer travel options, or makes genuine alternatives to migration available.

Belachew Gebrewold is Professor of international relations and head of department of social work and social policy at Management Center Innsbruck, an Entrepreneurial School. His research areas are international security, conflicts and migration.

Tendayi Bloom co-edited this book as a Research Fellow at the United Nations University Institute on Globalization, Culture and Mobility in Barcelona, Spain. She is currently a Postdoctoral Associate at Yale University's Macmillan Center, in the Global Justice Program, exploring aspects of noncitizenship, statelessness, migration and justice.

Cover image: R.M., Barceloneta, Barcelona, 2015. © Tatiana Diniz Abud.

R.M. has been living in Spain for four years now and he works in a restaurant. When I told him that I wanted to take pictures for this project at the beach he was really excited and actually he was the one who took me to this spot in Barceloneta. He told me that when he needs peace he comes to this pier just to sit down and look at the sea. He started trying to get his papers in order a while back but was denied because he has two fines for being undocumented. He's going to pay the fines and start the process again. He wanted his story to be told.

Understanding Migrant Decisions

From Sub-Saharan Africa to the Mediterranean Region

Edited by Belachew Gebrewold and
Tendayi Bloom

LONDON AND NEW YORK

First published 2016
by Routledge
2 Park Square, Milton Park, Abingdon, Oxon OX14 4RN

and by Routledge
711 Third Avenue, New York, NY 10017

Routledge is an imprint of the Taylor & Francis Group, an informa business

© 2016 selection and editorial matter, Tendayi Bloom and Belachew Gebrewold; individual chapters, the contributors

The right of Tendayi Bloom and Belachew Gebrewold to be identified as the authors of the editorial material, and of the authors for their individual chapters, has been asserted in accordance with sections 77 and 78 of the Copyright, Designs and Patents Act 1988.

All rights reserved. No part of this book may be reprinted or reproduced or utilised in any form or by any electronic, mechanical, or other means, now known or hereafter invented, including photocopying and recording, or in any information storage or retrieval system, without permission in writing from the publishers.

Trademark notice: Product or corporate names may be trademarks or registered trademarks, and are used only for identification and explanation without intent to infringe.

British Library Cataloguing in Publication Data
A catalogue record for this book is available from the British Library

Library of Congress Cataloging in Publication Data
A catalog record for this book has been requested.

ISBN: 978-1-4724-8276-1 (hbk)
ISBN: 978-1-3155-4915-6 (ebk)

Typeset in Baskerville
by Swales & Willis Ltd, Exeter, Devon, UK

Contents

List of Figures and Tables vii
Acknowledgements ix
List of Contributors xi

Introduction: Understanding Migrant Decisions: From Sub-Saharan Africa to the Mediterranean Region 1
BELACHEW GEBREWOLD AND TENDAYI BLOOM

1 **Insecurity and Migration from the Horn of Africa** 17
BELACHEW GEBREWOLD

2 **Liminality and Migrant Decision-Making in the Aftermath of the Political and Refugee Crises in the Mediterranean, 2010–2013** 37
PEDRO MARCELINO, MARIA FERREIRA AND NATALIA LIPPMANN MAZZAGLIA

3 **Contested Views of the Causes of Rural to Urban Migration amongst Pastoralists in Niger** 59
JULIE SNOREK

4 **Autonomy in Times of War? The Impact of the Libyan Crisis on Migratory Decisions** 80
DELF ROTHE AND MARIAM SALEHI

5 **Privatised Migration Management in the Mediterranean Region and Sub-Saharan Migration Decision-Making** 99
TENDAYI BLOOM

6 Navigating the Eastern Mediterranean: The
   Diversification of Sub-Saharan African Migration
   Patterns in Turkey and Greece   120
   MARIEKE WISSINK AND ORÇUN ULUSOY

7 Morocco as a Destination for Labour Migrants?
   Experiences of Sub-Saharan Migrants in the Call
   Centre Sector   139
   SILJA WEYEL

8 Gendered Differences in Migration and Return:
   Perspectives from Ethiopia   156
   SARAH LANGLEY

9 'Living without Possibility': The Implications of the
   Closure of an Autonomous Space Created by
   Undocumented Sub-Saharan Metal Scrap Collectors
   in Barcelona, Spain   175
   SOPHIE RAMLØV BARCLAY AND ANN LAUDATI

10 'You make a decision and you start your journey':
   Reflections of a Ghanaian Economic Migrant and
   Founder of the NGO, CEHDA   194
   IDDRISU WARI

11 Conclusions and Recommendations   219
   BELACHEW GEBREWOLD AND TENDAYI BLOOM

Index   232

Figures and tables

Figures

I.1	An installation at El Manar University, Tunis, created by the Forum Tunisian pour les Droits Economiques et Sociauxn	4
I.2	Number of migrants from the Sub-Saharan region in Mediterranean countries	12
I.3	Proportion of migrants globally originating from Sub-Saharan Africa compared to other regions in 2013	13
I.4	Global geographic distribution of migrants from the Sub-Saharan region in 2013	13
3.1	Trucks of Libya returnees arriving at the transit center in Dirkou, Niger	59
3.2	Pre-colonial West Africa	62
3.3	Modern-day Niger	62
3.4	Process of sedentarization of nomadic groups	64
3.5	Main research sites in Niger	66
5.1	Proportion of Mediterranean states imposing carrier sanctions	102
5.2	Proportion of Mediterranean states imposing punishments on migrants for irregular entry	102
5.3	Proportion of Mediterranean states imposing ancient on civil society assistance of irregular immigrants	103
5.4	Number of attendees from each sector at the EOS High Level Roundtables	107
7.1	Number of official call centres in Morocco 2001–2013	144
7.2	Number of call centres in Moroccan cities 2013	144
10.1	Logo of the organization, CEHDA	202
10.2	Classes in Sawla with CEHDA's first teacher	203
10.3	Adults of Sawla involved in cultural and literacy activities organized by CEHDA	205
10.4	Iddrisu Wari with Catalan volunteers and dedicated farm manager	207
10.5–10.8	Community engagement in CEHDA farm project in Sawla	208

10.9	Iddrisu Wari described this as his former 'Teraza'	209
10.10–	CEHDA farm project in Catalonia, from building latrines,	
10.12	to ploughing the land, to celebrating successful crops	214

Tables

I.1	Countries of the Mediterranean, by sub-region	11
I.2	Sub-Saharan countries according to sub-region	12
3.1	Typology of migrants	69
3.2	Coping and adaptation strategies for pastoral households	73
5.1	Some ways migration management is privatised in the Mediterranean Region	104
5.2	Frontex detection of irregular border crossing	108
8.1	Perceptions of time abroad by gender	168
8.2	Perceptions of return within the household by gender	169
8.3	Perceptions of return within the wider community by gender	169

Acknowledgements

This book acknowledges first and foremost those who migrate *in extremis* from the Sub-Saharan Region to and through the Mediterranean and suffer unacceptable hardships en route. There is a risk that work in this field could become voyeuristic discussion of misfortune. That is not our intention. This book celebrates migrant decision-makers and aims to contribute to bringing the discussion of how individuals make migration decisions into policy-making and thereby contribute to more humane and indeed effective policy in this area.

The editors would like to thank each of the project's contributors. Every person involved has been extremely dedicated. This includes fitting childbirth around chapter completion, crossing international borders to get better internet, managing broken bones, ill health, and all manner of other impediments, and all without financial support or reward. The book was made possible by everyone's commitment, good spirit, flexibility and team work. It has been wonderful to work with people so dedicated to the project and to the widening of questioning and understanding which hopefully comes across in the book. Part of this is also seen in the cover image, and the editors would like to thank the generosity of Tatiana Diniz Abud, Olga Amaya, Silvia Giménez and Raihan Mulla. They created this image especially for the book and did so within tight time constraints.

The first inkling of an idea for this project emerged from conversations at the World Social Forum for Migrations in Quezon City in the Philippines in 2012, and the project was developed within the Research Programme on Sociocultural Impacts of the Global Economic Crisis on Migration at the United Nations University Institute on Globalization, Culture and Mobility (UNU-GCM) in Barcelona, Spain.

Particular thanks go to several UNU-GCM staff members. Àngels Fabregues and Anna Franzil facilitated the gathering of contributors to discuss the project in Barcelona in 2014. Valeria Bello introduced the editors to each other and created the UNU Migration Network, which brought in four of the contributors. Megha Amrith, Alex Lazarowicz, Parvati Nair and Janina Pescinski supported the project in different ways. Particular acknowledgement must also go to those who gave their time to discuss our work at the UNU-GCM Conference on Statelessness and Transcontinental Migration in Barcelona in 2014.

All of us involved in this book also thank most warmly those at the publishing house whose belief in the project and work have been crucial to ensuring its successful completion. In particular, we would like to thank those with whom we have worked directly: Tamsin Ballard, Amanda Buxton, Kirstin Howgate, Brenda Sharp and Amy Thomas, as well as all those involved in the formatting and indexing of the final book project.

Contributors

Sophie Ramløv Barclay is currently a political anthropology student at Copenhagen University. She holds an MA in Anthropology from the University of Edinburgh and an MA in Political Science from the University of Pompeu Fabra. Previously she has worked in the Council of Europe with policy-making and has extensive experience advocating and disseminating the personal lived experiences of various migrant groups across Europe through enthnography, photography, film and theatre.

Tendayi Bloom is a researcher exploring the relationship between noncitizens and states and the implications of migration. She co-edited this book as a Research Fellow at the United Nations University Institute on Globalization, Culture and Mobility (UNU-GCM) in Barcelona, Spain. It falls within the UNU-GCM Research Programme on 'Sociocultural Impacts of the Global Economic Crisis on Migration'. She is currently a Postdoctoral Associate in Yale University's Global Justice Program.

Belachew Gebrewold is professor of international relations and head of the Department of Social Work and Social Policy at the Management Center Innsbruck, an Entrepreneurial School. His research areas are international security, conflicts and migration. His recent publications include, besides various scientific articles in peer reviewed journals, *Africa and Fortress Europe* (Ashgate 2007); *Anatomy of Violence* (Ashgate 2009); *Global Security Triangle* (Routledge 2013).

Maria Joao Ferreira is an Assistant Professor at the School of Social and Political Sciences (ISCSP) of the University of Lisbon, Portugal. She has worked extensively on European migration policy, biopolitics, critical discourse analysis, the politics of security and the state of exception.

Sarah Langley is a Researcher at UNU-MERIT's Migration and Development research cluster. Since beginning her position, she has worked on migration themed research initiatives for various institutions including the German Development Cooperation, the Dutch Ministry of Foreign Affairs, IOM, KNOMAD, and the Inter-American Development Bank. She holds an MSc in Public Policy and Human Development from

Maastricht Graduate School of Governance (MGSoG)/UNU-MERIT and an MPA from Northern Arizona University.

Ann Laudati is a lecturer of human-environmental relations in the School of Geographical Sciences at the University of Bristol. Her work aligns with the broader sub-fields of natural resource conflicts, war and informal economies, political ecology, conservation and development, and Sub-Saharan Africa. She was first introduced and afforded the opportunity to work with Barcelona's migrant scrap metal collectors as an instructor for a field immersion unit on the politics of waste in Barcelona.

Pedro F. Marcelino is a researcher, producer and policy consultant affiliated to Longyearbyen Consulting and Media, in Toronto, Canada. He has worked on migrant identities, migrant rights and border narratives, and has been developing film projects to bring these subjects to a wider audience.

Natalia Lippmann Mazzaglia is an Argentine human rights lawyer, based in Buenos Aires, where she works in the Innocence Project Argentina. During her work with the International Human Rights Clinic at the University of Quebec in Montreal in 2011–2012, she has been party to a pivotal case brought before the Inter-American Court of Human Rights against the Dominican Republic, on the rights of Haitian migrants.

Delf Rothe is a post-doctoral fellow at the Institute for Peace Research and Security Policy, Hamburg. He is co-editor of the volume *Euro-Mediterranean Relations after the Arab Spring* (Ashgate 2013). In addition, he has published articles on climate-induced migration, renewable energy policy in the MENA region, and international political theory and methodology in journals such as *International Relations*, *Security Dialogue* and *International Relations and Development*.

Mariam Salehi is a research fellow in the research network 'Re-Configurations: History, Remembrance and Transformation Processes in the Middle East and North Africa' and a doctoral candidate in political science at the Centre for Conflict Studies at the University of Marburg. Within the network, she contributes to the research field "Political Transformation Processes and Transitional Justice", researching Transitional Justice in Tunisia. Prior to joining 'Re-Configurations', she worked as a researcher at the Chair for Political Science, especially International Relations at Helmut Schmidt University, Hamburg. She holds an MSc in Global Politics from the London School of Economics and a BA in Integrated European Studies from the University of Bremen.

Julie Snorek is a practitioner and researcher of social ecological system transitions in the Sahel and Sahara. She has led research programs for the United Nations University: Institute for Environment and Human Security (UNU-EHS), Foundation for Environmental Security and Sustainability, and is currently a doctoral candidate at the Institute for

Environmental Science and Technology at the Autonomous University of Barcelona (UAB). Her research addresses linkages between social vulnerability, uneven development, polycentric governance, ecological change and conflict and cooperation in the context of climate change.

Orçun Ulusoy coordinates research at the VU University Amsterdam in the programme 'Border policies, sovereignty, human rights and the right to life of irregular migrants'. He studied law at Dokuz Eylül University in Izmir, Turkey. As a lawyer he worked on human rights-related cases with a focus on LGBT rights, asylum and migration. He was a founding member of the Association for Solidarity with Refugees in Izmir and of 'Kayiki'; a network of Turkish and Greek human rights activists, researchers and lawyers working on asylum and migration issues.

Iddrisu Wari (Rashid) finished his secondary school in Ghana, and followed a course in socio-cultural mediation in health in Barcelona. He has worked as assistant for vulnerable and homeless African people in Barcelona and in social houses for immigrants. He has conducted staff training sessions based on the health perception of African people and about the situation of African people in the street, also delivering training on cultural diversity at the Institute of the Catalan Police Academy. Rashid Abubakar Iddrisu is the founder of the NGO CEHDA and now monitors Spanish volunteers in Ghana with CEHDA. He also works as a songwriter and has won the 2011 SGAE music contest in Madrid.

Silja Weyel is a PhD student at the Maastricht Graduate School of Governance and UNU-MERIT and is currently finalizing her dissertation on experiences of labour market integration of Sub-Saharan migrants in the Moroccan call centre sector. She holds an MA in Migration Studies from the University of Sussex, UK and an MA in Sociology from the University of Marburg, Germany. Before integrating into the PhD programme in Maastricht, Silja worked for the International Organization for Migration in Switzerland and Germany and conducted freelance research for the Swiss Refugee Council.

Marieke Wissink is a PhD candidate at Maastricht University in the Netherlands, where she studies the interaction between the transnational social networks and migration processes of Sub-Saharan migrants in Turkey and Greece. Originally trained as a social worker, she obtained a bachelor's degree in Cultural Anthropology and Development Studies and a research master's degree in Social Cultural Sciences at Radboud University Nijmegen. She has worked for the Association for Solidarity with Refugees in Turkey and currently works at the Dutch Council for Refugees.

Introduction

Belachew Gebrewold and Tendayi Bloom

As this book goes to press, towards the end of 2015, the urgency of understanding migration to and through the Mediterranean region is increasing daily. The focus has moved beyond migrants from Sub-Saharan Africa to include, increasingly, those travelling from Middle Eastern countries, particularly Syria. Indeed, the most recent discussions can often ignore the Sub-Saharan movements that have not stopped as migration from other regions increases. It is also becoming increasingly widely acknowledged that the policies governing migration in the Mediterranean region are inadequate – both because of the ever higher death toll and because of their impotence in meeting the stated policy aims, largely of reducing migration flows. The contributors to this volume call for policy development based on an understanding of migrant decision-making, and this project provides a stepping-off point for such work. The complexity of individual decision-making can be left unacknowledged in debate about migration in the Mediterranean and policy responses draw upon simplified models. In *Understanding Migrant Decisions*, individual decision-making takes central stage.

This book considers how changing conditions in the Mediterranean region have affected the decisions of those migrating from Sub-Saharan Africa to or through the region. As such, it represents an important and overdue contribution to international policy-making and academic discourse. The volume brings together contributions demonstrating very different types of decision-making frameworks from across the context of Sub-Saharan movement to and through the Mediterranean. It describes persons moving for a variety of reasons, sometimes acting as individuals, sometimes as heads or members of households, sometimes as members of communities, though usually as some mix of these. It includes discussion of persons affected by conflict and insecurity, by economic pressures, and by desire for economic, cultural and other enrichment. Throughout, the book's contributors find that events in the Mediterranean cannot be taken alone in understanding migration decision-making of persons from Sub-Saharan Africa, but as part of an increasingly complicated global system that cannot be encompassed by one simplified theory or explained by looking at one regional context in isolation. There is a long history of migration in the Mediterranean region and today's developments are part of a bigger dynamic. It was not possible to address all dynamics in this book. Crucially, that of the generations of highly skilled Sub-Saharan migrants filling Northern skills shortages, particularly in health and transport sectors, are not examined in any detail. This book does not advocate a single way of understanding migration from Sub-Saharan Africa to and through the Mediterranean. Instead, it argues for a policy framework that places an understanding of the complexity of individual decision-making at the centre.

For the contributors and editors of this volume, the currently high volume of movement of persons from Sub-Saharan Africa to and through the Mediterranean is a phenomenon that is of interest not just to one or two regions, but globally. The privations and dangers which the persons involved currently experience on their journeys are of global concern and policy responses must be developed through joined up global dialogue and collaboration. Yet, it cannot do this without taking into account diverse individual, local and national experiences and relationships. Central to this will be understanding how people themselves are deciding whether to move and how to move in the first place, and then how people make the decision whether to move onwards, to remain or to return. Knowing why individual people are moving and how they decide upon which routes to take can help to ensure the development of policy that promotes safe travel options or makes genuine alternatives to migration available but that also successfully meets the goals of the states involved. It also helps to reconstruct the migrants under discussion as individuals rather than merely defined within broad theories and trends.

This book does not offer a single solution as such. Instead, it advocates abandoning the search for a simple 'solution' and promotes recognition that the migration of Sub-Saharans and others to and through the Mediterranean is not itself a 'problem' to be solved. Rather, it is a complex phenomenon that currently carries a number of problematic ramifications, particularly for the migrants, that need a collaborative global approach in order to be resolved. The chapters do not aim to provide anything near a complete picture. Instead, they are intended to provoke further thinking in this area. Some core suggestions for how such a collaborative approach could be developed are presented in the conclusion to this volume, which also brings together the necessarily diverse threads of the book as a whole.

A Period of Change

Many parts of the world have been affected by economic downturn. In Europe, it started, arguably, in around 2008, with EuroGroup and IMF bailouts offered to Greek banks in 2010 and 2011 and to Spanish banks in 2012. Unemployment and poverty have risen significantly across the Northern Mediterranean since this time, with unemployment in Spain reaching 27% of the active population in the first quarter of 2013 (e.g. El País 2014).

Meanwhile, on the Southern shores of the Mediterranean, 2010 saw the beginning of protests in Tunisia and Algeria, and 2011 saw more protests in Egypt, Morocco and Libya, leading to regime change in some cases. In the Eastern Mediterranean, unrest in Syria also started around that time and has become increasingly violent, so that at the time of writing it is hard to see the situation as other than catastrophic. Aegean states, Turkey and Greece have also been affected by both political unrest and economic downturn. During the writing of this book, this has only become exacerbated, with emergency discussions about Greece's future within the Eurozone and European leaders failing to agree upon a unified response to Mediterranean migration. The Northern African countries have long acted as a 'buffer zone' against Sub-Saharan African migrants trying to cross into European states. During the Al-Gaddafi era, individual European states such as Italy, as well as the EU itself, had strong relations with the Libyan leadership in terms both of oil and of keeping African migrants from the European territory, for example. This led many Sub-Saharan migrants to be trapped in Libyan prisons before regime change and then to be stranded in encampments afterwards. There are several contested sites across the region particularly affecting migrants of Sub-Saharan origin, including, for example, the Spanish territories Ceuta and Melilla and the Tunisian camp of Chouchan. The changes in government in the Southern Mediterranean has put Northern Mediterranean states under renewed migration pressures from Sub-Saharan Africa as has the extreme violence to the East. Alongside this, Sub-Saharan countries have also been substantially affected by the global economic downturn.

It is becoming increasingly obvious that discussion about the 'Arab Spring'[1] or the 'European Economic Crisis'[2] needs to be tempered by informed analysis of how these events impact migration. Fears of terrorism and domestic political concerns can lead under-examined assumptions to drive domestic and regional migration policies. Such policies in fact lead to tragic death in the Mediterranean Sea, make persons unable to flee untenable situations, and give rise to the existence of a population without basic rights on all sides of the Mediterranean. This is made particularly clear, for

---

1 The terminology of 'Arab Spring' to describe the series of uprisings that have taken place across the Southern and Eastern Mediterranean is problematised in this volume. The origin of the phrase to describe the recent uprisings is unclear, but one apparent source is the American journal, *Foreign Policy* (e.g. see discussions of Haschke 2011; Keating 2011; Massad 2012). While some contributors to this project use the phrase where its use locates the discussion within the prevalent discourse of the time, the project as a whole is careful to avoid referring to specifically ethnic aspects of the unrest, and to avoid conflating diverse events occurring across the Southern and Eastern Mediterranean region as a single movement without demonstrating this complexity and diversity. Consequently, where possible, the phrasing, 'Arab Spring', is avoided.
2 The 'European economic crisis' refers to an economic downturn that is certainly not European, or even focused around Europe. It arguably began in the United States and has been felt globally.

example, in an extensive 2014 International Organization for Migration (IOM) report, *Fatal Journeys* (Brian and Laczko 2014) and is demonstrated graphically by an installation created by the Forum Tunisien pour les Droits Economiques et Sociaux in Figure I.1.

The installation lists the 16,175 migrants who have been established to have died en route to Europe between 1993 and 2012. The installation was set up in the El Manar University, Tunis on the occasion of the World Social Forum, March 2013, and started at the Law Faculty, extending through the university complex. This image shows just under a third of the installation.

As this book goes to press, the concern has been made even more vivid by controversial images of children washed ashore in Libya and Turkey, for example. It is important to note also that changes in the region have led to new opportunities for migrant workers and revised concepts of which destination countries are desirable, and Chapter 7, for example, presents

Figure I.1 An installation at El Manar University, Tunis, crated by the Forum Tunisian pour les Droits Economiques et Sociaux (Photo: Tendayi Bloom)

the developing francophone call centre industry in Morocco, largely hiring French-speaking migrants from the Sub-Saharan region. This book offers an analysis of this situation in order to open debate about migration decision-making of Sub-Saharan Africans in the light of changing conditions in the Mediterranean region.

A New Approach

Over this period of change and increased focus on Mediterranean migration policy, one crucial dynamic has received insufficient coverage: individual decision-making. For a long time, the Mediterranean Sea has represented a crucial corridor and destination for persons from Sub-Saharan Africa to Europe and elsewhere. However, little has been published about how recent developments in the Mediterranean Region have affected individual decision-making of those migrants originating from Sub-Saharan Africa. *Understanding Migrant Decisions* addresses this. It examines whether migration decisions made by persons from Sub-Saharan Africa have been affected by changing conditions in the Mediterranean and if so, how. Some chapters offer high-level analyses of conditions and migration patterns in subregions; others focus on localised contexts. As a whole, they provide a new perspective, specifically looking at whether and how changing conditions in the Mediterranean Region have affected the migration decisions of persons from Sub-Saharan Africa – the decisions regarding whether to move, to move on, to stay, or to return. Crucial to the approach in this book is not only the diversity of contexts discussed but also the diversity of analytical approaches.

The so-called *new economic theory of migration* suggests that migration-related decisions are made by households rather than by individuals. Accordingly, migration is a strategy to diversify the economies of households as an instrument to manage risk at the household level, and not necessarily to maximise benefits (Stark and Bloom 1985). However, the underlying approach taken in this book is to see migrants as individuals and their decisions as the decisions taken by individuals. Nevertheless the chapters throughout the book find that such individual decision-making needs to be understood within the context of family and community, as well as of information available. There are systems of trust and of familiarity affecting how people decide to move, but there are also the effects of incidental experiences and media as well as individual priorities. All of these need to be taken into account in order to understand how individuals make decisions, even if such decision-making is understood at the individual level.

In migration research the processes of decision-making are usually explained from various theoretical perspectives. Migration is often defined as the physical transition of an individual or a group from one society to another; or human spatial movements whereby people, individually or collectively, change their place of abode (Saunders 1956: 221; Eisenstadt 1954: 1). Against this background we can see that there are usually two categories of analysis: push and pull factors. The most common push factors are economic or demographic (poverty, unemployment, low wages, high fertility rates, lack of basic health and education); political (conflict, insecurity, violence, poor governance, corruption and human rights abuses); social and cultural (discrimination on the basis of ethnicity, religion, gender or caste); and environmental (harvest failure, resource depletion, and natural and/ or man–made disasters) (International Development Committee 2004: 18–19). Pull factors are economic opportunities such as jobs, an increase in living standards, and personal opportunities such as family reunification or pursuing non-economic personal goals. In this context migration is caused by an imbalance in the "standard of living" (the level the population desires) and the actual "scale of living" within a society.

Lee differentiates between hard (humanitarian crisis, armed conflict, environmental catastrophes) and soft (poverty, social exclusion, unemployment) factors. The favorable pull factors at destination tend to attract migrants who are positively selected in terms of human capital or motivation, whereas this might not be the case when the unfavorable push factors at origin play a crucial role in instigating the migration process (Lee 1966). But the hard and soft factors are not always separate. Those who are pushed by hard factors are usually pulled by destinations where the soft factors will be addressed. This means that the economic factors are important also for those who flee conflicts and violence. It is obvious that asylum seekers are less influenced by economic factors than the so-called "economic migrants", because their main reason to emigrate is persecution. But, as soon the decision to leave is made, economic factors may affect the choice of a certain host country and route. Thus, the possibilities of income maximisation and risk minimisation explain why asylum seekers try to gain asylum more frequently in some countries rather than in others (Thielemann 2003: 14–15). This is the main reason why in this volume we purposely do not separate the hard and soft factors or focus too much on either of them as these factors are barely separate once the decisions to migrate are taken.

This book moves away from attempts to provide an overarching descriptive theory to understand the movement. Instead, it seeks to draw out overlapping dynamics that affect how people are making decisions. This is not to deny that such generalisations and theories could serve a purpose further down the line, but to recall that these generalisations concern only trends and patterns and are not speaking to the individual reasons for migration decision-making. This is emphasised in Chapter 1, which shows how traditional theorisations of migration decision-making interplay with the realities of movement associated with insecurity, particularly in the Horn of Africa, but also beyond. It presents migration decisions as part of a system of decision-making within a context of state collapse and rise of Islamic fundamentalism and experience of drought. This complexity is not only found in the Horn of Africa, for example, Chapter 3 presents the movement of Niger's agriculturalists to Libya and beyond as crucially affected by the large rural-urban migration in Niger, as well as the impact of events in Libya upon Niger's population. Chapter 4 finds that those from Nigeria, Ghana, Togo, Senegal and Mali who have moved through Libya, ending up in Germany, have followed a number of decision-making routes, with different processes affecting their initial migration decision from those driving their secondary decision to move from Libya. There are also a range of other, larger, forces in place. For example, private sector activity along the migration routes to and through the Mediterranean affects migration decision-making in unpredicted ways. While European states focus on public campaigns against trafficking and smuggling, Chapter 5 argues that these make up one aspect of a much wider system of private entities making money out of the migration phenomenon described in this book – and indeed, a private sector that has powerful influence, both on the way individuals make decisions about moving, and how states make decisions about stopping them moving. This needs to be read alongside and in contrast to Chapter 2's analysis of the construction of the rhetoric of 'crisis' to describe this phenomenon and the interplay of policies of control with individual freedom and individual decision-making.

While the first half of this book focusses on initial decision-making, the second half considers more the secondary decision-making of persons already in the Mediterranean Region whether to return, to remain, or to move onwards. It finds that this is also characterised by complexity. For example, Chapter 6 finds that changes in Turkey and in Greece are leading to the development of new and interconnected patterns of migration within the Aegean Region. A very different dynamic is discussed in Chapter 7, which explores a migration system that has developed within the francophone nexus between French-speaking Sub-Saharan countries, Morocco and France, such that workers from countries in West and Central Africa work in call centres in Morocco, servicing companies in France through new forms of global labour interaction. Such workers mention that they are less affected by changes in North Africa than they are by changes in European countries and refer also to the small number of European call worker staff travelling to Morocco for work. This represents one of a range of new forms of mixed modes of quasi-migration, where individuals work in one country (in this case France), while based in another (in this case Morocco), which may itself be a country of physical immigration for the employees. Chapter 8 offers another set of contexts and another set of explanations. It discusses the reflections of migrants returning to Ethiopia from the Middle East, considering their experiences of migration and how this has affected their return decision-making process. Some of their conclusions are predictable, while others are more unexpected. In particular, the impact of gender roles, both traditional and evolving, in how people make decisions is highlighted.

In order to emphasise the complexities and diversity of experience at even a very micro level, the final two chapters of this book offer in-depth holistic analyses of the decision-making processes throughout their migration experiences of Sub-Saharan migrants in one Mediterranean city, Barcelona, Spain. Barcelona provides a useful example, as it is a major city of Sub-Saharan immigration and through-migration, in a country hit by the economic difficulties of recent years. However, it is not one of the 'extreme crisis' locations of the current migration phenomenon. As such, the analysis of the decision-making processes of Sub-Saharan migrants now in Barcelona, and of the mechanisms that they have developed to cope with the changing regional conditions can help in the development of wider understandings of the situation in the region, but also in acknowledging the specificity in individual migration experiences and hence decision-making. These chapters examine how migrants' decision-making brought them to Barcelona in the first place, and how they are thinking about whether to stay, to move on, or to return. What becomes clear is that, even in the context of Sub-Saharan migrants into one city, the situation is far from simple and in fact involves a complex network of interests, needs and drivers.

Chapter 9 provides an analysis of the scrap metal collection industry, or 'chatarra', that has grown up among the Sub-Saharan community in Barcelona and how it has been sculpted by a changing policy environment (local, national and regional) and by changing economic conditions. It charts how, in 2013, in the east of Barcelona, 300–600 undocumented migrants, largely of Sub-Saharan African origin, were living in an abandoned building with no running water or electricity, had developed a metal-collecting cooperative and informally supplied local businesses with cheap metal. In late 2013, following an eviction and sustained campaign from the local police, the large cooperative was disbanded. This chapter follows the group over the period from 2011 until 2014, looking at how changing conditions in Barcelona and in Spain more generally have affected their decision-making, in terms of how they now view their initial migration decisions, how they see possible onward or return migration, and the sorts of activities and organisations in which they engage while in Barcelona. Chapter 10 then homes in on the autobiographical experience of one such migrant. Crossing the Mediterranean from Ghana to Spain before Spain's economic downturn, the author of the final piece examines both his own decision-making process and describes the decision-making of those with whom he now engages as part of his Ghanaian-Spanish development NGO. He looks at the potential role of leaders in both Sub-Saharan and Mediterranean countries in affecting positive policy and suggests that the current context is full of misinformation, both among migrants and potential migrants and among host communities and their governments.

The conclusion draws together the threads developed throughout this book and offers some recommendations for how to move forwards. It emphasises the nature of the complexity and what this means for global policy responses to the developing phenomenon of migration to and through the Mediterranean Region. It engages with existing contemporary discourses and looks at ways in which these could be redirected to ensure a global policy framework that better responds to the realities of how and why people are making decisions whether to migrate and how to migrate to and through the Mediterranean.

This volume represents a key opening to crucial discussions in this area. It provides contributions from a range of disciplines, and with a range of perspectives. This includes experts in governance, human geography, international relations, law, migration, politics, security studies and sociology. Overall, the contributors argue that there has been a shift in migration decision-making. However, they offer a range of analyses of this change, critiquing a simplistic wholesale attribution of this directly to the conditions in the Mediterranean often referred to as the 'Arab Spring' and as the 'European Economic Crisis' without acknowledging wider regional as well as global dynamics. The book demonstrates the interaction of changes in the Mediterranean Region with the other regions with which it intersects: Africa, Asia, Europe and the Middle East. As such, as well as representing a first attempt to bring research in this area together in one place, this volume provides a critical overview of the debate as it currently exists in Chapter 1 and builds upon this throughout the volume, and presenting a set of recommendations arising from the book's new approach in the Conclusion.

There has been a surge of work examining the situation in the Mediterranean Region as a result of recent complex and intersecting changes, both economic and political, affecting wealth, development and human security. This has also included work looking at the impact on these regions of the increasing levels of migration across the sea. However, there is currently insufficient debate regarding the impact of these changing conditions on the *migrants* and *potential migrants* themselves. More specifically, policy considerations have not tended to include the impact on their migration decision-making. This book, *Understanding Migrant Decisions*, builds on a tradition of locating Sub-Saharan African migration within wider contexts (e.g. De Bruijin *et al.* 2001; Adepoju *et al.* 2008), to offer a revised perspective in the light of dramatic recent events in the Mediterranean Region. It is unique in re-aligning the focus and applying an interdisciplinary approach to examining decision-making among Sub-Saharan African migrants throughout the migration process. In this way, as well as providing a rigorous and original contribution to the academic literature, it will be of interest to a wider policy-making and informed general audience. *Understanding Migrant Decisions* leads the way in considering recent developments in the Mediterranean and their effects on how migrants and potential migrants moving from the Sub-Saharan Region view their migration options.

No book can hope to do everything, and this book certainly has many limitations. The perspectives of certain types of entities have not been included – in particular, NGOs, international organisations and labour movements. It has also been impossible to examine all sub-regional systems and the migration contexts in all countries in the Mediterranean Region and all those countries of Sub-Saharan Africa. Instead of giving a comprehensive analysis of migration decision-making of those travelling from Sub-Saharan Africa to and through the Mediterranean, this book aims to provide a range of perspectives and approaches to the migration decision-making. Important to this has been the contribution, in Chapter 10, of analysis by someone with personal experience of the migration process. The author of Chapter 10 presents a very personal examination of economic migration, but this is not to suggest that there is not also a large body of individuals, discussed in other chapters, moving with urgency through the region under discussion.

Who Are the Migrants?

Simply put, the migrants described in this volume are those moving from Sub-Saharan Africa to and through the Mediterranean Region. These include persons moving for a range of reasons, often reasons which compete, intersect, overlap, and perhaps conflict. This includes well-paid skilled workers moving on visas through to those finding irregular routes. Some may move initially for economic reasons, but then make secondary movements to avoid violence (as in the examples in Chapter 4, for example). It includes persons whose experiences of poverty and drought are driven by problems of security and war (as in the case of some of those described in Chapters 1 and 3, for example) and persons whose specific skills make them attractive in emerging labour markets (e.g see Chapter 4) and those who are well-placed to participate in changing business environments (see Chapter 6). The commonly perceived need to categorise persons into distinct categories is found to be problematic in the contexts discussed in this volume. For example, some highlight the pressure put on people to construct their reasons for moving in simplistic ways in order to fit within policy frameworks and frameworks of public understanding (e.g. see Chapter 10), while others are illegalised or legalised depending on changing policy frameworks (e.g. see Chapters 6 and 9). While the protections offered by global and domestic humanitarian statuses like refugee are vital to uphold, the lines between these categories of migrant are greyer than can sometimes appear. This is also the case with definitions of class, ethnicity and tribal membership. As Chapter 9 argues, individuals' ethnic and tribal affiliations became differently expressed in response to changes in host country policy and consequent differences in coping strategies, even including divergences in how an individual may choose to self-identify. This is particularly marked in Chapter 4's analysis of onward migration from Libya in the context of civil war in that country. Meanwhile, Chapter 6 finds that economic and social changes in Greece and Turkey have led people to move between class brackets and identifications. Individuals' migration status, their ethnicity and their social class are crucial to understanding migration, yet the complexities apparent in the way in which these categorisations interact, alter and are constructed are also vital to understand in this changing and multifarious context.

Before continuing with the main content of the book, it is necessary to set up and problematise some of the language used. Debate about migration, and about unfolding events in the Mediterranean Region, can be contentious and the language loaded. When talking about migration outside the regulatory framework of the states concerned, this book, where possible, prefers the word 'irregular' over 'illegal'. This is to distinguish those actions that take place outside administrative regulations from those actions that break laws directly. It prefers 'irregular' to 'undocumented' because this covers the wider range of migration processes intended in this volume. For further analysis of the available terminology, the reader is referred to core texts in this area (e.g. Ghosh 1998: 34; Dauvergne 2008; Van der Valk 2003: 323; de Genova 2002: 420; Koser 2007).

The Mediterranean Region refers here to all countries with a Mediterranean coastline. These are listed in Table I.1, according to broad sub-region. As is touched upon in some of the chapters in this volume, these sub-regions can be contested. In fact, as is made clear in this book, there is significant complexity in the overlapping of regions in the Mediterranean, and some chapters indeed focus on further sub-regions *within* these. The Mediterranean also sits at an overlapping of other global regions, with Europe to the north, Asia to the east and Africa to the south. It also includes the Middle East, which overlaps with some of these, and is an important aspect of the Mediterranean dynamic. Sub-Saharan Africa is the large region composed of those countries to the south of the Sahara. These can also be considered according to broad sub-regions, as shown in Table I.2, and chapters in this book also look at dynamics between these regions, and at further sub-regions within them.

Levels of migration to the Mediterranean have been (depending on your perspective) high and growing for some time. Figure I.2 shows this, using the 2013 Statistics and Projections data set of UNDESA (UNDESA 2013). It includes only those countries of the Mediterranean Region which record more than zero persons from Sub-Saharan Africa in the mid-year data for at least one of the years 1990, 2000, 2010 and 2013. However, it is crucial to recognise that, while Sub-Saharan migrants represent an important group in the

Table I.1 Countries of the Mediterranean, by sub-region

Northern Mediterranean	Southern Mediterranean	Eastern Mediterranean
Albania	Algeria	Cyprus
Bosnia and Herzegovina	Egypt	Greece
Croatia	Libya	Israel
France	Morocco	Lebanon
Italy	Tunisia	Malta
Monaco		Palestinian Territories
Slovenia		Syrian Arab Republic
Spain		Turkey

Table I.2 Sub-Saharan countries according to sub-region

Western Africa		Eastern Africa		Southern Africa
Benin	Angola	Burundi	South Sudan	Botswana
Burkina Faso	Cameroon	Comoros	Uganda	Lesotho
Cape Verde	Central	Djibouti	United	Namibia
Côte d'Ivoire	African	Eritrea	Republic of	South Africa
Gambia	Republic	Ethiopia	Tanzania	Swaziland
Ghana	Chad	Kenya	Zambia	
Guinea	Congo	Madagascar	Zimbabwe	
Guinea-Bissau	Democratic	Malawi		
Liberia	Republic of	Mauritius		
Mali	the Congo	Mozambique		
Mauritania	Equatorial	Rwanda		
Niger	Guinea	Seychelles		
Nigeria	Gabon	Somalia		
Senegal	Sao Tomé	(Sudan)		
Sierra Leone	and			
Togo	Príncipe			

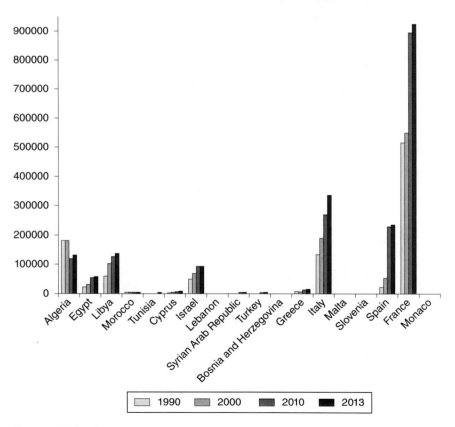

Figure 1.2 Number of migrants from the Sub-Saharan region in Mediterranean countries from 1990 to 2013 according to DESA data

Introduction 13

Mediterranean Region, as shown by Figure I.4, they in fact represent only 7% of the region's migrants. This is slightly lower than the global percentage of migrants originating from Sub-Saharan Africa, as shown in Figure I.3.

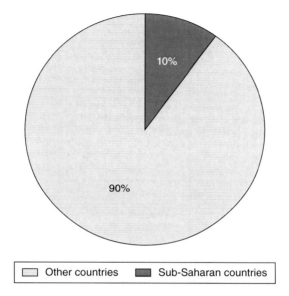

Figure I.3 Proportion of migrants globally originating from Sub-Saharan Africa compared to other regions in 2013

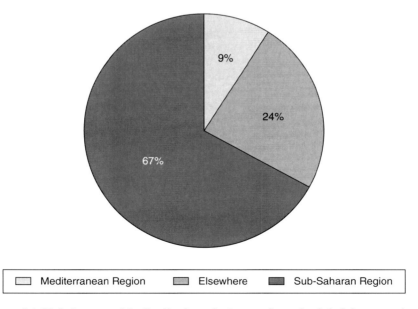

Figure I.4 Global geographic distribution of migrants from the Sub-Saharan region in 2013

14   Belachew Gebrewold and Tendayi Bloom

Furthermore, while the Mediterranean Region is an important location for migrants from Sub-Saharan Africa, Figure I.4 demonstrates that the vast majority remain in Sub-Saharan Africa (67%) and 24% move elsewhere.

How this Book Came Together

This book was developed under the auspices of the United Nations University Institute on Globalization, Culture and Mobility (UNU-GCM) Research Programme on Sociocultural Impacts of the Global Economic Crisis on Migration. It arose from a joint concern among the contributors to bring together different and interrelated notions of how people are making decisions in order to feed into more effective and just policy-making. The project developed and was presented as a conference section in July 2014, at the UNU-GCM conference on Statelessness and Transcontinental Migration. The debates held at that event, as well as the comments made before and afterwards on the papers presented, were crucial to shaping the current volume. There is a risk that those considering this area focus only on one approach, one context, one theoretical framework and one community of voices. What has become clear from the collaboration behind this book project is that this is not only intellectually problematic but is leading to a policy environment that is inadequately suited to the lived reality of migration to and through the Mediterranean. At the time of writing this introduction, this is becoming tragically more true than ever.

For this reason, effort has been made in the final selection to ensure diversity of context and diversity of disciplinary focus. For example, there are contributions focussing on migration to and through the Northern Mediterranean, the Southern Mediterranean and the Eastern Mediterranean. There are also contributions addressing migration from specific contexts in Western Africa, Central Africa, Eastern Africa and Southern Africa. Moreover, there are attempts to ensure that differing approaches within these regions are addressed. The book is not intended to be comprehensive, but to draw attention to major debates and analyses and to provide an overview analysis of the sorts of processes involved in the decision-making of migrants and potential migrants from Sub-Saharan Africa to and through the Mediterranean Region. It argues that policy-makers and analysts need to take into account many factors and a vast regional complexity in the development of policy responses to changing conditions. It is hoped that this book can act as a catalyst to new ways of thinking about these migration dynamics and to an on-going engagement with migration decision-making as an important research focus.

Most people do not migrate (UNDESA estimates suggest that 97% of the world's population has stayed put), and this is also the case in Sub-Saharan Africa. Moreover, as Figure I.4 shows, the vast majority of Sub-Saharan international migrants migrate within the Sub-Saharan Region (67%). This book is focussed on that minority of persons migrating from

Sub-Saharan Africa to and through the Mediterranean Region. It looks at their decisions to be movers, and then their secondary decisions whether to move onwards, to stay where they are, or to move back. As such, this book looks specifically at whether the decisions of such individuals are affected by changing conditions in the Mediterranean Region. It argues that they are, to an extent, but that this is part of a much more complex system of decision-making, an understanding of which must be central to any related global policy formation.

References

Adepoju, Aderanti, Ton van Naerssen and Annelies Zoomers (eds) (2008) *International Migration and National Development in Sub-Saharan Africa*, Brill, Leiden.

Attias-Donfut, Claudine, Joanne Cook, Jaco Hoffman and Louise Waite (eds) (2012) *Citizenship, Belonging and Intergenerational Relations in African Migration*, Palgrave Macmillan, Basingstoke.

Brian, Tara and Frank Laczko (eds) (2014) *Fatal Journeys: Tracking Lives Lost During Migration*, International Organisation for Migration, Geneva.

Crépeau, François (2013) *Regional study: management of the external borders of the European Union and its impact on the human rights of migrants*, Report of the Special Rapporteur on the human rights of migrants, François Crépeau, Human Rights Council, Twenty-third session, United Nations General Assembly A/HRC/23/46.

Cross, Catherine, Derik Gelderblom, Niel Roux and Jonathan Mafukidze (eds) (2010) *Views on Migration in Sub-Saharan Africa: Proceedings of an African Migration Alliance Workshop*, HSRC Press, Cape Town.

Dauvergne, Catherine (2008) *Making People Illegal: What Globalization Means for Migration and Law*, Cambridge University Press, Cambridge.

de Bruijn, Mirjam, Rijk van Dijk and Dick Foeken (eds) (2001) *Mobile Africa: Changing Patterns of Movement in Africa and Beyond*, Brill, Leiden.

de Genova, Nicholas (2002) 'Migrant "Illegality" and Deportability in Everyday Life' *Annual Review of Anthropology* 31: 419–47.

Eisenstadt, S.N. (1954) 'The Absorption of Immigrants', London.

El País (2014) 'Evolución del mercado laboral', *El País* Newspaper, online edition 24 July 2014, http://elpais.com/elpais/2014/07/24/media/1406211787_263475.html [30/07/2014].

Ghosh, Bimal (1998) *Huddled Masses and Uncertain Shores: Insights into Irregular Migration*, Martinus Nijhoff Publishers, The Hague.

Haschke, Paloma (2011) 'Yes, Mubarak is gone. But now what?', UNAOC blog post, 2 November 2011, http://www.unaoc.org/2011/11/yes-mubarak-is-gone-but-now-what/ [30/07/2014].

International Development Committee (2004) 'Migration and development. How to make migration work for poverty reduction', Sixth report of session 2003–04, Volume 1, House of Commons, http://www.publications.parliament.uk/pa/cm200304/cmselect/cmintdev/79/79.pdf [20/12/2006].

Keating, Joshua (2011) 'Who first used the term Arab Spring?', *Foreign Policy* blog post, 4 November 2011, http://blog.foreignpolicy.com/posts/2011/11/04/who_first_used_the_term_arab_spring [30/07/2014].

Koser, Khalid (2007) *International Migration: A Very Short Introduction*, Oxford University Press, Oxford.
Lee, E.S. (1966) 'A Theory of Migration', *Demography* 3(1): 47–57.
Massad, Joseph (2012) 'The 'Arab Spring' and other American seasons', *Al Jazeera Opinion*, 29 August 2012, http://www.aljazeera.com/indepth/opinion/2012/08/201282972539153865.html [30/07/2014].
Saunders, H.W. (1956) 'Human Migration and Social Equilibrium', in Spengler, J.J./Duncan, O.D. (eds) "Population Theory and Policy", 219–29, Glencoe.
Thielemann, E. (2003) 'Does Policy Matter? On Governments' Attempts to Control Unwanted Migration', *European Institute Working Paper* May 2003 http://www.lse.ac.uk/collections/europeaninstitute/pdfs/Eiworkingpaper2003-02.pdf [05/05/2005].
Stark, O. and Bloom, D.E. (1985) 'The new economics of labour migration', *American Economic Review* 75(2): 173–8.
UNDESA (2013) Trends in International Migrant Stock: The 2013 Revision. UNDESA data set: http://www.un.org/esa/population/migration/index.html [30/07/2014].
Van der Valk, Ineke (2003) 'Right-Wing Parliamentary Discourse on Immigration in France', *Discourse and Society* 14: 309–50.

1 Insecurity and Migration from the Horn of Africa

Belachew Gebrewold

Introduction

The Horn of Africa has been experiencing various political, economic and security crises for decades. The state collapse of Somalia, the rise of Islamic fundamentalism in the whole region, recurrent drought affecting the livelihoods of subsistence farmers as well as nomads, and political repression especially in Eritrea have been driving various segments of the regional population into regional and international migration. Eritreans attempting to flee their country are being persecuted by the authorities if caught before leaving the country, or are being enslaved or tortured by smugglers such as those in Egypt on their way to Europe. Many Somalis have been fleeing conflicts and violence in their country and heading for Europe. Many more Somalis have also migrated within the Horn of Africa such as to Ethiopia, Kenya and Djibouti as guest workers fleeing their country. The main objective of this chapter is to explore whether the changing conditions in the Mediterranean have affected migration from the Horn of Africa to Europe. Given the particularly complex context in the Horn of Africa, it provides a useful model within which to expand upon the theoretical frameworks that will emerge in this book as a whole, as well as demonstrate the inadequacy of trying to characterize this movement within a singular theory

The chapter starts with a theoretical discussion on causes and decisions for migration. Though the main focus of the chapter will be on conflicts in the Horn of Africa, as main causes it is important to stress that the decisions of migrants can have at the same time economic, political or sociological reasons. Be it migration from the Horn of Africa or from other regions of Africa, the theories and explanations of migration can overlap, and it is usually difficult to limit the migration decisions to purely economic, sociological, etc. theories. One of the key arguments in this book as a whole is that there is not just one theory which explains all migration push and pull factors; and that migration decisions are not linear. That is, none of the theories alone can explain a migration decision as the migrants' decisions are caused by different circumstances and factors. Decisions and strategies change and are adapted all the time depending on the situations the migrants experience on their way to their destinations. Even those who flee persecution not only look for physical safety but also for a place where they can meet their economic needs.

Using this as a vehicle for examining the theoretical frameworks more broadly, the section after the theoretical discussion focuses on the causes of migration in the Horn of Africa. Because conflicts have been destroying the economic infrastructure, livelihoods and job opportunities, they are considered in this chapter as the main driving factors. Though many countries in the Horn of Africa are affected by various forms of conflict, the main focal countries of the section will be Eritrea and Somalia. Eritrea, since its formal independence from Ethiopia in 1993, has been going through a brutal dictatorship which pushes many Eritreans to flee their country and be exposed to human trafficking, torture, detention and agony on their way to Europe mainly through Egypt, Libya and Israel. Similarly, Somalia has been devastated since 1991 by unending civil war, state collapse and radical Islamists cooperating with Al-Qaeda. Based on this background analysis the chapter addresses the impacts of the changing conditions in the Mediterranean region on the migration decisions of these two Horn of Africa countries.

Theoretical Reflections on Migration Decisions

For this chapter as well as for the book in general, it is important to stress that, *first*, addressing the causes and consequences of migration requires a multidisciplinary approach from human rights, humanitarian, economic, political, ecological, security, etc. points of views. *Second*, different migration theories can give helpful insights for policy makers as well as researchers and civil society into why and how migration decisions are taken. However, it is important to stress from the outset that migrants' decisions are caused by different circumstances and factors. This non-linearity and 'flexibility' of decisions is one of the core concepts of this volume. Keeping this in mind, this section discusses briefly the different migration theories.

In general in the sociological and economic discussion of migration and population, migration is understood to be caused by an imbalance in the desired 'standard of living' (the level the population desires) and the actual 'scale of living' within a society. Saunders defines migration as human spatial movements whereby people, individually or collectively, change their place of abode (Saunders 1956: 221). Samuel N. Eisenstadt examines the determinants of migration, the social structure of the migration process and the absorption of migration by using Talcott Parsons' model of explanation according to which the establishment of a general theory in the social sciences should focus on codification of existing concrete knowledge by providing a generalized hypothesis for the systematic reformulation of existing facts and insights (Talcott/Shils 1951: 3). The point of reference is the action of an individual actor or of a collectivity. The theory is interested in the actor's orientation to a situation (ibid.: 4).

Eisenstadt defines migration as the physical transition of an individual or a group from one society to another, moving from a familiar world to an unfamiliar world (Eisenstadt 1954 1). It consists of three phases: firstly, formation of the motivation of the migrant after having considered the advantages and disadvantages of migration; secondly, the migration phase, i.e. leaving the country of origin and arriving in a new environment, the process of 'de-socialisation' – the movement from a life based on known social roles to a life without structures and orientation (new forms of interaction and participation); thirdly, the 'process of absorption': insertion of migrants in the new society. The success of absorption is dependent upon three sub-processes (institutionalisation of role expectations and behaviour in everyday life, the migrants' adjustment to host society, and institutional participation). When former identity is given up and replaced by identification with the host society and when emotional forms of expression and symbols are integrated, it is called full absorption. Such a full absorption can only be achieved if participation in institutions such as economy, politics and culture is possible (Han 2000: 46ff).

The migration theory analysis of Hartmut Esser focuses on the integration process of migrants through re-socialization and reorganization. This process entails three further aspects. The first aspect is *acculturation*, according to which adaptation of behavior, orientation pattern and characteristics of the host society are seen as learning processes; secondly, *integration*, which is only possible as a consequence of learning processes. Esser differentiates between the personal, social and systemic integration. The third aspect of the integration process is *assimilation*, which happens in four forms: cognitive assimilation (knowledge), social assimilation (interaction), structural assimilation (institutions), and identificative assimilation (values) (ibid.: 58ff).

Everett S. Lee (1966) defines migration as a permanent or semi-permanent change of residence. The general scheme of Lee's analysis contains four types of factors: firstly, factors associated with the home country; secondly, factors associated with the potential host country; thirdly, intervening obstacles; and finally, personal factors. However, according to Lee, the number of factors is as infinite as the methods of individual estimation and therefore it is not possible to precisely understand them. It is generally possible to set forth a few factors which seem of special importance and note the general and average reaction of a considerable group. Based on the most important factors, Lee deduces 19 hypotheses (six concerning the scope of migration, six concerning migration streams and counter streams and seven concerning the characteristics of migrants) (Lee 1966: 50).

Lee differentiates within those factors between hard or immediately life-threatening (humanitarian crisis, armed conflict, environmental catastrophes) and soft or gradual and structural (poverty, social exclusion, unemployment). The favourable pull factors at destination tend to attract migrants who are positively selected in terms of human capital or motivation, whereas this might not be the case when the unfavorable push factors at origin play a crucial role in instigating the migration process (ibid.).

There were some suggestions made by then British Prime Minister Tony Blair in 2003 to establish 'transit processing centers' or reception centers in countries outside the European Union (EU) to which EU member states would return asylum seekers and where UNHCR would screen them for refugee status. Libya was one of the potential countries for such centers. An EU summit of June 2003 found the idea worth considering and important for a 'more orderly and managed entry in the EU of persons in need of international protection' even if later Blair's idea of 'transit processing centers' or reception centers could not be supported by all interior ministers at the October 2004 meeting in the Netherlands. The idea of 'offshoring' EU's responsibilities for asylum seekers through 'transit processing centers' or reception centers could not be adopted though detention centres were introduced. An interesting irony of the issue is that the then Libyan leader Mu`ammar al-Gaddafi had denied that there were migrants in Libya, either heading through Libya to Europe or seeking asylum. He called the issue of asylum 'a widespread lie.' During his visit to Italy on June 11, 2009, he even said, 'Do we really think that millions of people are asylum seekers? It is really a laughable matter.' He characterized the African migrants as people 'living in the desert, in the forests, having no identity at all. Let alone a political identity' (Human Rights Watch 2009: 47).

According to Thielemann, two very significant aspects in the deterrence factor are, namely the prohibition from work and the above-average rejection rate. Further, for him the most significant pull factors are a low unemployment rate, liberalness factor and a large number of foreigners belonging to a certain community, hence existing historical ties and networks (Thielemann 2003: 25–30). The argument of Thielemann concerning existing historical ties and networks is viable and convincing. However, the 'liberalness factor' has a weak aspect. Many migrants from conflict regions do not always have enough knowledge about their destination countries, the political systems and traditions there. Many come to know only upon their arrival, having been smuggled by human traffickers or just travelling, that such a country where they are brought to exists. So the GDP or liberalness factor is true in the case of the well-educated migrants. Many migrants affected by conflicts belong unfortunately not to this privileged category. This issue is discussed in Chapter 10 in this volume.

J.E. Taylor (1986) emphasises the importance of personal migrant networks in the envisaged host country as pull factors. Such networks decrease monetary, psychological and other similar costs and migration risks. As Heisler says, these networks create a kind of ethnic enterprise through 'reactive solidarity'. This ad hoc solidarity is a solidarity which did not exist before immigration but which becomes a resource for members of the group after immigration. Technological revolutions such as easier and faster global transportation systems facilitate transnational and transcontinental networks of migrants (Heisler 2000: 81, 87; Brettell 2000: 106–18). As discussed above, Thielemann examined push and pull factors related to migrant networks based on historical ties. For Taylor as well as Thielemann colonial relations play a big role because linguistic, economic and cultural ties cause migrants to move to the industrialized countries of former colonizers. The more the relatives and friends move there, the more ties and networks emerge in the receiving countries and the more migrants follow. A good example is the case of Pakistanis and Bangladeshis in the United Kingdom (UK). The cultural, education and linguistic system will be very much influenced by the former colonial power. This helps the Bangladeshis or Pakistanis easily integrate. As the large number of Pakistanis and Bangladeshis in the UK shows, historical ties are important pull factors with a high positive correlation to the number of asylum seekers in a country. Similarly, it is not by chance that many Eritreans and Somalis head for Italy, the former colonial power. Somalis (2,775) and Eritreans (2,110) were two of the five main citizenships of non-EU asylum applicants in Italy in 2013.

Besides the colonial relationships, personal migrant networks also play a role. According to Eurostat, the following number of Eritreans applied for asylum in 2013: 4,880 in Sweden, 2,560 in Switzerland, 3,250 in Norway. Similarly, the number of asylum applicants from Somalia was: 3,940 in Sweden, 1,695 in Norway, 3,260 in the Netherlands, and 920 in Denmark. Meanwhile, Italy is becoming a transit country, not only a destination country, like Malta where 1,015 Somalis and 475 Eritreans applied for asylum in 2013 (Eurstat 2014). The number of Somali asylum seekers in the EU-28 increased from 14,280 in 2012 to 18,560 in 2013 (30% increase); and that of the Eritreans from 6,400 in 2012 to 14,580 in 2013 (127.8% increase) (Eurostat 2014). Whereas the high number of Somali and Eritrean asylum applications in Italy can be explained by the colonial background, the high number in the Netherlands, Norway, Sweden and Switzerland is certainly due to networking among family members and friends. This means that those who are already there are an invaluable source of information for those who attempt to immigrate. During the Eritrean independence war until 1991, and the Somali civil war since 1991, many Eritreans and Somalis fled their countries and migrated to various European countries. Given the fact that the Somali civil war and Eritrean government's dictatorship remained constant, it is fair to conclude that this rapid increase in the number of Somali and Eritrean asylum seekers in the past years is due to the changing conditions in the Mediterranean.

The economic factor is the leading factor in the analysis of migration theories. Accordingly, even politically persecuted asylum seekers or refugees take into account the economic dimension while taking decisions for migration. As such, asylum seekers prefer to apply for asylum in richer countries, not always in safer countries. What they look for is not only political security, but also economic gain such as job opportunities in the host countries, income maximization and risk minimization. However, people affected by extreme poverty are least likely to have the means to migrate. Their migration movements, if at all, take place predominantly within their respective states, moving from the countryside to cities. As various studies show, migrants from remote areas are often not from the poorest regions or from the poorest households because migration is too difficult and the cost too high (Haan and Yaqub 2009: 5). In many cases it happens that family members sell their properties to enable the would-be migrant to finance his journey abroad. Such individual and family decisions of migration depend further on their information about the GDP of the destination country. According to this risk minimization and profit maximization approach, 'relative number of asylum applications in a country will be positively correlated with its GDP, and negatively with its unemployment rate' (Thielemann 2003: 19). Networking and information gathering through modern media are invaluable resources for migration decision-making.

The decision theory of migration (Thielemann 2003) maintains that migration is caused by a variety of individual decisions that aim at benefit maximisation. As a consequence, we would be able to predict the scope of migration if we were able to know when the benefits of migration are deemed higher than those of staying (Besher 1967: 75). That means that the accuracy of prediction is dependent upon the ability of science to predict individual decisions. Besher assumes that the 'mode of orientation' is very important for decisions. He differentiates between the 'purposive-rational' type of orientation (long-term perspective concerning the evaluation of action possibilities and its alternatives; decision mostly dependent on information), the 'traditional' type of orientation (decision depends on traditions), and the 'short-run hedonistic' type of orientation (decision depends on short-term emotional aspects). Finally, he categorised persons on the basis of their profession, their age and the duration of their education. On the basis of this categorization, it is possible to predict that in certain groups the probability for migration is higher than in others (Besher 1967: 134–5). For example, immigrants into EU-27 Member States in 2012 were, on average, much younger than in destination countries of the immigrants. As Eurostat shows, in early 2013, the median age of the EU population was 42 years, while the median age of immigrants in 2012 ranged from 26 years (in the United Kingdom) to 40 years (in Bulgaria) (Eurostat 2014).

According to the dual labour markets theory in labour economics (Piore 1979), migration is the product of permanent demand for migrant labour at the destination countries whose economy depends upon the migrant workers (Piore 1979; Massey 2006: 36; Todaro 1976). With increasing economic development, the labour shortages at the bottom of the hierarchy increase. This causes entrepreneurs to search for immigrant workers who are willing to take dirty, difficult and dangerous jobs. This economic behavior of the employer is more profitable than to raise wages in order to attract a local labour force. For the employer, increasing wages to preserve the local labour force is economically irrational. Whereas the immigrant workforce is a more flexible production factor, the local workforce is protected by institutions such as trade unions and regulations of working conditions. This factor petrifies the labour market dualism (Massey et al. 1993: 441–3).

According to the world systems theory (Wallerstein 1974), international migration is associated with the advances of the capitalist system and global markets in the globalized world of today. Economic actors from the industrialized world are increasingly searching for land, raw materials, labour and new consumer markets in poorer countries (Massey et al. 1993: 445), whereas labour flows in the opposite direction. Hence, migration is a natural product of disruptions and dislocations as a consequence of capitalist development (Massey et al. 2006 : 42).

Another economic approach to migration theories which comes very close to Besher's decision theory is the neoclassical macroeconomic theory of migration, according to which migration is the result of a decision depending on a cost-benefit-analysis (Massey et al. 2006: 37). Migrants calculate migration benefits as a sum of net income over a certain period of time. Net income means expected income in the receiver state minus expected income in the sender state; whereas expected income means that the potential income needs to be multiplied by the probability of work. Migration costs are important when taking decisions. Migration costs include direct costs such as travel expenses and indirect costs such as those that emerge when looking for a new job or while adapting to a new environment. This is an investment in travelling, learning a new language and culture, adapting to a new market, cutting old ties and forging new ones (Massey et al. 2006: 37; Todaro 1976). A quantitative evaluation of costs, such as adaptation costs, is of course difficult. Finally, the cost-benefit analysis calculates migration benefits minus migration costs. In the case of a positive result, migration brings benefits and will be realized (Sjaastad 1962: 87).

According to the so-called new economic theory of migration, migration-related decisions are made not only by individuals who migrate but also by households. Migration is a strategy to diversify the economies of households as an instrument to manage risk at the household level, and not necessarily to maximize benefits. It is households that take migration decisions, as individuals are usually embedded within families/households. The money coming from abroad is used for investments in productive activities (which should lead to additional income) (Stark 1991).

The institutional theory of migration maintains that the imbalance between a large number of people who would like to enter a developed country and the strict visa policies of these countries facilitates the emergence of entrepreneurs ('immigration black market') and institutions that promote the international movement of people. Voluntary humanitarian organizations also arise to address the exploitation and victimization of migrants and to enforce the rights and improve the treatment of regular or irregular migrants (Massey et al. 2006 : 45).

According to cumulative causation theory (Myrdal 1957) 'each act of migration alters the social context within which subsequent migration decisions are made, typically in ways that make additional movement more likely'. One component of this cumulative causation is the distribution of income: 'as a household's sense of relative deprivation increases so does the motivation to migrate'. The migration of some from a village or neighborhood results in an increase of income for those who have moved and for their families. The consequence of this migration is income difference and further migration of the other members of the community. Another factor in the migration decisions is that a taste for consumer goods and styles of life that are difficult to attain through local labour creates a new culture of migration. Moreover, raising educational levels in peripheral areas increases the potential returns to migration and attracts more and more educated people to urban areas abroad or at home. Finally, immigration produces 'immigrants' jobs': 'once immigrants have been recruited into particular occupations in significant numbers, those jobs become culturally labelled as "immigrants' jobs" and native workers are reluctant to fill them, reinforcing the structural demand for immigrants' (Massey et al. 2006: 46–9).

As some studies show, the decision to migrate is negatively correlated to geographical distance. The number of persons going a given distance is directly proportional to the number of opportunities at that distance and inversely proportional to the number of intervening opportunities (Stouffer 1962: 69–91). As asylum seekers usually do not have the necessary finances at their disposal to undertake long-distance travel, a positive correlation of geographic proximity with the dependent variable is assumed (Haun 2007: 26).

According to the unified migration systems theory, similar migratory patterns and continuous interplay of historical, economic, cultural and political linkages between sending and receiving countries determine migration systems (Kritz et al. 1992; Mabogunje 1970; Zlotnik, 1998: 12–13). Migration leads to a unified space that contains home and host countries and although distance plays a role, it is not decisive (Massey et al. 2006: 49). Therefore, migration is often between those regions that are already connected culturally, historically, politically or economically. This is the case, for example, concerning existing ethnic networks that facilitate migration of individuals. A similar aspect was discussed regarding historical ties and networks that facilitate further migration.

Krippendorf describes the impact of tourism to countries of the south to be mainly negative; for example, tourists often have alternative modes of behavior and consumption than the host society. As a consequence, the local population wants to imitate the culture of the tourists or they react with discontent and resignation, or it tries to adapt local traditions based on the commercialization within the tourism region (Krippendorf 1988: 22). Moreover, the mass media of modern society function as linkages in the social fabric (Rosengren 1988: 91). The main direction of the information flow is from the North to the South, which has a variety of consequences for the countries in the South, such as an increasing cultural heteronomy (Hinterleitner 1996: 26). There is certainly a problem that the information dispersed by the media does not correspond to reality. As a consequence, the media has a positive impact on the African migration decision only because it gives a distorted image of Western reality. Chapter 10 in this volume is a perfect explanation of this. Moreover, the media's messages might be interpreted in very different ways depending on one's environment and social background. Audiences are active in various ways. How they select from and reinterpret, for their own purposes, the media materials they consume influences their decision to migrate. Improved modes of transportation, modern telecommunication, television, e-mail and the internet not only make transnational, transcontinental and transcultural communications easier, but they also contribute to the increasing fascination with the modern lifestyle in the industrialized world (Brettell 2000: 102–4).

In this section, different theories of migration are discussed. We have seen in those theories that there are various causes and theoretical explanations of migration. However, it is important to stress that the decision of migrants can have at the same time economic, political or sociological reasons. As a result, theories and explanations can overlap, and it is usually difficult to limit analysis of migration decisions purely to one or another theory. In today's asylum and migration debate in Europe, there is a perceived need in the media and policy discourse to differentiate between economic migrants and 'real' asylum seekers who are fleeing conflicts and war. The idea behind this differentiation is to give asylum to those who are physically threatened, whereas those who take the migration journey for economic reasons will be repatriated. European politicians as well as citizens seem to see a clear distinction between economic migration decisions and those decisions caused by physical insecurity. But the migrants themselves do not seem to see such a clear distinction. And the different migration theories which we saw above seem to corroborate the understandings of the migrants. Even those who flee persecution do not always look only for a safe place where they will not be killed. Understandably, since all they own has been destroyed, they look for a place where they can comfortably meet their economic needs as well as where their physical safety is guaranteed. Here we can see how freedom from fear and freedom from want go together. However, it is important to underline that freedom from fear and freedom from want are not the only push and pull factors.

Even the freedom from fear and/or freedom from want cannot explain everything about the current migration decisions and the movement of the migrants across the Mediterranean or southeastern Europe. Cumulative causation theories, institutional theories, unified migration theories, economic theories, world system theory, etc. play their role in each migration decision of any migrant risking her life. Against this background, in the following section I try to show that even though the dictatorship in Eritrea and conflicts and state collapse in Somalia are prominent push factors of migration from these two countries, the aspects discussed in the theories above are equally valid in the explanation of migration. Hence in the Horn of Africa the causes of emigration are not only economical but also political and humanitarian, due to different types of violent conflicts as shown in the following section.

Conflict System in the Horn of Africa

Migration has different causes: economic, ecological, political, sociological and so forth. Therefore, firstly, the fact that the Horn of Africa is highly affected by conflicts does not necessarily lead us to the conclusion that all migrants from this region are physically persecuted. Secondly, even those who are physically persecuted not only seek physical safety. Most migrants are certainly pushed by the need for physical security but they are also pulled by physical safety and economic prospects in the destination. In addition, it would be inadequate to limit the causes of migration only to physical safety and economic prospects. The different factors discussed in the migration theories in the above section are equally important for the migration decision from the Horn of Africa. Be it cumulative causation theory, world system theory or sociological theory, each plays its role. However, in this section I focus on conflicts in the region and show how they became an important push factor from the Horn of Africa

Conflicts and violence have prevailed in the Horn of Africa for a long time. Conflict has occurred within states, between states, among proxies, between armies. The magnitude of violent conflict in the Horn of Africa, taken over time, is greater than in any other African region (Healy 2008: 9). Since 1991, Somalia has become the theatre of unending civil war, brutal violence, warlords, displacement, refugee exodus, drought and famine, and Islamic radicalism. The Transitional Federal Government is completely overwhelmed by the situation in spite of the support it gets from AMISOM (African Union Mission in Somalia). Intense fighting between government-allied forces and radical Islamists has been inflicting dramatic casualties among civilians. The Somali situation contradicts the common assumption that ethnically, religiously and culturally homogenous states were less prone to civil war.

The decades-long liberation war of Eritrea against Ethiopia ended in 1991, but Eritrea has mutated into one of the most brutal dictatorial regimes in the world. Ethiopia continues to face different rebel groups. Conflicts between the Ethiopian government on the one hand, and Oromo rebels, Ogaden liberation groups, Afar armed groups – to mention just a few – on the other hand, have been affecting Ethiopia's political and socio-economic security and facilitating the proliferation of arms across the region. These conflicts are leading to violation of human rights, suppression of press freedom and an undermining of democratic values. In spite of clan differences, Somalia is usually considered as ethnically homogenous. Clan heterogeneity has substituted ethnic heterogeneity and, consequently, has exacerbated the brutal civil war.

Ethiopia, Kenya and Djibouti are fighting Al-Shabaab (a radical Islamist group linked to Al-Qaeda) in Somalia unilaterally as well as through AMISOM. Moreover, the unending tension with Eritrea has taken advantage of the conflict between the ONLF (Ogaden National Liberation Front) and Ethiopian government, and it is supporting ONLF and Al-Shabaab in Somalia against Ethiopia. Ethiopia's counter-insurgency in Ogaden as well as its invasion of Somalia in 2006 and 2011 is justified by a 'necessity of counter-terrorism'. This has led to a revival of Somali national sentiment and sense of common destiny that cuts across the clan divide and national borders. Eritrea appears to struggle to trust anyone in the region but also could ally with anyone, and institutionalize its isolation (Healy 2007; 2008). The tension between Eritrea and Ethiopia is exacerbating the conflict in the Horn of Africa in general and in Somalia in particular. Eritrea in the meantime is known as one of the most repressive, rogue and belligerent regimes in the world. Eritrean national service and its concomitant Development Campaign are designated as forced labour (Kibreab 2009). Provisions of the constitution of 1997 are still not implemented. Eritreans are seeking refuge abroad, fleeing the oppression, imprisonments and disappearances imposed by their own government (Hedru 2003). Eritrean Islamic Jihad (EIJ), an armed radical Islamic front, is engaging in Eritrea. Because of its conflict with Ethiopia, the Eritrean government argues that national security must always come first, not elections or democratic change.

Ethiopia and Eritrea have been increasing their military support to rival proxies in Somalia, spreading instability to northern Kenya, re-legitimizing warlords and destroying hopes for internal peace efforts. Somali militias have been launching cross-border attacks into Ethiopia and supporting Ethiopia's armed rebels. Ethiopian troops have launched assaults at different times into Somalia. With each new act of violence and cross-border arms transfer, the regional dimensions of these conflicts deepen (Pendergast 1999). Borders are porous, governments are weak, national security systems are ineffectual. Small arms and light weapons are difficult to control; among the cross-border pastoralist community, arms are acquired overtly and facilitate livestock raiding (Griffiths-Fulton 2002). A shared security approach to resolve these conflicts is not employed; military solutions have taken precedence, and the conflicts have been treated individually. In this regional conflict, the dictatorial regime of Eritrea is justifying its existence by indicating that the Ethiopian government is keen to destabilize it. Poverty, human rights violations and an unending conscription is forcing Eritreans to leave their country. In the same way, Somalia has become another Afghanistan. Economic destruction, Islamic radicalism and poverty have been pushing thousands of Somalis into different parts of the world each year. In the following section, I show how the changing conditions in the Mediterranean region have been exerting an impact on the migration decisions of Eritreans and Somalis affected by the conflict system in the Horn of Africa. This means emigration due in part to the conflict system in the Horn of Africa has been taking place for decades. Now, the question is, what have the changing conditions in the Mediterranean contributed to this phenomenon?

Migration from the Horn of Africa in Light of the Changing Conditions in the Mediterranean Region

It is not easy to clearly identify the *direct* impacts of the changing conditions in the Mediterranean region on the migration decisions from the Horn of Africa. However, the *indirect* impacts, such as human trafficking have substantially increased since 2011 (Shelley 2014). The collapse of Libya and the uncontrolled conflict-laden northern regions of Egypt have been facilitating human trafficking of migrants, including from the Horn of Africa. Due to hunger, poverty, compulsory and indefinite military service, and systematic human rights abuses, including arbitrary arrest and detention, torture, forced labour, severe restrictions on freedom of movement and expression, and persistent religious persecution, a massive number of Eritrean refugees has been leaving Eritrea for countries including Ethiopia. Only in the first half of 2013, the UNHCR and the Ethiopian Administration for Refugee and Returnee Affairs (ARRA) have registered more than 4,000 Eritrean refugees, including a large number of unaccompanied minors who require special protection, as well as young educated men from cities. As of the end of May, Ethiopia was hosting 71,833 Eritrean refugees in four camps in Tigray region and two others in the Afar region in north-eastern Ethiopia. By mid-2013 the total number of Eritrean refugees in Sudan was more than 114,500 (Gebre-Ebziabher 2013).

Eritrean refugees who are returned face indefinite detention and torture. But those who flee also risk a perilous journey that includes risk of torture, capture, imprisonment and death. Human traffickers exploit the situation, profiting from Eritreans paying to be smuggled across the border. Three refugee camps near Shire, Ethiopia are home to about 45,000 refugees, with as many as 1,000 Eritrean refugees arriving each month. The camps, in the northern part of Ethiopia, not far from the Eritrean border, include Shimelba (established in 2004), Mai-Aini (2008) and Adi Harush (2010) (Center for Victims of Torture 2014).

By 2011, there were 17,175 Eritreans in Israel, with nearly a thousand crossing the Sinai to Israel every month. According to some sources, in 2013 there were 35,895 Eritreans and 15,210 Sudanese out of the more than 60,000 irregular African migrants believed to be in Israel (Tobia 2013). Though asylum seekers who return to Eritrea are in danger of persecution or even death at the hands of the Eritrean regime, Israel has been searching for ways to fly them back to Eritrea. In response to the growing number of African migrants entering its territories, Israel has built a wall on its southern border with Egypt (Berman 2013). On their way from Sudan or Eritrea to Israel the threat of kidnap and torture at the hands of Bedouins who control the Sinai is ever present, and many do not survive the journey. Some members of Israel's parliament have called the migrants from the eastern African countries 'a cancer' on Israeli society, 'a plague', or yelled 'Blacks out!' (Tobia 2013).

Since President Mubarak of Egypt was ousted in February 2011 there has been a significant increase in attacks in the country on persons including: Israelis, Egyptian police officers and soldiers, tourists, and migrants such as those from the Horn of Africa (Agence France-Press 2013). The Bedouin kidnappers grabbed one migrant, Winnie Beyene, in Sudan as she fled Eritrea in late 2011 after her husband was imprisoned. They brought her to the Sinai desert and threatened to kill her three young children for organ trafficking unless she could hand over $30,000. She was forced to call her family back home in Eritrea and beg them to save her children by sending the money (Tobia 2013). A clan of Bedouins called Rashaida are notorious for snatching migrants fleeing Sudan, Ethiopia and Eritrea, and chaining, raping, torturing and dismembering body parts for ransom from their families back home. Different Bedouin groups sometimes fight over the refugees. Usually, once the ransom has been paid, they will be brought near the Israeli border, but the Egyptian security forces have a policy to shoot on sight (Tobia 2013).

Especially after the fall of Mubarak the lawless Sinai Peninsula has become a living hell for thousands of refugees, mostly from Eritrea, Ethiopia and Sudan, who are being kidnapped and tortured by human traffickers. The traffickers chain together groups of men and women, pour molten plastic on their bodies, deprive them of food, water and sleep, subject them to vicious beatings and electric shocks, and rape them (Washington Post 2013). They give them their mobile phones and begin to torture them while their families are listening on the other end. Security in the Sinai has worsened since Egyptian President Mohammed Morsi was ousted by the military on July 3, 2013. Israel constructed a fence on the border with Egypt to keep out African migrants, and the flow of asylum seekers into Israel from the Sinai slowed significantly. As a result the Bedouins started to lose money, so they began to kidnap refugees from camps inside Sudan; and some Sudanese soldiers guarding the United Nations' Shagarab refugee camp in eastern Sudan often work with the kidnappers (Shen 2013). The traffickers keep the migrants as slaves, sell, chain, beat or torture them and demand a ransom sometimes of up to $50,000; they beat children, even a six-month-old baby, to force the parents to beg for ransom money (Shen 2013).

The tragedy of the migrants in the Mediterranean is not new and had been happening even before the more recent changing conditions in the region related to the protests against dictators of the Northern African countries. For instance, in March 2009 more than 200 African migrants drowned after their boat sank off the coast of Libya. Such developments have increased continuously after the changing political and security conditions in the region. In the first four months of 2013, 30,000 refugees and migrants arrived from the Horn of Africa (especially from Ethiopia and Somalia) compared to 33,634 arrivals over the same time period in 2012 in Yemen. Since 2006 when UNHCR began gathering data, 477,000 have arrived in Yemen (UNHCR 2013). According to the UNHCR in 2012, around 107,500 people made the journey from the Horn of Africa to Yemen, which is frequently used as a transit point by Ethiopians traveling to the Gulf States and beyond. Those asylum seekers and migrants, including women and children, are exposed to torture, exploitation, violence and sexual abuse. Yemen hosts more than 242,000 refugees, of which some 230,000 are Somali (UNHCR 2013).

A Somali Olympic athlete, Samia Yusuf Omar, drowned while attempting to reach Europe on a migrant boat trying to cross from Libya to Italy in April 2012, after she arrived in Libya in September 2011 and was detained there. The athlete faced death threats and intimidation by Islamist militia al-Shabab when she returned to Somalia after the 2008 Olympics (BBC 2012b). According to Eurostat, Somalia is the leading African country of origin from which the highest number of asylum applications are made in the EU, more than 14,000 in 2012 (Eurostat 2014).

According to the UNHCR around 3,000 Eritreans try to flee each month from a country which, with some 10,000 political prisoners, is becoming a giant jail. Moreover, Eritreans flee their country mainly due to forced, indefinite military conscription, a system which requires all citizens to serve in the army for an unlimited amount of time, a practice akin to slavery. According to the UNHCR, there were 363,077 Eritrean refugees in the Horn of Africa as of November 2014 (UNHCR 2015). Most of them wait for an opportunity to start their journey to Europe, North America or Canada. There is also a lack of freedom of press and expression, and widespread arbitrary detention and torture. Similarly, much of Somalia is controlled by Al-Shabaab Islamist militants and ravaged by two decades of war (BBC 2012a).

Horn of African migrants travel often through Yemen, with at least 50 people arriving daily in the northern town of Haradh, en route to the Gulf. These migrants, suffering severe abuse and economic and sexual exploitation, are stranded at the Saudi border. About 90% of them are men in search of job opportunities in the Gulf States (OCHA 2013a). The UNHCR estimated that more than 100 migrants either drowned or went missing in 2011. The influx of migrants and refugees from the Horn of Africa to the Gulf doubled from around 53,000 in 2010 to over 107,000 in 2012 (IOM 2013).

Many African migrants who fled persecution and conflict back home in Eritrea and Sudan survived their ordeal on their route through North

Africa and reached Israel only to face mistreatment by the Israeli government, such as detainment for a year without trial (The Washington Post 2013b). The Libyan authorities do not deport Eritreans and Somalis to their countries due to widespread human rights abuses in Eritrea and the conflict in Somalia, but they do keep them for months or even for more than a year in detention (Human Rights Watch 2014b).

In early February 2014, Italy's navy rescued 1,123 people from inflatable boats. As a result of the continuous influx of migrants from Sub-Saharan Africa through North Africa to Europe, Italy has been patrolling Libya's coast. In mid-June 2014, at least 39 people drowned some 65 km off the coast of Libya (BBC 2014a). According to Frontex, the EU border agency, from January to April 2014, 42,000 migrants were detected on routes from North Africa, with 25,650 of these crossing from Libya. According to the Italian government the number of refugees and other migrants arriving at its shores had reached more than 39,000 by the end of May 2014, and the total for 2014 at the time of writing was more than the equivalent period in 2011, the year of the Arab Spring, which eventually saw 140,000 make clandestine crossings into Europe mainly from Syria, Afghanistan and Eritrea (Adams 2014). For years before the demise of Al-Gaddafi, the main route through Libya was closed and migrants from Sub-Saharan Africa have been building up and waiting for the very first opportunity to move for a couple of years (Düvell and Düvell 2011).

Due to state collapse, war and violent Al-Shabab militia, Somalia is one of the main senders of migrants and asylum seekers throughout the world. In 2012 more than 14,000 Somalis applied for asylum in the EU, and about 18,000 in industrialized countries in general. Similarly, around 12,500 Eritreans applied for asylum in industrialized countries. As of January 2014, Somalia had 1,121,738 refugees, 35,472 asylum seekers, 36,100 returned refugees, 1,133,000 internally displaced peoples (IDPs), and 104,706 returned IDPs (UNHCR 2014a). Regarding Eritrea, as of January 2014 there were 308,022 refugees and 30,038 asylum seekers. In general in the East and Horn of Africa countries highly affected by conflict and displacement, the number of people in the region requiring humanitarian assistance has risen significantly, and access to those in need is very limited. At the time of writing there are some 6 million people of concern to UNHCR, including 1.8 million refugees and more than 3 million IDPs (UNHCR 2014b).

According to the deputy Interior Minister of Italy Filippo Bubbico, in 2013, a total of 2,925 vessels of various shapes and sizes landed on Italian shores, carrying about 43,000 people, including nearly 4,000 children, through the routes Libya, Egypt and Turkey, mainly from Syria (11,307) and Eritrea (9,834 – an increase of 400%). On 19 July 2014, 19 migrants died by suffocating aboard a crowded boat carrying some 600 people travelling from North Africa to Italy. Immigration charities estimate that between 17,000 and 20,000 migrants died at sea trying to reach Europe between 1993 and 2013 (BBC 2014c). According to the UN more than 130,000 migrants arrived in

Europe by sea in 2014, compared with 80,000 in 2013; more than half of those arriving by boat were refugees from Syria and Eritrea. From January to September 2014, Italy received more than 118,000 migrants (UNHCR 2014c).

The experiences of the migrants are appalling and include: an exhausting journey across the Sahara, slave-like working conditions such as in Libya while trying to earn the money for the sea crossing, overloaded boats, migrants in distress ignored by fishing boats or coast guard vessels going by and helicopters flying overhead, and Frontex border patrol actors more interested in pushing migrants and asylum seekers back than in rescuing those in distress. They may drift in the Mediterranean for days until they are finally rescued. Many die or suffer from thirst and hunger to the point of drinking their own urine, and boats run out of fuel or sink. Migrants experience the deaths of friends and family members, and are required to part with huge sums of money. They are cheated and mistreated by the traffickers (OSCE 2013). There is also the agony of family members left behind who sold their property to enable them to make this journey and the consequent pressure on the migrants to pay this back and enable a better future for their relatives back home.

Conclusion

Thanks to its geostrategic position, the Horn of Africa has been suffering from different conflicts for the past several decades and beyond. There are four points important to highlight in the conflict-migration nexus in the Horn of Africa: *first*, the main push factor for the Somalis and Eritreans to leave their countries and risk their lives is the physical insecurity they have been facing in their countries. The conflicts without borders in the region have exacerbated the situation. Islamic fundamentalism, various internal conflicts and interstate tensions constitute a conflict system that has posed a great challenge to making peace in the region. The peoples of those countries have suffered for decades; they are in such a desperate situation that the only option that remains is to leave the country and save their lives and look for opportunities abroad. *Secondly*, as a result of the conflict, the economic infrastructure is massively destroyed. Investment is rare, job opportunities are out of sight. Therefore, there is no other option but emigration, as the economic theories of migration explain. *Thirdly*, in such a grim situation the politically and economically induced decision to migrate is a household decision, not only an individual decision as the new economic theory of migration suggests. Those who emigrate need a lot of money by local standards to reach their destination. Since as individuals they rarely have such a high amount of money to pay the travel or the human traffickers, they have to borrow from their friends and/or sell, in most cases, the property of the family members in the hope that they may pay them back in the future. Here it is important to stress that their migration decisions are not only about freedom from fear and freedom from want. Even if they are fleeing physical insecurity and poverty, it is important to take into account the different explanations of the migration theories we have seen in the first section. *Fourthly*, the changing conditions in the Mediterranean have proliferated human traffickers who know how to exploit the desperate migrants fleeing conflicts and economic misery (OSCE 2013). This is an entrepreneurship that has emerged due to the fall of the North African dictators and changing conditions in the region, further augmented by an increasing supply of emigrants fleeing appalling situations in their home countries. Addressing the causes and consequences of these tragedies requires a multilevel and concerted action from human rights, humanitarian, economic, political, and security points of view. The different migration theories discussed above can provide helpful insights for policy makers into why and how migration decisions are taken. It is also important to note that none of the theories taken alone can explain a migration decision, since migration decision-making is caused at the same time by different circumstances and factors.

References

Adams, Paul (2014) 'Migration surge hits EU as thousands flock to Italy', http://www.bbc.com/news/world-europe-27628416 [10/07/2014].

Agence France-Press (2013) 'Fighting in the Sinai since Mubarak's fall', http://www.globalpost.com/dispatch/news/afp/130819/fighting-the-sinai-mubaraks-fall [18/07/2014].

BBC (2012) 'Somalia Olympic runner drowns trying to reach Europe', http://www.bbc.com/news/world-africa-19323535 [25/07/2014].

BBC (2012a) 'Lampedusa boat disaster: Divers recover more bodies', http://www.bbc.com/news/world-europe-24418779, [23/03/2014].

BBC (2014a) 'Italy warns Mediterranean migrant rescues may end', http://www.bbc.com/news/world-europe-27878346 [19/07/2014].

BBC (2014b) 'Italy migrant influx incessant and massive, says minister', http://www.bbc.com/news/world-europe-26043057 [12/07/2014].

Berman, Lazar (2013) 'Eritrean refugees assail Israeli deportation policy', http://www.timesofisrael.com/eritrean-refugees-assail-israeli-deportation-policy/ [17/07/2014].

Besher, James M (1967) *Population Processes in Social Systems*, The Free Press, New York, London.

Brettel, Caroline B (2000) 'Theorizing migration in Anthropology: the social construction of networks, identities, communities, and globalscapes', 97–135 in Caroline B Brettell and James F Hollifield (eds) *Migration Theory: talking across disciplines*, Routledge, London.

Center for Victims of Torture (2014) 'Eritrean Refugees in Ethiopia', http://www.cvt.org/where-we-work/africa/ethiopia [17/07/2014].

Düvell, Franck and Bastian Vollmer (2011) 'Improving EU and US Immigration Systems for responding to Global Challneges: Learning from Experience', Background paper, EU-US immigration systems 2011/01, Center on Migration, Policy and Society, University of Oxford.

Eisenstadt, Shmuel N (1954) *The Absorption of Immigrants*, Routledge and Kegan Paul, London.
Eurostat (2014) 'Five main citizenships of (non-EU) asylum applicants, 2013' (number, rounded figures), http://epp.eurostat.ec.europa.eu/statistics_explained/images/b/b5/Five_main_citizenships_of_%28non-EU%29_asylum_applicants%2C_2013_%28number%2C_rounded_figures%29_YB15.png [18/09/2014].
Gebre-Ebziabher, Kisut (2013) 'Eritrean refugees in Ethiopia get new camp in north of country', UNHCR, http://www.unhcr.org/51b9b66b9.html [17/07/2014].
Griffiths-Fulton, Lynne (2002) 'Small Arms and Light Weapons in the Horn of Africa', *The Ploughshares Monitor* Summer 2002, 23(2), http://ploughshares.ca/pl_publications/small-arms-and-light-weapons-in-the-horn-of-africa/ [12/09/2014].
Haan, Arjan de and Shahin Yaqub (2009) 'Migration and Poverty, Linkages, Knowledge Gaps and Policy Implications', United Nations Research Institute for Social Development, Social Policy and Development Programme Paper Number 40 June 2009
Han, Petrus (2000) *Soziologie der Migration*, UTB, Stuttgart.
Haun, Elizabeth (2007) *The Externalisation of Asylum Procedures. An Adequate EU Refugee Burden Sharing System?*, Peter Lang, Frankfurt.
Healy, Sally (2008) 'Eritrea's regional role and foreign policy: Past, present and future perspectives', Chatham House, London.
Healy, Sally (2007) 'Conflict in the Ogaden and its regional Dimension', A Horn of Africa Group Seminar Report, Chatham House, London.
Hedru, Debessay (2003) 'Eritrea: Transition to Dictatorship, 1991–2003', *Review of African Political Economy* 30/97, 435–44.
Hoffmann-Nowotny, Hans-Joachim (1970) *Migration. Ein Beitrag zu einer soziologischen Erklärung*, Ferdinand Enke Verlag, Stuttgart.
Hollifield, James F (2000) 'The politics of international migration: how can we "bring the state back in"', 137–86 in Caroline B Brettell and James F Hollifield (eds) *Migration Theory: taking across disciplines*, Routledge, London.
Human Rights Watch (2009) 'Pushed Back, Pushed Around: Italy's Forced Return of Boat Migrants and Asylum Seekers, Libya's Mistreatment of Migrants and Asylum Seekers', http://www.hrw.org/sites/default/files/reports/italy0909webwcover_0.pdf [21/07/2014].
Human Rights Watch (2014b) 'Libya: Whipped, Beaten, and Hung from Trees', http://www.hrw.org/news/2014/06/22/libya-whipped-beaten-and-hung-trees [23/07/2014].
IOM (2013) 'Lack of Funds Limiting IOM Assistance to Stranded Migrants in Yemen', http://www.iom.int/cms/en/sites/iom/home/news-and-views/press-briefing-notes/pbn-2013/pbn-listing/lack-of-funds-limiting-iom-assis.html [10/07/2014].
Kibreab, Gaim (2009) 'Forced labour in Eritrea', *Journal of Modern African Studies* 47/1 41–72.
Krippendorf, Jost (1988) *Für einen anderen Tourismus. Probleme-Perspektiven-Ratschläge*, Fischer RB, Frankfurt.
Kritz, Mary, Lin Lean Lim and Hania Zlotnik (eds) (1992) *International migration systems: A global approach*, Clarendon Press, Oxford.
Lee, Everett (1966) 'A Theory of Migration', *Demography* 3/1 47–57.

Mabogunje, Akin L (1970) 'Systems Approach to a Theory of Rural-Urban Migration', *Geographical Analysis* 2/1 1–18.
Massey, Douglas S, Joaquín Arango, Graeme Hugo, Ali Kouaouci, Adela Pellegrino and J Edward Taylor (2006) 'Theories of international migration: A review and appraisal', 34–62, in Anthony Messina and Gallya Lahav (eds) (2006) *The Migration Reader: Exploring Politics and Policies*, Lynne Rienner, Boulder.
Massey, Douglas S, Joaquin Arango, Graeme Hugo, Ali Kouaouci, Adela Pellegrino and J Edward Taylor (1993) 'Theories of International Migration: Review and Appraisal', *Population and Development Review* 19/3 431–66.
Myrdal, Gunnar (1957) *Rich Lands and Poor*, Harper, New York.
OCHA (2013a) 'Yemen: Addressing the plight of migrants from the Horn of Africa', http://www.unocha.org/top-stories/all-stories/yemen-addressing-plight-migrants-horn-africa-0 [12/01/2014].
OSCE (2013) 'Office of the Special Representative and Co-ordinator for Combating Trafficking in Human Beings, Enhancing Co-operation to Prevent Trafficking in Human Beings in the Mediterranean Region', November 2013.
Parsons, Talcott and Edward Shils (eds) (1951) *Toward a general theory of action*, Harper, New York.
Piore, Michael J (1979) *Birds of passage: Migrant labour in industrial societies*, Cambridge University Press, Cambridge.
Prendergast, John (1999) 'Building for Peace in the Horn of Africa: Diplomacy and Beyond', http://reliefweb.int/report/eritrea/building-peace-horn-africa-diplomacy-and-beyond [23/03/2009].
Rosengren, Karl Erik (1986) 'Linking Culture and Other Societal Systems', 87–98 in Sandra J Ball-Rokeach and Muriel G Cantor (eds) *Media, Audience, and Social Structure*, Sage, Beverly Hills.
Saunders, H W (1956) 'Human Migration and Social Equilibrium', in Joseph J Spengler and Otis Dudley Duncan (eds) *Population Theory and Policy*, The Free Press, New York.
Shelly, Louise (2014): Human smuggling and trafficking into Europe: a comparative perspective, Washington DC: Migration Policy Institute, http://www.migrationpolicy.org/ [18/08/2015].
Shen, Ashish Kumar (2013) 'Egypt: 'In Sinai, I saw hell'; refugees are easy prey for brutal human traffickers', http://www.washingtontimes.com/news/2013/jul/21/in-sinai-i-saw-hell-refugees-are-easy-prey-for-bru/?page=all [10/09/2014].
Sjaastad, Larry A (1962) 'The costs and returns of human migration', *Journal of Political Economy* 70/5, 80–93.
Stark, Oded (1991) *The Migration of Labor*, Basil Blackwell, Cambridge.
Stouffer, Samuel Andrew (1962) *Social Research to Test Ideas*, Free Press, New York.
Taylor, J Edward (1986) 'Differential migration, networks, information and risk' in Oded Stark (ed.) *Research in Human Capital and Development*, Vol. 4 *Migration, Human Capital, and Development*, JAI Press, Greenwich.
Thielemann, Eiko (2003) 'Does Policy Matter? On Governments' Attempts to Control Unwanted Migration', *European Institute Working Paper*, May 2003, http://www.lse.ac.uk/collections/europeaninstitute/pdfs/Eiworkingpaper2003-02.pdf [05/05/2005].
Tobia, P J (2013) 'Unpromised land: Eritrean Refugees in Israel', http://www.pbs.org/newshour/spc/unpromised-land/ [17/07/2014].
Todaro, Michael P (1976) *Internal migration in developing countries*, International Labour Office, Geneva.

UNHCR (2015): Eritrea: 2015 UNHCR subregional operations profile – East and Horn of Africa, http://www.unhcr.org/pages/49e4838e6.html [07/09/2015].

UNHCR (2014a) '2014 UNHCR country operations profile – Somalia', http://www.unhcr.org/pages/49e483ad6.html [20/07/2014].

UNHCR (2014b) '2014 UNHCR regional operations profile – East and Horn of Africa', http://www.unhcr.org/cgi-bin/texis/vtx/page?page=49e4838e6&submit=GO [20/07/2014].

UNHCR (2014c) 'UNHCR alarmed at death toll from boat sinkings in the Mediterranean', http://www.unhcr.org/54184ae76.html [19/09/2014].

UNHCR (2013) 'More than 30,000 refugees and migrants make risky sea crossing to Yemen this year', http://www.unhcr.org/517aa1c16.html [26/06/2014].

Washington Post, The (2013a) 'Egypt: 'In Sinai, I saw hell'; refugees are easy prey for brutal human traffickers', http://www.washingtontimes.com/news/2013/jul/21/in-sinai-i-saw-hell-refugees-are-easy-prey-for-bru/?page=all [20/07/2014].

Washington Post, The (2013b) 'Israel says it won't forcibly deport illegal African migrants, but it wants them to leave', http://www.washingtonpost.com/world/israel-says-it-wont-forcibly-deport-illegal-african-migrants-but-it-wants-them-to-leave/2013/12/20/1c81d8be-5cf2-11e3-8d24-31c016b976b2_story.html [23/07/2014].

Zlotnik, Hania (1998) 'The theories of international migration. Paper for the Conference on International Migration: Challenges for European Populations', Bari, Italy, 25–27 June 1998.

2 Liminality and Migrant Decision-Making in the Aftermath of the Political and Refugee Crises in the Mediterranean, 2010–2013

Pedro Marcelino, Maria Ferreira and Natalia Lippmann Mazzagali

Introduction[1]

Tragic shipwrecks in the Mediterranean Sea are not a novelty. Yet, the sheer number of migrants traversing in increasingly unseaworthy vessels, following civil unrest in Libya, caught segments of civil society in Europe completely unaware (e.g. Popp 2014) – and riled up others (e.g. Walker 2011a; 2011b). As early as 2010, the liminality of daily life generated by the civil unrest in Libya facilitated a renewed elasticity of the maritime border (Marcelino and Farahi 2011), which had previously been stamped out by an agreement between Gaddafi's regime and the European Union (Sherwood 2011). This newly reopened migratory channel to Europe quickly summoned Trans-Saharan migrant routes back to Libya (and out of it). With the country's institutional collapse and rampant corruption, there was little fear of repercussions. Within a year, the Mediterranean space between the Libyan and the Tunisian coasts to the south, and Malta and Italy to

---

1 Since this chapter was finished, a sequence of transformative events have been unfolding in Europe, dramatically shifting the central issues and tenets of this text from a focus on Mediterranean migration routes, and overall migration to Europe, to an increasingly tragic theatre of inhumanity. To the thousands of migrants trying to reach Europe through the Mediterranean, we must now add migration flows that come by land through Southeastern Europe through Turkey, Greece, Macedonia, Serbia, Hungary and Austria. From a discursive perspective, the reinforcement of a securitarian approach to migration flows has never been clearer. This is best represented by Hungary's decision to build a wall along its Serbian border. Subsequently, the Hungarian government argued that only militarized patrols could ensure the efficiency of this wall. Such a proposal is accompanied by the mobilization of discourses that cast migrants as a threat to European identity. But the mobilization of an ecological approach is visible also in the discourses uttered by governments and groups of citizens across the continent. To a certain extent, alternate (more measured) approaches have been taken by decision-makers in countries such as France and Germany. On the media front there is at last a glimmer of understanding about the complexity of the issues: we are no longer talking about migrants; 'the word [*migrant*]', McKernan (2015) says, 'has become a largely inaccurate umbrella term for this complex story'. We are now looking at the biggest refugee crisis Europe has faced since World War II – and the continent is not only ill prepared, but also ill-at-ease to deal with it.

the north, became a hotspot for the smuggling of irregular migrants (IRIN 2011; IOM 2014).

The 2011 civil war in Libya further enabled the situation. By the time Syrian refugees started to flock out of that country's own conflict, in 2012, adding to a growing contingent of Sub-Saharan Africans exploring this new route for economic reasons and Eritreans and others seeking asylum in Europe, Libya was squarely re-established as a transhipment hub for migrants (Gates of Vienna 2011). Transnational criminal networks operating in the country explored the despair of thousands for profit, with even less consideration for human life than they typically showed. Ships were overloaded, people thrown overboard, and boats sunk with shocking frequency, leaving thousands to drown. With few other options on the table, bona fide refugees accepted the risk – despite the likelihood of their detention and repatriation, at best, or death, at worse (BBC News 2014; Sherwood 2011).

Meanwhile, in Europe, a traditional political divide over immigration deepened, pitting those incensed by what they called a 'flood' or an 'invasion' against those whose moral compass could not accept the shocking reality of hundreds of human beings perishing daily on their doorstep, as if nothing happened (BBC News 2014; IRIN 2011; Sherwood 2011). Europe faced a moral conundrum of gigantic proportions, and one that is far from being resolved (Economist 2013).

This chapter addresses a grossly under-explored category of analysis on European migration: the conditioning of migrant decision-making processes by the 'host' society. It focuses on the on-going human catastrophe occurring off the Mediterranean coasts, where the lives of Sub-Saharan and Middle Eastern migrants moving across the region appear to have lost value – and where, under the idle gaze of the international community, categories such as 'asylum seeker' and even 'refugee' appear to have lost their meaning, and the sense of solidarity they deserve – although the question about who is, in fact, a bona fide asylum seeker or refugee had been latent for a long time (Cohen 2006 145–8).

The chapter is divided into three sections. Firstly, we look at the migration crisis as explored in European political discourse and practices. We discuss this ongoing human catastrophe by addressing how political discourse translates into concrete policies. We also argue that Europe has adopted purely securitarian tactics to curtail migrants' 'substantial freedoms', and demonstrate how the EU's migration narratives devalue human dignity.

Secondly, we examine the social and juridical normativity responsible for dehumanising migrants and creating a state of exception that is tacitly assigned to *the other*. The theoretical approach of this section reviews *de facto* and *de jure* policies and practices under which migrants are analysed as the receivers of normative dispositions that severely condition their individual, familiar, and collective growth, thus stipulating *ad initium* a social belonging politically characterized as structural pathology in the EU.

Finally, we take a brief look at the cross-pollination of political discourses, media discourses, and public opinion, and how this fluidity of terms and ideas affects life at sea by ultimately conditioning the reactions of civil society in 'host' countries.

The Migration Crisis and European Political Discourse

European political discourse on Mediterranean migration can be discussed bearing in mind the distinctions between two main narratives on the articulation between migration and European public policies: a securitarian narrative and an ecological narrative (Huysmans 2006; Gibson 1986; Gibson 1986; Morozov 2011).

Securitarian Narrative

A securitarian narrative to a policy problem represents that policy problem as a security question and, more specifically, as a security threat (Huysmans 2006). Consequently, the policy instruments employed to 'manage' those questions and its policy discourses are drawn from the security arena (Huysmans 2006).

The discursive strategies employed by both the securitarian and ecological narratives, namely the normalisation of the belief that migrants constitute risks for their European host societies, should be interpreted as 'forms of anticipatory knowledge' (Aradau and van Munster 2013), for they instruct audiences on how to think about migration and they form the discursive basis for the legitimation of European public policies in the migration arena (ibid. 2013).

The securitarian narrative to migration and European public policies highlights how migrants constitute threats to the security of host countries (Huysmans 2006). Migration is represented as a question that has to be politicised as a risk and dealt with through security measures located mainly at the border and on transit and origin countries (van Munster 2009). Migrants are represented as a 'burden' that has to be shared among states (Boswell 2003). A strong emphasis is put on the need to distinguish between regular and orderly migration and irregular and criminal migration flows (European Commission 2004). In public policy terms, border patrolling, expulsion and the conclusion of readmission agreements with transit and origin countries are the preferred mechanisms to deal with migration flows (Frontex 2014; 2013). The southern border of the European Union is discursively argued as the most vulnerable in terms of risk assessment (Frontex 2013: 6). Migrants have to be prevented from arriving and/or settling in European countries (see Arens 2009). This explains why the criminalisation of trafficking, repatriation and the creation of detention centres on the fringes of the European continent assume a fundamental importance for the securitarian narrative (Frontex 2013; Frontex 2014). It should be taken into consideration that the securitarian narrative privileges discursive practices in the migration arena based on images of quantity and on the need for containment, namely, maritime images of 'waves', 'floods' and 'tsunamis' (Charteris-Black 2006; Musolff 2011).

European discourses on the Mediterranean political and refugee crisis of 2010–2013 reveal the clear adoption of a securitarian narrative (Frontex 2013; 2014). EU agencies like Frontex have undoubtedly adopted such an approach (see Frontex 2013; 2014; Pop 2011). In a 2011 Human Rights Watch (HRW) Report that assessed Frontex's ill treatment of migration detainees in Greece, HRW Refugee Program Director Bill Frelick is adamant when he argues that '[a]s new migration crisis emerge in the Mediterranean basin and as Frontex responsibilities expand there is an urgent need to shift EU asylum and migration policies from enforcement-first to protection-first' (HRW 2011:2). However, the European Union's (EU) response to the Mediterranean political and refugee crisis of 2010–2013 has clearly prioritised enforcement measures, namely to ensure efficient repatriation operations (Frontex 2014). The institutional discourse concerning Frontex was centred not on the need to humanize its procedures but, instead, around the discussion of how to strengthen the capabilities of the Warsaw-based agency (Pop 2011).

Like other EU foreign operational missions, Frontex-run operations are subject to the bottom-up approach, which means that Frontex is dependent on national resources (Pop 2011). Frontex Executive Director Ilkka Laitinen has argued, however, that the agency should be endowed with its own operational resources in order to avoid the need for 'bilateral negotiations with each country with parliaments giving their approval' (Pop 2011, no pagination). In order to strengthen his plea for operational autonomy, Laitinen also said that 'countries impose all sorts of conditions when we want technology and equipment' (Schult 2011, no pagination). Laitinen's words can be understood as a 'securitisation manoeuvre' since he argued in favour of the lifting of the normal procedures that regulate the legitimation of foreign enforcement operations in member-states, namely, parliamentary control procedures (Balzacq 2011). In May 2014, when the discussion surrounding European migration policies was already intense due to the elections to the European Parliament, Frontex issued its *2014 Annual Risk Analysis* where it warns of a possible surge in the number of asylum-seekers entering European countries through the southern border (Frontex 2014; Cowell and Bilefsky 2014). The same document also warns that the numbers of irregular migrants going to Europe in the first five months of 2014 was already higher to the total amount of irregular entries in the whole of 2013 (Frontex 2014; Cowell and Bilefsky 2014). Fuelling the narrative of an 'escalation' of migration flows, particularly in the EU southern border, Frontex *Annual Risk Analysis* cautioned that summer months facilitate irregular migration flows (Frontex 2014; Cowell and Bilefsky 2014).

The fact that Frontex makes forecasts on present and future migration flows in a document strategically designated as *Annual Risk Analysis* demonstrates the representation and politicisation of migration as a risk and, consequently, the adoption of a securitarian narrative (Huysmans 2006; van Munster 2009). In addition to this practice of Frontex, the practice in member-state decision-making responding to Mediterranean migration flows also privileges a securitarian narrative (Huysmans 2006; van Munster 2009).

Southern European member states have discursively 'europeanised' (Ifantis 2004 25) the Mediterranean migration question, which has paved the way for more enforcement policies centred on Frontex and on the mobilisation of military means – 'gunboat surveillance' (de Lucas 2013) – in order to curb migration flows. Since 2011, the main response of southern European countries, such as Italy, to Mediterranean migration flows has been the deployment of naval and air patrols (Cowell & Bilefsky 2014; Marcelino and Farahi 2011). Greece, on the other hand, has opted for the construction of a fence on its border with Turkey (Cowell and Bilefsky 2014; Popp 2011). Greece and Turkey as destinations and transit hubs are specifically addressed in Chapter 6.

Europeanisation – here understood as the impact of the European Union in its member states' public policies (Börzel and Risse 2000) – in the migration arena is mainly visible at a discursive level since it serves as a way for southern European member states to claim more financial resources from the European Union (Arens 2009). However, at a policy level, integrating EU member states' policies concerning migration is difficult due to high domestic pressures coming mainly from right-wing parties which wish to maintain national sovereignty on migration and asylum (EurActiv 2013).

Member states' responses to the Mediterranean migration 'crisis' was, in fact, argued by some media to have empowered a generalised indifference concerning the fate of migrants at sea and, in particular, concerning the maritime duties to save individuals in distress (Arens 2009). Arens designates the public policies enacted by European leaders as a 'contemptible monthslong campaign against African refugees' (Arens 2009, no pagination). The construction of a securitarian narrative concerning Mediterranean migration flows is particularly employed by two strategic EU member states: Italy and France (see Arens 2009; Day 2011).

The Italian government led by Prime Minister Silvio Berlusconi (2008–2011) empowered the belief that intercepted migrants should be returned to Africa without an opportunity to request asylum (The Scottsman 2009; Arens 2009). The Italian government stance on migration was widely debated within the country (The Scottsman 2009; Arens 2009). Institutional voices related with the Catholic Church accused Western governments of ignoring the human tragedy occurring in the Mediterranean (The Scottsman, 2009; Arens 2009). The Catholic journal *Avvenire* compared the contemporary human tragedy of boat people in the Mediterranean to the Holocaust (The

Scottsman, 2009; Arens 2009). Ironically, on May 2009, Berlusconi tried to justify his government's policies towards Mediterranean migrants, arguing that since Italian detention centres had such poor conditions that they could be compared to concentration camps, it would be 'more humane' to repatriate them (Arens 2009). In March 2011, Silvio Berlusconi employed a 'natural disaster' image to classify the impact of migration flows: the then Italian chief of government compared Mediterranean migration flows to a 'human tsunami' (Sauer 2011). He made such remark when the international community was still trying to assimilate the consequences of the real Japanese tsunami of 11 March 2011 (Sauer 2011). Franco Frattini – Italian Foreign Minister between 2008 and 2011 — also classified Mediterranean migration flows as an 'exodus of biblical dimension' (Sauer 2011, no pagination). The securitarian approach to migration control assumed particular significance when Italian Interior Minister Roberto Maroni argued in favour of the employment of 'private civilian militias' to control migration (Arens 2009).

Despite an initial disagreement on the management of Mediterranean migration flows, on April 2011 the French and Italian governments jointly argued in favour of the overhauling of the EU free travel system due to the Mediterranean migration crisis (Day 2011). At a joint summit in Rome, Berlusconi and the then French President Nicolas Sarkozy called for the introduction of more severe border control policies and the consequent 'watering down' of the goals of the Schengen free movement system (Day 2011). In a joint letter to the EU, the two leaders employed a discourse based on the argument of exceptionality in order to uphold the need to reform the Schengen legal regime and to strengthen Frontex (Day 2011). A discursive approach based on exceptionality also constitutes a narrative strategy frequently employed by the securitarian and the ecological narratives in the migration arena (see Huysmans 2014).

The French political discourse on migration has also been marked in recent years by an increasing radicalisation (see Borrud 2012). In the aftermath of the Franco-Italian joint summit and letter to the EU, 2012 presidential candidate Nicolas Sarkozy reiterated that France would be the first member state to interrupt its participation in the Schengen area if tougher measures concerning migration control would not be taken (Borrud 2012). Particularly from 2007 onwards, Sarkozy's political discourse was heavily centred on the need to curtail irregular migration (Borrud 2012). During the 2012 presidential elections, Sarkozy vowed to take action at domestic and European levels, which was considered as a clear reinforcement of his anti-migration 'drive' with the goal of competing with the Front Nationale for far-right voters (Borrud 2012). Sarkozy's political agenda was adamant in proving the ability of his government to drastically reduce, through deportation, the number of irregular migrants on French territory (Borrud 2012). The political performance of the Sarkozy-led French cabinet was discursively represented as depending, among other factors, upon deportation numbers (Borrud 2012). In 2011, then French Interior Minister Claude Gueant proudly announced that France had deported more 'illegal immigrants' than 'ever before' (Borrud 2012). Gueant's political rhetoric also included the politicisation of migrants as risk, namely by claiming that migrants 'are two to three times more likely to commit crimes than average French nationals' (Borrud 2012).

Ecological Narrative

An ecological approach to a public policy question highlights how the social perception of such a question is constitutive of the policy options that are designed for it (Gibson 1986). When a particular phenomenon is perceived as a threat, that perception affects the ecological fabric of a community since what is at stake is communitarian sustainability (Gibson 1986).

The ecological narrative constitutes a most extreme version of the securitarian approach, since it considers that migrants endanger the nature of their host states understood as political communities (see Hope 2014; on the ecological approach see Gibson 1986; Morozov 2011). Migrants are discursively constructed as 'others' that can no longer be integrated in the social, economic and political tissue of their European host communities (Front Nationale 2014). It is not only border security that is at stake (Huysmans 2006). It is the very essence of the host state(s) as a political and cultural community that is perceived as being endangered (see Huysmans 2006; Bauman 2000).

Contrary to the securitarian narrative, the ecological narrative employs metaphors associated not with the menace of quantitative flows but with the qualitative threat coming from migration flows (Hope 2014). This explains why migratory flows are represented following the militarised image of 'invasion' that threatens to impinge on the identity core of host states (Charlemagne 2010; see also Charteris-Black 2006). The ecological narrative puts forward the argument that migrants play a constitutive role in the unfolding of the economic, political and moral crisis that has been taunting European states (Hope 2014). This ecological narrative develops a line of reasoning consistent with economic nationalism (Korkut et al. 2013). In fact, to represent migration through an ecological terminology can be achieved through a political as well as through an economic framework (Kuisma 2013). In this context, an ecological narrative to the articulation between migration and public policies frames migrants either as economic menace or as a political and communitarian threat to the cultural and social cohesion of particular societies (Kuisma 2013).

The political option of the ecological narrative is to reduce drastically the presence of migrants, regular and irregular, in host countries (Front Nationale 2014). It is important to note that according to an ecological narrative, there should not be a trade-off between an instrumentalist approach to migration and the preservation of the identitarian essence of a host country (Hope 2014). This means that even when migrants bring economic prosperity they should be treated as potential ontological, and therefore ecological, threats (Hope 2014).

Mediterranean migration flows were very intensely present on the discussion agenda of the political parties competing in the recent elections for the European Parliament (Cowell and Bilefsky 2014). The European Parliament elections constituted a fundamental ground to understand the discursive nature of the ecological narrative applied to the migration arena (Cowell and Bilefsky 2014).

Some of the extreme right-wing political parties that performed very well in those elections, namely in France and the United Kingdom (UK), have a clear anti-migration agenda (Cowell and Bilefsky 2014). The electoral results of European extreme right-wing political parties will have clear spill-over effects on European mainstream and traditionally moderate political parties that are being pressured to adopt harder stances on migration questions (see Cowell and Bilefsky 2014). The far-right political parties, backed by 'euroskeptic media', are constantly fuelling the perception that migration flows are 'spiralling out of control' even when concrete data does not consubstantiate such perception (Cowell and Bilefsky 2014, no pagination; *The Economist* 2010). Marine Le Pen, the current leader of the French Front Nationale, in 2011, referred to Tunisian migrants arriving at Lampedusa as 'the vanguard of a gigantic migratory wave' (Perrault 2011). The homepage of the French Front Nationale states that both regular and irregular migration should be halted since assimilation is not possible on a context of 'mass migration' (Front Nationale 2014, no pagination). The idea that assimilation is not possible derives from the belief that migrants, more than a quantitative risk, constitute a qualitative risk to the cultural cohesion of host countries (see Huysmans 2006). The current leader of Front Nationale, when accused of manipulating the fears of the French people, has also explicitly stated that: '[f]ear can be useful sometimes ... when we are about to fall on a precipice, it is normal to be afraid of falling. It is what we learn as children' (Perrault 2011, no pagination).

Fear-mongering is crucial as a discursive practice among anti-migration political platforms (Charteris-Black 2006). Nigel Farage, the leader of the UK Independence Party, has compared migration flows to the United Kingdom to a 'disaster' (Wintour 2014). Opting for an ecological approach to migration, Farage has stated that 'mass migration has turn (*sic*) Britain into an "unrecognisable" country' (Hope 2014). The leader of UKIP declared that he supports a ban on migration even at the cost of British prosperity (Wintour 2014). In Farage's words: '[i]f you said to me do you want to see another five million people come to Britain, and if that happened we would all be slightly richer, I would say, do you know what, I would rather we were not slightly richer' (Wintour 2014). The 'disaster' and 'invasion' narratives are also employed by Humberto Bossi, the historic leader of the Lega Nord (Northern League), which once claimed that migration can only be stopped through the use of extreme force: '[a]fter the second or third warning, boom ... the cannon roars. The cannon that blows everyone out of the water. Otherwise this business will never end' (BBC 2003). In 2010, a poster of the Northern League displayed a boat loaded with brown and black faces and a slogan saying: '[w]e stopped the invasion' (Charlemagne 2010, no pagination).

Dehumanising the Migrant and Mainstreaming Bare Life

It seems important to discuss racism as a determining factor of the discursive practices that we have been addressing with regard to African migration to Western Europe. Racism performs a role as a constitutive phenomenon of those discursive practices and as a causal factor regarding contemporary migration political and normative public policies reform (see Guillaumin 1995).

It should be discussed if faced with the real fact of daily migrant arrival to European shores – the arrival of de Lucas' (2002) *fobotipo* of illegal immigrants – whether there are concrete spaces, at social and institutional levels, at which it is possible to know specific data about the subjective and particular identity of *newcomers* (de Lucas 2002). The knowledge of such data may favour migrants' swift integration and participation in host societies (de Lucas 2002). However, one should be aware that the interaction between migrants and their host societies is fundamentally asymmetrical and hierarchical since the presence of migrants – 'the others' – in host societies is perceived as inferior, precarious and temporary (see Bauman 2000). A walk through some of the main cities in Europe will demonstrate the existence of hundreds of people, presumably of African origin, attempting to sell objects and to offer their services (e.g. see the discussion on scrap metal collection in Spain in Chapter 9). The picture postcard of young migrants, men and women, running from urban police patrol units is not strange, even if it may be indifferent, to European cities' tourists.

In some situations, these non-citizens have access to precarious jobs in non-qualified segments of the food and lodging industries, in construction companies and in household service. However, outside these identified areas, it is vastly unknown how migrants live. Throughout Europe, it would appear as if there is a certain ignorance, or a tacit choice to ignore, how migrants live, what their religion is, and which schools their children attend. This extends to migrants' opinions on subjects like politics, art or corruption – which they certainly have. In some less fortunate cases, European host societies receive as anecdotal the regrettable news of another shipwreck that causes uncertain numbers of fatalities (see Ward 2014). The death or disappearance of men, women and children causes sympathy, commiseration and moral compassion from the European public (Ward 2014). However, those feelings are temporary and dissolve with the passing of time. The temporary nature of public opinion and compassion empowers the normalisation of boat tragedies involving Mediterranean migrants, which leads to the intensification of norms and measures aiming at the control of migratory movements coming from the African shores through 'gunboat surveillance' (Ward 2014; de Lucas 2013). The intensification of 'gunboat surveillance' has visible consequences for both European states and EU public policies in the migration arena (de Lucas 2013).

As de Lucas notes, migration questions are not approached from a human rights perspective but from instrumental, securitarian and humanitarian/compassion perspectives (de Lucas 2002). An instrumental perspective considers migration in the context of market policies (de Lucas 2002). The securitarian perspective aims to manage and control migration flows (de Lucas 2002). The humanitarian/compassion perspective emerges in contexts of emergency and situations of extreme gravity (de Lucas 2002). The impact of such a perspective is limited since restricted to exceptional circumstances and confined to particular groups and cases benefiting from occasional humanitarian intervention (de Lucas 2002).

It should be noted, whilst not discussing the questions concerning the existence of human races as a pre-requisite for the conceptualization of racism, that the authors are approaching the latter from a social/ideological perspective, and not from a biological perspective (see Wieviorka 1991). This means that racism is discussed here through the observance of the practices of the group or agent that is responsible for racist acts the consequences of which affect particular groups (see Wieviorka 1991). We agree with the concise and simple definition of racism given by Wieviorka that argues that racism is 'the belief in the idea that there is a link between the physical, genetic or biological attributes and heritage of an individual (or group) and his intellectual and moral qualities' (Wieviorka 1991: 18). Xenophobia can be defined in the same terms and as an extension of the concept of racism whenever national origin can be argued as a determining factor of an individual's moral attributes and heritage (see Wieviorka 1991).

When discussing racism and xenophobia we do not consider these concepts as a problem of relation between races, cultures and nationalities (see Wieviorka 1991). We argue, on the contrary, that it is possible to address the contemporary social and political context of Western Europe through the scapegoat theory (see Wieviorka 1991; Girard 1989; Colman 2005). This theory, and as it is mentioned by Wieviorka, emerges in contexts of crisis and implicates particular human groups represented through ideal and degrading stereotypes and as a risk for their host societies who should, at best, tolerate them (Wieviorka 1991: 37).

In this context, the Foucauldian (1997) thesis on the cyclical historical discourse that has legitimised the structure of power established during the French Revolution can serve as the backdrop through which we can understand current southern European countries' policies in the migration arena. Southern European countries have, in fact, faced the migratory, racial and ethnic conflicts by developing three particular power strategies through which they intend to fight the supposed barbaric occurrence of migratory flows: a first strategy concerns nationalities and the phenomenon of language; a second strategy concerns the social and economic consequences of migratory flows; a third strategy, finally, concerns race politics understood as the biological component of the contemporary articulation between power and knowledge (Foucault 1997: 155–6).

The lack of knowledge concerning the 'other' plays a performative role in the construction of migrants as scapegoats (see Wieviorka 1991). It empowers the normalisation of rigid stereotypes, of a frequent biological and forensic nature, that give unity and coherence to popular anti-migration feelings (see Wieviorka 1991). A clear example is given by the anti-migration discourse employed by the French Front Nationale that, through its ideological leader Jean Marie Le Pen, argued that 'Ebola epidemics would be the solution to control African immigration' (Le Monde.fr/AFP 2014, no pagination). Faced with such an outrageous declaration, and far from punishing a clear demonstration of racism and xenophobia, the latest elections for the European Parliament represented a significant triumph for Marine Le Pen's Front Nationale (Le Figaro.fr/Le Monde.fr/AFP 2014). It is clear that the discursive reference to a homogeneous foreigner, represented through fixed stereotypes, is fundamental for the emotional and distorted construction of an unified, impersonal and collective *other* as well for the psychological normalisation of migrants' exclusion and for the adoption of such exclusion on states' public policies in the migration arena (Wieviorka 1991: 63).

Racism is, therefore, strongly empowered and institutionalised by discursive practices employed by both the media and political decision-makers (Wieviorka 1991). When the ideological criteria that support racist practices are unified, segregation, discrimination and violence (Wieviorka 1991 129–71) – or other serious human rights' violations – become imbedded in states' normative discourses and public policies with serious consequences for Mediterranean migrants.

In the context of the discussion concerning migrant detention centres, the debate does not revolve around the physical well-being and integrity of the individuals, nor the fact that children are lodged in the same conditions as the adults, and not even on the omission of legal procedures concerning refugee applications. It is assumed that people in detention centres are violent and, therefore, violence becomes a legitimate resource to be used by the state's apparatus. Racism and xenophobia are so well articulated that they become instrumental concerning states' economies and public policies (Wieviorka 1991). The immediate consequence of this performative role of racism and xenophobia concerning states' economies and public policies is the displacement of the non-citizen individual concerning the reach of supposedly universal human rights (see Benhabib 2004). The consequence of such displacement is, in practice, the non-acknowledgement of the human being (individual) as a legal category (for a discussion see Benhabib 2004).

The increase in migratory flows is frequently represented as a security question (Huysmans 2006). This kind of representation empowers the normalisation and mobilisation of the belief that migration flows are potential causers of chaos (namely urban chaos) and, consequently, the invocation of states of exception, a political status that historically has brought brutal costs for humankind (for a discussion see Huysmans 2006).

European political practices concerning migration are framed by two opposing moral discourses, namely a securitarian narrative (discussed above) and a humanist narrative. Western societies, worn-out by economic austerity and crisis, *buy* the right-wing political narratives that uphold more restrictions concerning migration policies and the criminalisation of migration flows, despite a recent and much contested Italian legislative proposal, in the context of the Lampedusa tragedy of October 2013, to bring to a halt the consideration of irregular migration as a legal felony (Italian Internal Affairs Ministry 2014). Opposing such a narrative, Pope Francis has recently argued for the need to respect the figure of the migrant (La Stampa.it 2014). Simultaneously, the humanitarian crises in Syria, Sudan and Palestine are lamented and less strict migration and asylum laws are called for. In practice, the introduction of reforms in migration policies was delayed due to the 2014 European Parliament elections and their expected results (Bárbulo 2014). Some new regulations concerning the figure of the refugee were introduced. However, those regulations have, essentially, a precarious nature and the virtues of their introduction become doubtful if compared with the intensity of 'gunboat surveillance', and if compared with the fact that individuals that do not reach the European shores do not, in fact, get to exercise their right to claim refugee status (de Lucas 2013). The increasing involvement of the private security sector in this process is discussed in some detail in Chapter 5.

Faced with the scenario described above, it is pertinent to establish a parallel between the contemporary context of European migration with the figure of the *relationship of exception* identified by Agamben in his work *Homo Sacer*, as 'an extreme type of a relationship in which something is only included through its own exclusion' (Agamben 1998 31).

Focusing attention on Mediterranean migration flows indicates that 'gunboat surveillance' (de Lucas 2013) has very diffuse consequences and a very diffuse reach in what concerns the patrolling of the European territorial sea. Such diffused reach is concomitant with the figure of the relationship of exception whereby

> 'the situation created in the exception has the peculiar characteristic that it cannot be defined either as a situation of fact or as a situation of right, but instead institutes a paradoxical threshold of indistinction between the two. It is not a fact, since it is only created through the

suspension of the rule. But for the same reason, it is not even a juridical case in point, even if it opens the possibility of the force of law' (Agamben 1998: 18).

In this context, an alarming relation of similarity can be established among the Nazi execution camps and the maritime territory adjacent to Europe since, in both, the exception as a feature of sovereignty has become the rule. In Agamben's words, the state of exception that constituted the execution camps was 'a portion of territory located outside of the normal legal order' (Agamben 1998: 216). It is visible how in both the historical and the contemporary examples, the same elements are present, namely, 'the absolute independence regarding any kind of judicial control and every reference to the normal legal framework' (Agamben 1998: 215–17), which creates and empowers 'an area of indistinction between the inside and the outside, the exception and the rule, the legal and the illegal' (Agamben 1998: 215–17). The ideological impetus of nationalist ideology – proposed as a 'nationalist revolution' during the Third Reich and contemporarily introduced through more subtle discursive practices – and the *de facto* stripping of citizenship status and rights[2] have reduced individuals to a bare life, whose existence is dependent on the sovereign will and is deprived of all human rights protection (Agamben 1998).

The Cross-Pollination of Political Discourse, Media Discourse, and Public Opinion

While the previous sections alluded to a diversity of legislated and socialised practices detrimental to migrants in the European context, a glaring aspect should be acknowledged: negative discourses surrounding migration, refuge and asylum often circulate across multiple platforms, such that the source of terms and ideas may be difficult to ascertain. For instance, did the tarnished term 'invasion' originate in civil society discourse, did it come from a political level or was it co-opted after an introduction by the media? This would require, no doubt, a completely separate study on language usages in the context of migration.

We do know, however, that the pervasive discourse is oftentimes inflammatory, misguided or simply false (e.g. The Australian Times 2011; Daily Mail 2011; This is Africa 2014; Walker 2011a; 2011b). During the Libyan uprising, for example, it was startling to find frequent reports associating

---

2 In this context, it is clear that in Nazi extermination camps, Jews were stripped of citizenship due to Nuremberg laws. Although there are specific features characterizing Mediterranean migration, and the two cases are in all else not comparable, one element of comparison (and strictly this element) is, nonetheless, useful: in both cases, the subjects were unilaterally stripped of citizenship rights, thrown into a liminal state, and subjected to the rules and regulations imposed on them externally.

sub-Saharan migrants with Gaddafi troops across the media (BBC 2011). These reports almost immediately made the connection between this 'fact' and the decision-making processes through which many migrants and refugees accepted the risk of crossing the sea, out of fear of reprisals. It is difficult to pinpoint whether media reports or political leaders initiated this idea, or whether street-speak climbed through the grapevine and made it to the front pages, becoming a version of the 'truth'; in war, as Phillip Knightley (2003) reminds us, truth is often the first casualty. Either way, it was soon a generalized statement seen on the media, and uttered by politicians and civil society alike. African migrants during the Libyan uprising thus became, by and large, '*murtazaka*', or mercenaries (e.g. BBC 2011; Mensah 2011). This particular subject is comprehensively explored in Chapter 3.

Popular assumptions about refugees and asylum seekers as 'queue jumpers', made in some member states, are such that authorities have, at times, gone out of their way to dispel the myth that these individuals somehow get priority at the border or in accessing social services (e.g. Green 2009, Hammersmith & Fulham Council 2011; Salford Council 2014). While fringe sections of society might harbour such feelings, it is likely they are mostly fostered by repeated allusions to the subject in the press, and certainly by inflamed mention in the speeches of controversial anti-immigration politicians.

Incidentally, when the arguments should go the other way, the transmission of thoughts does not appear to function as efficiently. Two such examples were the riots in Lampedusa and the protests in the Safi Barracks detention centre in Malta. In the former case, migrants called for better conditions in the overcrowded centres (see, for example, Business Insider 2011; Day 2011; Middle East Online 2011; Pisa 2011). In the latter case, protestors called for their release as asylum-seekers under European law, but were met by the Maltese Government's abusive use of force and media muzzling (Peregin 2011; Times of Malta 2011). This event was certainly not an isolated incident: Malta has long been criticized for being heavy-handed in the treatment of detainees (Times of Malta 2005). In a convenient twist, political discourse across the board ignored the root causes of the riots and protests, instead focusing on some misguided form of entitlement the migrants supposedly had (Times of Malta 2011). In both cases, civil society activists and media voices came to their defence.

Perhaps more shockingly, reports about shipwrecks and boats turned away from Europe (and eventually sinking with passengers on board), and about the sheer tragedy of thousands of deaths appear not to capture the attention of anyone except the few reporters and activists blowing the whistle and appealing to public consciousness (e.g. Gates of Vienna 2011; Popp 2014). Public engagement, however, had tended to be lukewarm at best, and easily forgotten amid the flurry of international tragedies that always appear too distant, and too foreign. Politicians are either mute about them or use these horrible events as an opportunity to turn the argument on its head (i.e. stopping the flow of migrants); and civil society has generally ignored all but the most appalling incidents.

Yet, the reality is difficult to hide: according to the International Organization on Migration (IOM) (2014), between January and September 2014, at least 3,072 migrants died unnecessarily in the Mediterranean. Most drowned. These numbers are four-fold those of 2013, and six-fold those of 2012. At least 22,000 migrants have died at sea trying to cross to Europe since the year 2000 (IOM 2014). With these numbers prominently disseminated (Zerrouky 2014), it is almost unbelievable that neither the media, nor politicians, nor civil society – with the exception of a small but loud activist minority – appeared to take notice. Under these circumstances, it must be asked if the glaring indifference of so many Europeans to the dramas unfolding right on their doorstep may be partially justified by the growing influence of extreme right-wing anti-immigrant views in some political quarters, which may have, in turn, contaminated the mainstream (Castles and Miller 2003: 264–6), thereby treating immigrants, refugees, and asylum seekers as objects of politics and helping normalise indifference to the suffering of others. One must surely wonder, in the aftermath of these constant tragedies, and the apparent indifference of so many (Economist 2013), how much is an African life worth? Are certain lives, as Judith Butler (2006) posited, 'worth' more than others, more deserving of mourning and respect?

Conclusions

This chapter has looked at the migration crisis as portrayed in political discourse and practices in Europe and argued that Europe has adopted a set of securitarian tactics to restrict migrants' freedoms, namely their freedom to move, and even to migrate. It has demonstrated that, through a calculated securitisation of migration policies, the EU has been implementing a perspective on migration as a threat, and that this policy is conducive to the devaluation of human dignity, by reducing migrant and refugee lives to precariousness (Butler 2006; see also Huysmans 2006), and influencing decision-making processes among their peers.

The chapter has also examined a selection of social and juridical norms that gradually dehumanized migrants and created an overarching, pervasive state of exception (Agamben 1998). It has shown that this Kafkesque state of exception is assigned to them, whether or not they agree to the norms. They are, in this way, the subject of regulations drafted for them but about which they have no say. The chapter has demonstrated that migrants and refugees are, in this process, relegated to a state Agamben (1998) dubbed 'bare life', unilaterally subjected to and analysed as the mere receivers of normative dispositions, which severely conditions their individual, familiar and collective growth. The chapter has shown these are *de facto* and *de jure* policies and practices adopted broadly across the EU. Those policies and practices are based on an asymmetrical relation between migrants and host countries' authority.

The chapter has also reflected on how the blurring of the lines between political, media and public opinion discourses creates the conditions to substantiate aggressive policies at sea. These, in turn, affect the lives of individuals on board apprehended (or shipwrecked) vessels, and thus ultimately serve as a deterrent to others in source states.

At its core, this chapter addressed the feelings of the *other* as pivotal missing datasets in post-modern societies, and namely in Europe. Using a theoretical framework derived from Wieviorka's analysis of North American race relations, we emphasized that, as an ideology, racism is less a consequence of knowledge about the other and more of a lack of knowledge about the identity of the other (see Wieviorka 1991). As such, diffuse feelings are transformed into conviction and emboldened political action, which perhaps explains the vitriolic nature of the social subtext surrounding migration (Castles and Miller 2003: 266).

This discourse is, no doubt, fuelled by misconceptions, does not seek to understand motivations and identities, and pushes migrants and refugees to stigmatized spaces of foreignness, precariousness, illegality and criminality. This scarcity or total absence of points of contact between migrants and host societies, strengthened by a structural institutional state of unbelonging is, we argued, a functional tool of biopolitics and a Trojan Horse helping to establish the normality of a *permanent* state of exception applicable only to irregular migrant populations, whose consent was never sought, and who, thus, involuntarily send home a message of discouragement. However, as is evident by the increasing number of migrants and refugees trying to reach Europe, this strategy is neither successful in subduing migrants living in a liminal state – such as detention centres – nor in deterring peers from joining them. Ironically, while the former group looks forward to life outside the centres, the latter willingly dreams of a life inside them, seen as a stepping stone to the liminality which, in time, may bring about the expected result: legal recognition. Such is the Kafkesque reality of Europe in the twenty-first century.

Network and migrant experience theory indicates, as Robin Cohen (2006: 131) reminds us, 'that once someone has migrated internationally, he or she is likely to do so again, leading to repeated movements over time'. However, in the current environment along the shores of the Mediterranean, this choice is tantamount to jumping from the frying pan to the fire. With conflict and extremist violence looming all across the Middle East and in parts of Sub-Saharan Africa, and affecting the safety and the livelihood of millions of people, it is reasonable common-sense that any human being with dreams, aspirations and a family to protect, would, given the choice, consider leaving. Many – particularly the young, on whose shoulders the well-being of an extended family often rests – have been shown to consider this option in spite of the hazards along the way (Charlemagne 2013; IRIN 2011). Risk itself is arguably not a significant deterrent (Wittmeyer 2013) in the face of a lack of the conditions for safety and fair livelihood at home. In the greater scheme of things, many will arguably continue to take the risk (IRIN 2011).

And, if they do, the chapter contends that Owen Fiss' argument on integration applies, at least to those who are already within the political community: 'My point is not to subvert the administration process or otherwise open the borders', but to 'insist that laws regarding admission cannot be enforced or implemented in ways that would transform immigrants into pariahs' (Fiss 1999: 16).

References

Agamben, Giorgio (1998) *Homo Sacer. Sovereign Power and Bare Life*, Stanford University Press, Stanford.
Aradau, Claudia and Rens van Munster (2012) *Politics of Catastrophe: Genealogies of the Unknown*, Routledge, London.
Arens, Marianne (2009) 'Italy: Xenophobic immigration policy leads to hundreds of deaths in the Mediterranean', *World Socialist Web Site*, International Committee of the Fourth International, http://www1.wsws.org/articles/2009/aug2009/ital-a27.shtml [20/05/2014].
The Australian Times (2011) 'Gaddafi's migrant invasion plan revealed', *The Australian Times*, 3 October 2011, http://www.theaustralian.com.au/news/world/gaddafis-migrant-invasion-plan-revealed/story-e6frg6so-1226156947214?nk=0745e623fc2ac098dc2cb15a1b82e1a8 [10/2014].
Balzacq, Thierry (2011) *Securitization Theory: How security problems emerge and dissolve*, Routledge, Abingdon.
Bárbulo, Tomás (2014) 'Los Estados son hipócritas con la UE en asuntos de inmigración', *El País*, 19 May 2014, http://politica.elpais.com/politica/2014/05/19/actualidad/1400531142_204821.html [05/06/2014].
Bauman, Zygmunt (2000) *Liquid Modernity*, Polity Press, Cambridge.
BBC (2003) 'Italy on fire on migrants' row', *BBC News*, 16 June 2003, http://news.bbc.co.uk/2/hi/europe/2993718.stm [07/2014].
BBC (2014) 'Libya migrant boat sinks with more than 170 on board', *BBC News*, 23 August 2014, http://www.bbc.com/news/world-africa-28913436 [10/2014].
Benhabib, Seyla (2004) *The Rights of Others*, Cambridge University Press, Cambridge.
Borrud, Gabriel 2012, 'Sarkozy intensifies anti-immigration rhetoric', *Deutsche Welle*, 12 March 2012, http://www.dw.de/sarkozy-intensifies-anti-immigration-rhetoric/a-15703843-1 [06/2014].
Börzel, Tanja and Thomas Risse (2000) 'When Europe hits home: Europeanization and Domestic change', *European Integration Online Papers* 4/15.
Boswell, Christina (2003) 'Burden sharing in the New Age of Immigration', *Migration Policy Institute, Migration Journal*, 1 November 2003, file:///D:/Mig/Burden-sharing%20in%20the%20New%20Age%20of%20Immigration%20_%20migrationpolicy.org.htm [06/2014].
Butler, Judith (2006) *Precarious Life: The powers of mourning and violence*, Verso, London.

Camilleri, Ivan (2005) 'UNHCR "shocked" with Safi Barracks incidents', *The Times of Malta*, 19 January 2005, http://www.timesofmalta.com/articles/view/20050119/local/unhcr-shocked-with-safi-barracks-incidents.101758 [10/2014].

Castles, Stephen and Mark Miller (2003) *The Age of Migration: International population movements in the modern world*, third edition, The Guilford Press, New York.

Charlemagne (2013) 'Adrift about boat people: The deaths off Lampedusa highlight Europe's contradictions about immigration', *The Economist*, 12 October 2013, http://www.economist.com/news/europe/21587802-deaths-lampedusa-highlight-europes-contradictions-over-immigration-adrift-about-boat [10/2014].

Charlemagne (2010) 'No boatloads but still trouble. Sometimes what does not happen is the real news', *The Economist*, 12 August 2010, http://www.economist.com/node/16797747 [07/2014].

Charteris-Black, Jonathan (2006) 'Britain as a container: immigration metaphors in the 2005 election campaign', *Discourse & Society* 17/5 563–81.

Cohen, Robin (2006) *Migration and its enemies: Global capital, migrant labour and the nation-state*, Ashgate, Aldershot.

Colman, Arthur (2005) *Up from Scapegoating: Awakening Consciousness in Groups*, Chiron Publications, North Carolina.

Cowell, Alan and Dan Bilefsky (2014) 'European Agency reports surge in illegal migration, fuelling a debate', *The New York Times*, 30 May 2014 file:///D:/Mig/Burdensharing%20in%20the%20New%20Age%20of%20Immigration%20_%20migrationpolicy.org.htm [06/2014].

Daily Mail (2011) 'Asylum seekers from Arab spring pour into Europe', *Mail Online*, 27 September 2011, http://www.dailymail.co.uk/news/article-2042240/Asylum-seekers-Arab-spring-pour-Europe.html [10/2014].

Day, Michael (2011) 'Police beat Tunisian migrants as "refugee island" is hit by clashes', *The Independent*, 22 September 2014, http://www.independent.co.uk/news/world/europe/police-beat-tunisian-migrants-as-refugee-island-is-hit-by-clashes-2358759.html [10/2014].

Day, Michael (2011b) 'Sarkozy and Berlusconi find a common cause: keep immigrants out', *The Independent*, 27 April 2011, http://www.independent.co.uk/news/world/europe/sarkozy-and-berlusconi-find-a-common-cause-keep-immigrants-out-2275210.html [06/2014].

De Lucas, Javier (2013) 'Between Repression and Paternalism: European Asylum and Immigration Policy after the Lampedusa Tragedy', *Critical Legal Thinking*, 14 December 2013, http://criticallegalthinking.com/2013/12/14/repression-paternalism-european-asylum-immigration-policy-lampedusa/ [06/2014].

De Lucas, Javier (2002) *La herida original de las políticas de inmigración. A propósito del lugar de los derechos humanos en las políticas de inmigración*, Universidad de Valencia, Valencia.

EurActiv (2013) 'EU threatened by "rampant right-wing populism" warns German think tank', *EurActiv*, 5 December 2013, http://www.euractiv.com/eu-elections-2014/rampant-right-wing-populism-thre-news-532119 [06/2014].

European Commission (2004) *Communication from the Commission to the Council, the European Parliament, the European Economic and Social Committee and the Committee of the Regions: Study on the Links between Legal and Illegal Migration*, Commission of the European Communities, Brussels, http://eur-lex.europa.eu/legal-content/EN/TXT/PDF/?uri=CELEX:52004DC0412&from=EN [20/05/2014].

Fiss, Owen (1999) *A community of equals: The constitutional protection of new Americans*, New Democratic Forum, Washington, DC.

Foucault, Michael (1997) *Il faut défendre la société: cours au Collège de France (1975–1976)*, Seuil/Gallimard, Paris.

Front Nationale (2014) 'Stopper l'immigration, renforcer l'identité francaise', www.FrontNationale.com, Le site officiel du Front Nationale, http://www.frontnational.com/le-projet-de-marine-le-pen/autorite-de-letat/immigration/ [06/2014].

Frontex (2014) *Annual Risk Analysis 2014*, European Agency for the Management of Operational Cooperation at the External Borders of the Member-States, Warsaw, http://frontex.europa.eu/assets/Publications/Risk_Analysis/Annual_Risk_Analysis_2014.pdf [06/2014].

Frontex (2013) *Annual Risk Analysis 2013*, European Agency for the Management of Operational Cooperation at the External Borders of the Member-States, Warsaw, http://frontex.europa.eu/assets/Publications/Risk_Analysis/Annual_Risk_Analysis_2013.pdf [06/2014].

Gates of Vienna (2011) 'Camp of Saints: Revised numbers, yet again', *Gates of Vienna*, 3 October 2011, http://gatesofvienna.blogspot.ca/2011/10/camp-of-saints-revised-numbers-yet.html [10/2014].

Gibson, James (1986) *The Ecological Approach to Visual Perception*, Lawrence Erlbaum Associates Publisher, New Jersey.

Girard, René (1989) *The Scapegoat*, Johns Hopkins University Press, Baltimore.

Green, Andrew (2009) 'At last, the truth about immigration and council house queue jumping', *MigrationWatch UK*, 30 June 2009, http://www.migrationwatchuk.org/press-article/64 [10/2014].

Guillaumin, Colette (1995) *Racism, Sexism, Power and Ideology*, Routledge, London.

Hammersmith & Fulham Council (2014) 'Dispelling myths: Questions most asked about people who apply for housing and who are not local residents', 26 April 2011, http://www.lbhf.gov.uk/Directory/Housing/Housing_advice/General_housing_information_and_advice/115629_Dispelling_myths_Housing_non_local_residents.asp [10/2014].

Hope, Christopher (2014) 'Mass Immigration has left Britain 'unrecognisable', says Nigel Farage', *The Telegraph*, 28 February 2014, http://www.telegraph.co.uk/news/politics/ukip/10668996/Mass-immigration-has-left-Britain-unrecognisable-says-Nigel-Farage.html [06/2014].

Human Rights Watch (2011) *The EU's Dirty Hands: Frontex Involvement in Ill Treatment of Migrant Detainees in Greece*, HRW, New York.

Huysmans, Jef (2014) *Security Unbound. Enacting Democratic Limits*, Routledge, Abingdon.

Huysmans, Jef (2006) *The Politics of Insecurity: Fear, Migration and Asylum in the EU*, Routledge, Abingdon.

Ifantis, Kostas (2004) *Addressing Irregular Migration in the Mediterranean*, Center for European Studies, Brussels.

IOM (2014) *Fatal Journeys: Tracking lives lost during migration*, Tara Brian and Frank Laczco, http://www.iom.int/files/live/sites/iom/files/pbn/docs/Fatal-Journeys-Tracking-Lives-Lost-during-Migration-2014.pdf [10/2014].

IRIN (2011) 'Analysis: Why the "Arab Spring" matters to immigrants in Europe', *IRIN News*, 18 July 2011, http://www.irinnews.org/report/93258/analysis-why-the-arab-spring-matters-to-immigrants-in-europe [10/2014].

Italian Internal Affairs Ministry (no date) 'Irregular migration continues to be considered as a criminal felony', http://www.interno.gov.it/mininterno/export/sites/default/it/temi/immigrazione/sottotema002.html [10/08/2014].

Jardine, Nick (2011) 'Lampedusa ablaze as immigrants revolt', *Business Insider*, 21 September 2011, http://www.businessinsider.com/lampedusa-ablaze-as-immigrants-revolt-2011-9 [10/2014].

Knightley, Phillip (2003) *The First Casualty: The war correspondent as hero, propagandist and myth-maker from the Crimea to Iraq*. André Deutsch, London.

Kuisma, Mikko (2013) 'Good' and 'Bad' Immigrants: the economic nationalism of the True Finns' immigration discourse' in Korkut, Umut, Gregg Bucken-Knapp, Aidan McGarry, Jonas Hinnfors and Helen Drake (eds) (2013) *The Discourses and Politics of Migration in Europe*, Palgrave-Macmillan, New York.

Le Figaro.fr 2014, ' "Monseigneur Ebola": la solution de Jean-Marie Le Pen face à l'immigration', 21/05/2014, http://www.lefigaro.fr/pclitique/le-scan/couacs/2014/05/21/25005-20140521ARTFIG00054-monseigneur-ebola-la-solution-de-jean-marie-le-pen-face-a-l-immigration.php [10/08/2014].

Le Monde.fr/AFP 2014, 'Ebola pour "régler" les problèmes d'immigration, une simple "observation", selon M. Le Pen', 21-05-2014, http://www.lemonde.fr/europeennes-2014/article/2014/05/21/pour-jean-marie-le-pen-le-virus-ebola-peut-regler-en-trois-mois-les-problemes-d immigration_4422584_4350146.html [10/08/2014]

Marcelino, Pedro and Hermon Farahi (2011) 'Transitional African Spaces in Comparative Analysis: inclusion, exclusion and informality in Morocco and Cape Verde', *Third World Quarterly*, 32/5 883–904.

McKernan, Bethan (2015) 'Why Al Jazeera stopped using the word migrant (and we probably should too)', *The Independent*, August 2015.

Mensah, Nana (2011) 'Opinion: Libyan Crisis: What is Ghan running away from?', The Joy (Accra), 19 August 2011, http://opinion.myjoyonline.com/pages/feature/201109/73125.php [10/2014].

Middle East Online (2011) 'Riot police beat Tunisian migrants in Italy', *Middle East Online*, 21 September 2011, http://www.middle-east-online.com/english/?id=48155 [10/2014].

Ministero Dell'interno (no date) *Immigrazione clandestina e irregolare*, http://www.interno.gov.it/mininterno/export/sites/default/it/temi/immigrazione/sottotema002.html [08/2014].

Morozov, Evgeny (2011) 'After the Arab Spring: the Current State of the Internet & Democracy Debate', Stanford University. Center on Democracy Development and the Rule of Law, Program on Liberation Technology. 1 December 2011, http://liberationtechnology.stanford.edu/events/podcasts/page/3/ [05/2014].

Musolff, Andreas (2011) 'Migration, Media and 'deliberate metaphors'', *Methaphorik*, http://www.metaphorik.de/sites/www.metaphorik.de/files/journal-pdf/21_2011_musolff.pdf [20/05/2014].

Peregin, Christian (2011) 'Safi riot not entirely surprising - UNHCR', *The Times of Malta*, 18 August 2011, http://www.timesofmalta.com/articles/view/20110818/local/Safi-riot-not-entirely-surprising-UNHCR.380656 [10/2014].

Perrault, Guillaume (2011) 'Marine Le Pen s'invite à Rome et songe à Lampedusa', *Le Figaro*, 8 March 2011, http://www.lefigaro.fr/politique/2011/03/07/01002-20110307ARTFIG00650-marine-le-pen-s-invite-a-rome-et-songe-a-lampedusa.php [07/2014].

Pisa, Nick (2011) 'Dozens of police and immigrants injured as crowd of 1,000 Tunisians clash with authorities at Italian holding centre', *Mail Online* (London), 22 September 2014, http://www.dailymail.co.uk/news/article-2040343/Dozens-police-immigrants-injured-crowd-1-000-Tunisians-clash-authorities-Italian-holding-centre.html [10/2014].

Pop, Valentina (2011) 'EU border agency keen to send back more Tunisians', *euobserver*, 9 April 2011, http://euobserver.com/justice/32150 [20/05/2014].

Popp, Maximilian (2014) 'Europe's deadly borders: An inside look at EU's shameful Immigration policy', *Der Spiegel Online*, 11 September 2014, http://www.spiegel.de/international/europe/europe-tightens-borders-and-fails-to-protect-people-a-989502.html#spRedirectedFrom=www&referrrer= [10/2014].

Salford Council (2014) 'Asylum Seekers: Some myths and truths', 26 June 2014, http://www.salford.gov.uk/asylum-myths.htm [10/2014].

Samuel, Henry and Bruno Waterfield (2014) 'Jean-Marie Le Pen: Ebola epidemic would solve immigration problems', *The Telegraph*, 21 May 2014, http://www.telegraph.co.uk/news/worldnews/europe/france/10847344/Jean-Marie-Le-Pen-Ebola-epidemic-would-solve-immigration-problems.html

Sauer, Tobias (2011) 'Transit station for the 'human tsunami'', 29 July 2011, *The new federalist.eu*, http://www.thenewfederalist.eu/Transit-station-for-the-human-tsunami [06/2014].

Schult, Christoph (2011) '"The Situation is Escalating": Europe's Frontex Border Guard Stretched to Limit', *Spiegel Online International*, 21 February 2011.

Sherwood, Harriet (2011) 'Libya's detention centres accused of torturing migrants and refugees', *The Guardian*, 22 June 2014, http://www.theguardian.com/world/2014/jun/22/libyas-detention-centres-accused-torturing-migrants-refugees [10/2014].

This Is Africa (2014) 'Dutch cartoonist mocks African migrants', *This Is Africa*, 27 May 2014, http://thisisafrica.me/dutch-cartoonist-mocks-african-migrants/ [10/2014].

The Scottsman (2009) 'Split grows over Italy's crackdown on boat people as 73 are left to die', *The Scottsman*, 18 September 2009, http://www.scotsman.com/news/split-grows-over-italy-s-crackdown-on-boat-people-as-73-are-left-to-die-1-775580 [10/2014].

Times of Malta (2011) 'Riot no way to criticise detention policy, says government', *The Times of Malta*, 19 August 2011, http://www.timesofmalta.com/articles/view/20110819/local/Riot-no-way-to-criticise-detention-policy-says-government.380880 [10/2014].

van Munster, Rens (2009) *Securitizing Immigration: The Politics of Risk in the EU*, Palgrave Macmillan, Basingstoke.

Vatican Insider (2014) 'Tragedie dei migranti, il Papa: non basta rincorrere emergenze', *La Stampa.it*, 15 May 2014, http://www.lastampa.it/2014/05/15/esteri/vatican-insider/it/il-papa-limmigrazione-forzata-tragedia-epocale-non-basta-rincorrere-emergenze-uEAC0dbB8MB8fDSRB16aNO/pagina.html [08/2014].

Walker, Brenda (2011a) 'North Africans flee the Arab Spring', *Limits to Growth*, 3 April 2011, http://www.limitstogrowth.org/articles/2011/04/03/north-africans-flee-the-arab-spring/ [10/2014].

Walker, Brenda (2011b) 'Europe Faces Illegal Alien Tide as Gaddafi Revenge', *Limits to Growth*, 5 September 2011, http://www.limitstogrowth.org/articles/2011/09/05/europe-faces-illegal-alien-tide-as-gaddafi-revenge/ [10/2014].

Ward, Benjamin (2014) 'Europe's spectacle of compassion for migrants', *Open Democracy*, 15 May 2014, file:///J:/Europe%E2%80%99s%20spectacle%20of%20compassion%20for%20migrants%20_%20openDemocracy.htm [10/2014].

Wieviorka, Michel (1991) *L'espace du racisme*, Seuil, Paris.
Willsher, Kim (2014) 'Jean Marie Le Pen Suggests Ebola as solution to global population explosion' *The Guardian*, Wednesday 21 May 2014, http://www.theguardian.com/world/2014/may/21/jean-marie-le-pen-ebola-population-explosion-europe-immigration [08/2014].
Wintour, Patrick (2014) 'Nigel Farage: UKIP wants five-year ban on immigrants settling in UK', *The Guardian*, 7 January 2014, http://www.theguardian.com/politics/2014/jan/07/ukip-ban-immigrants-nigel-farage, [07/2014].
Wittmeyer, Alicia (2013) 'What's an African Life Worth? What crocodile-infested rivers and hovercrafts tell us about how people value their own safety', *Foreign Policy*, 9 December 2013, http://www.foreignpolicy.com/articles/2013/12/02/what_s_an_african_life_worth [10/2014].
Zerrouky, Madjid (2014) 'Déjà 3 000 morts cette année en Méditerranée'. *Le Monde*, 19 September 2014, http://www.lemonde.fr/les-decodeurs/article/2014/09/19/deja-3-000-morts-cette-annee-en-mediterranee_4489095_4355770.html?utm_source=dlvr.it&utm_medium=twitter#xtor=RSS-3208 [10/2014].

3 Contested Views of the Causes of Rural to Urban Migration amongst Pastoralists in Niger

Julie Snorek

Figure 3.1 Trucks of Libya returnees arriving at the transit center in Dirkou, Niger (IOM 2011).

Introduction

This chapter identifies and explores the linkages between the changing human security of societies in the Sahel and the decision by individuals and groups of these societies to embark upon the dangerous route across the Sahara and into the Mediterranean Region. Specifically, the lens is focused on those who live in the most fragile and marginal regions of the Sahel-Saharan band, in other contexts known as the pastoral zone in Niger, a country that shares its northern border with the currently politically unstable state of Libya. In this part of Niger, households are dependent upon a temporary form of rural-to-urban migration, which has been considered a tradition for more than a century. Yet, the key problems facing the rural system that dominates the nation's economy are being exacerbated by uncertain and variable rainfall, the precarious, unequal and haphazard development of the pastoral system, short-sighted governance and limited protection of ecosystems, and terms of trade that favour exploitation of smallholders. Drought emerges as the most critical factor to smallholders (pastoralists) who attempt to adapt to the climatic shocks through the only economic and institutional means available. For many, this means migration for some or all family members. In critical times, those who stay behind become 'trapped' in their home territories and dependent upon remittances from migrants and the trickle-in of humanitarian aid.

The desperation and exasperation of Sub-Saharan migrants has been evident in current times. These complex factors form the basis of the context in which we will present the perspective of the migrants from their 'trapped' families in Niger, exploring migration decisions and perceptions of the social and ecological changes to the rural system. The changes occurring in the Sahelo-Saharan zone indicate social and ecological tipping points for the rural populations, which foreshadow an increase of migration in the near future.

Movement of people has been unprecedented in recent years. At the global scale, many communities are experiencing multiple climate hazards, which have produced increasing human insecurities and enhanced the potential of individuals and groups to migrate, sometimes on a large scale, on a temporary or permanent basis. António Guterres, the United Nations High Commissioner for Refugees, points to the emergence of globalisation, unresolved poverty and enduring human insecurity as new trends in global displacement patterns (Guterres 2008). Nearly 17 million people were displaced by natural hazards (including drought) in 2009 and 42 million in 2010 (Foresight 2011), and evidence has emerged that more than 100,000 migrants landed in Europe during the first six months of 2015, over half of which crossed the Mediterranean from Libya (IOM 2015).

The questions pursued in this chapter are: *What is driving migration decisions of those leaving rural areas in the Sahel? More specifically, what are the social, demographic, economic, political, climatic/ecological, and psychological influences on households contributing to the decision to migrate? And, how important are environmental factors in migration decisions?* To explore these phenomena in light of the changing human security of the Mediterranean Region, this chapter examines the reasons for social and ecological change in rural areas, aiming specifically to understand if the environment is an important factor in migration from rural Sahel to urban areas in the Mediterranean Region. We propose that a more resilient ecological system has the capacity to better support rural livelihoods and thus contributes to lessen upheaval and migration. The chapter is divided into three parts: first, a description of the geopolitical and historical context of the region, then a depiction of current conceptual views on environmental push factors for migration, followed by the presentation of the data, and concluding with a general discussion of the findings and recommendations for managing migration and ecological resilience in Sahel societies. The information from this chapter provides the social and ecological context to current and future migration scenarios in light of continuing movement towards the Mediterranean Region and points to a need to establish greater resilience amongst rural groups.

Contemporary and Pre-Colonial Migration Trends

In the course of only seven months in 2011, more than 89,000 Nigeriens returned to Niger from the northerly neighbour Libya, escaping revolution, war and racial violence, some of which is based upon perceptions of Sub-Saharan Africans being 'Al Ghaddafi's mercenaries' (IOM 2011). The majority of these returnees had been supporting their families through the more plentiful economic opportunities in Libya prior to the civil war. The profiles of repatriated migrants reflected 99% males aged 20 to 40 years, not formally educated (82%) and working primarily in construction or agricultural labour while in Libya (IOM 2011). For the most part (93%), these individuals returned alone to their homes in Niger, those in which they had been supporting an average of five family members with the remittances from Libya (IOM 2011). Of registered returnees, 36.5% returned to areas in the pastoral zone of Tahoua in Niger, a region that experiences particularly high levels of out-migration (FEWSNET 2011). Approximately 384,400 Nigeriens were affected by the loss of remittances, and 137,386 of these are within the Tahoua region alone (IOM 2011).

The Libya crisis also permitted the filtering of arms into the arsenals of several latent non-state militant groups in the Sahel, including the Movement National pour la Liberation de l'Azawak (MNLA), the Movement for Unity and Jihad in West Africa (MUJAO), and Al Qaeda of the Islamic Maghreb (AQIM). Previous rebellions led by Tuareg leaders of groups similar to the MNLA took place from 1962–1964, 1990–1995, and 2007–2009 but never achieved the extent of success as this uprising in Mali. Since the civil war broke out in January 2012, over 470,000 refugees and internally displaced persons have been reported by UNHCR (2013). More than 23,000 of the refugees are being hosted in Tahoua (April 2013 UNHCR). This has exacerbated current problems in the region including food, water, and livelihood insecurity and has promoted remigration into neighbouring countries, including Libya.

To better understand this state of affairs, one must first examine history. The pre-colonial and colonial patterns of migration and governance frame the traditional modes of adaptation to drought. Prior to the period of French colonisation in the late nineteenth century, the area now considered to be Mali and Niger (Figure 3.3) was dominated by sedentary and nomadic Kel Tamashek (Tuareg) groups, who controlled the trade routes (Figure 3.2). From 1804 until the period of colonisation, the Sokoto Caliphate ruled from Burkina Faso to Cameroon, and across the southern border of Niger and Mali. The Tuareg controlled the trans-Saharan trade and, as a result, held stable relations with the leaders of the Sokoto Caliphate, receiving tribute and slaves in return for their transport of goods. During extended periods of drought that characterise the Sahel and Sahara, pastoralists and farmers in northern regions (Niger, Mali) migrated into the forests of their southern neighbours, staying until their herds were reconstituted. Pastoralists held tenure as far south as Kano and Katsina, but this changed during the colonial period (Snorek et al. 2014).

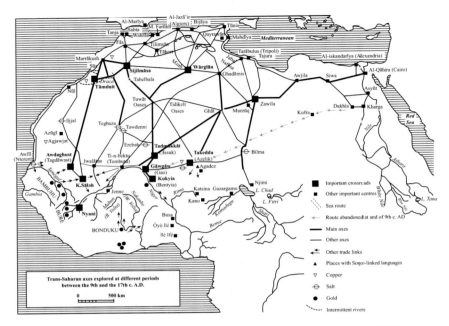

Figure 3.2 Pre-colonial West African trade routes (De Moraes Farias, 2003, Bentyia (Kukyia); http://afriques.revues.org/1174

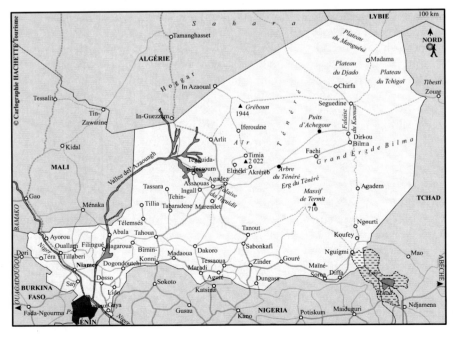

Figure 3.3 Modern-day Niger (Source: Hachette Tourism)

After the Berlin Conference of 1884–1885, Colonial West Africa was divided, drawing arbitrary borders separating the societies within the African Mediterranean Region from their southern neighbours in the Sahel (made up of Senegal, Guinea-Bissau, Gambia, Mauritania, Mali, Burkina Faso, Niger, and Chad) and preventing free movement (Figure 3.3). The adaptive systems of lengthy migration were no longer functional by the time colonisation ended in the 1960s. When the two great droughts hit the Sahel in 1974 and 1985, the populations no longer had the networks and systems that would allow them the same ease of access to southern lands (Snorek et al. 2014).

Instead, many pastoralists migrated North into the Sahara after the two periods of significant drought in the twentieth century, following offers from Al-Ghaddafi to provide labor visas to migrants, especially the Tuareg who, incensed by the Nigerien government's lack of attention to their needs in the recent drought crisis (Guichaoua 2008), sought military assistance to wage their own rebellion. Al-Ghaddafi used these migrants to fight in his wars as mercenaries. The income from this and other forms of work in Libya served to support the stabilisation of pastoral households after the droughts, pushing an ongoing northward migration. Despite the current continuing war in Libya, the governor of Agadez stated that in 2014, nearly 3,000 migrants per week make the treacherous journey across the desert, and the costs in both human lives and monetary value are increasing (Lewis 2014).

Vulnerability to Climate Change and Migration Decisions

Since the 1990s, a debate regarding the social and ecological reasons for migration, with climate change as a central factor, has dominated certain political and academic forums (Warner et al. 2008; Trolldalen et al. 1992; Richmond 1993; Rathgeber 2008). There is a dialectic relationship between the environment and the social, economic, cultural and political factors that condition and are conditioned by it. The decision to migrate is a result of social-demographic, psychological, economic, political, and climate/environmental push factors in the origin location and multiple personal and institutional pull factors in the host location (Figure 3.4), with environmental factors predicted to increase in influence (Renaud et al. 2011). Such pull factors contributing to rural-urban migration are generally assumed to be related to the supply of labor in the industrially-based economies, more often located in urban centres (Barrios et al. 2006). Push factors can include the loss of economies in the origin location, including rainfall variability in Sub-Saharan Africa (Barrios et al. 2006). Migration has emerged as a tool to both maintain the current livelihoods through remittances and adapt to an entirely new livelihood (Barrios et al. 2006; Boana et al. 2008; Barnett and Webber 2009; Black et al. 2011a), occasionally on a large scale to urban areas, contributing to the development of urban slums in mega-cities around the globe (Warner 2009; Parnell and Walawege 2011; Black et al. 2011b).

While many factors influence migration decisions, the influence of climate and environmental change should not be negated (Renaud 2011),

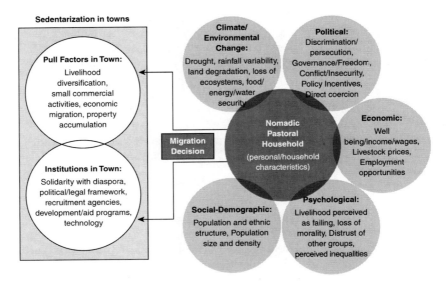

Figure 3.4 Process of sedentarization of nomadic groups, adapted from Black et al. (2011a) and Foresight Report (2011)

especially given the current high rates of ecosystem degradation (MA 2005) and frequency of climate change events (IPCC 2007). The terms *environmental migrants* and *environmental displacees* are used to describe voluntary or forced movement from their usual place of residence (Dun et al. 2007; Renaud et al. 2007). Environmental displacees migrate due to either rapid or slowly deteriorating environmental conditions and are forced to leave their usual place of residence because their lives, livelihoods and welfare have been placed at serious risk (Dun et al. 2007). Environmental migrants take a more proactive stance and migrate voluntarily due to the changing environmental conditions. Migrants are those individuals who have settled in towns or city centres (internally or through international migration) and non-migrants are those individuals who have remained in areas where some of the population has been pushed out.

These latter groups are often the extreme poor, members of marginalised groups, women, the elderly and children and are forced to stay in place because drought or other hazards have consumed any resources that could support mobility. These so-called 'trapped populations' are more likely to face multiple vulnerabilities because they are rendered unable to move away from environmental threats due to a lack of capital (Black 2011a). Trapped populations may increase in future decades because they are unable to move from locations that are extremely vulnerable to climate change.

Vulnerability and Migration in the Context of Tahoua, Niger

Niger provides an interesting case to examine vulnerability-based migration, as it is essentially a rural and agrarian economy. The UNDP's 2013 Human Development Report ranks Niger as 188th of 188 countries as the poorest country in the world (UNDP 2014). Of Niger's 19.1 million people (World Bank 2014), about half, or 48.9% are living below the poverty line (UNICEF 2012). Niger has one of the highest population growth rates in the world (3.6%), which aggravates the country's resource scarcity for its rapidly increasing population. All but 10% of the country's population lives less than 100 miles from the greener southern border with Nigeria, and 86% of the population lives in rural areas (République 2011). The country was divided geographically by the 1961 Decree into a southern cultivation zone and a northern pastoral zone, which was unofficially designated around the 350-mm (based on 1961 estimates) rainfall isohyets (Figure 3.5). Primary rain-fed crop production includes millet, sorghum, cotton and corn. Livestock (donkeys, sheep, goats, camels and cattle) are exported by the thousands to neighbouring Nigeria, where they demand a higher price than in Niger. The rate of urban growth is currently 4.3% (in 2012), and future projections expect the rate to increase to 5.7% by the year 2030 (UNICEF 2012). It is expected that urbanisation will be primarily due to demographic increases and rural-urban migration.

The greatest impact to the country's vulnerability is the weather. Slow-onset environmental change in the Sahel has already been widely documented (Hulme 1996; Nicholson et al. 1993; UNEP 1992; D'amato and Lebel 1998). Nicholson and Paulo documented changes in rainfall after the relatively wet 1950s (1993). Hulme (1996) assessed that there is little evidence of desiccation in any area on the globe except the Sahel. His conservative estimate of rainfall loss in the Sahel is 96.8 mm of rainfall per century (1 mm in annual rainfall since the 1900s). The 1990s showed a slight increase in rainfall (Brooks 2004), and this was followed by a higher frequency of drought events, in 2005, 2010 and 2012 and flooding events in late 2010 and 2013 (FEWSNET 2011; OCHA 2013). Other assessments point to high levels of rainfall variability as depicting long-term trends in the Sahel (Desanker and Magadza 2001; Hengsdijk and van Kuelen 2002; Giannini et al. 2013). The high frequency of drought and flood hazards in the Sahel is set to increase in the context of climate change (IPCC 2013).

Pastoral and Urban Case Study Areas

As stated by Lavinge Delville, 'immediate impacts can only be evaluated in their social context' (Warren et al. 2001: 84). Environmental change is rarely the main cause for rural to urban migration, but the value of understanding how ecological change relates to social decision-making is important to both policy and development leaders. By charting the case histories of internally displaced pastoralists who have settled in villages and towns of Niger over the course of the last ten years, we can understand the processes that are promoting this sedentarization of pastoralists as well as other factors that might be influencing this cultural shift. These histories define not only the reasons for their departure, but also what is shaping the current environment to make it uninhabitable and what makes the cities more appealing and desirable.

For the migrant sites, Niamey and Abalak provide the most interesting juxtaposition of internal migration sites based on the resources, cultural make-up and opportunities in both places. Niamey is the largest city and the capital and is located on the banks of the Niger River. According the National Institute for Statistics, Niamey held 750,000 residents in 2005, with an annual 4.8% growth rate. A melting pot of cultural groups from multiple countries, Niamey provides many opportunities for work, training and education. The city has also been an unfriendly host for many minority groups, such as Tuareg and Wodaabe pastoralists. Those former pastoralists who have little to no education or vocational training often take positions as guardians of infrastructure (where they also

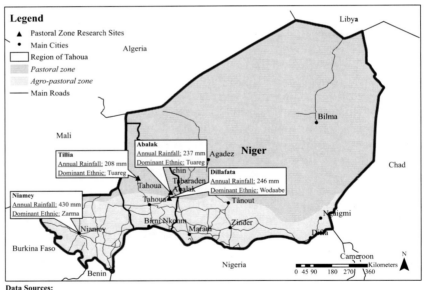

Data Sources:
FEWS NET (2011): Niger Livelihood Zones. (http://www.fews.net/sites/default/files/files/documents/reports/NE_Livelihoods_2011.pdf) World Bank: Climate Change Knowlewdge Portal (http://sdwebx.worldbank.org)

Figure 3.5 Main research sites in Niger (Livelihood zones: FewsNet (2011) and CILSS (2005); Rainfall data 1990–2009, World Bank Climate Change Knowledge Portal, map produced by Haas of UNU-EHS 2014)

sometimes receive housing) or many risk eviction living as squatters on underdeveloped land.[1]

The town of Abalak, located in the administrative region Tahoua is comprised primarily of former pastoralists and their families, though the town was merely a well and a school in the early 1970s. Today, population estimates for the city range from 13,555 to 39,000 persons[2]. Original migrants settled in Abalak in the aftermath of the 1973–1974 and 1984–1985 droughts, and concurrent droughts have brought successive waves of migrants. While Abalak has electricity, is located on a major road and hosts an important cattle market, finding work in Abalak is extremely difficult. Economic opportunities for unskilled workers in Abalak that require little or no capital investment include brick making, transporting water for construction, farming or selling items in a modest boutique. As a very last resort due to restrictive cultural norms, those who have no other choice will ask for alms or accept waiting in line to receive food aid, but such behaviour is considered highly shameful by residents of Abalak. Those with capital start small commercial ventures, construction companies, travel agencies, and non-governmental organisations. Others travel abroad to neighbouring countries where jobs are more plentiful and they can send remittances home. Women, who are typically not permitted to leave the home unaccompanied in Abalak, are particularly vulnerable when male relatives are absent.

Also in the pastoral zone, the commune of Tillia (located near the Mali border) and small hamlet (constituting too little infrastructure to be a village) Dillafata (approximately 23.3 km southwest of Abalak) were chosen as non-migrant research sites due to the prevalence of both increasing sedentarization and irrigated and rain-fed farming as well as pastoral activities in situ. Dillafata maintains a primary school, a cement well, a small boutique, a cement grain bank, and a cement fodder bank[3]. Of the approximately 110 households in Dillafata, 20 of these are living permanently in the village, while the remaining households maintain a state of semi-nomadicism. A major income for individuals in Dillafata is economic migration (30%) and their main challenge is the conflicts and degradation produced by transitory herders bringing cattle from southern farming villages.

Tillia on the contrary is a rural commune for which the inhabitants (31,175 individuals living in 22,000 km² or 1.5 inhabitants per km) comprise

---

1 I observed the destruction of one particularly important squatted area in a neighbourhood called Chateau Un. In 2007, the nearly 1000 squatters lost their belongings and livelihoods when arsonists started a fire late in the evening in Chateau Un. Now, the area is being developed by the owners.
2 This disparity is due to the large numbers of itinerant herding families who exit the pastoral plains to settle in Abalak during the dry season when water and food is scarce.
3 Most of the infrastructure was built since 1999 with the support of JEMED (Jeunesse en Mission Entraide et Developpement), a Tearfund-funded non-governmental project working in the pastoral zone with a headquarters in Abalak.

primarily Tuareg (70%) and Fulani (22%, includes also Wodaabe) pastoralists (Reform 2009). Tillia hosts 278 villages, hamlets and camps and possesses 129 wells, 80% of which are not fully functional or defective. Other water sources are minimal, including four pastoral wells (*contre puit*) and three borehole wells, which constitutes a 37.6% rate of coverage for the entire population of Tillia. Tillia also has a health centre, maternity centre, five primary schools that convene 60% of the students, and one middle school. The economic activities are primarily pastoral with some irrigated and rain-fed agriculture.

Three Types of Migrants

The first phase of research was conducted over a period of two months from May to June 2010 in Abalak, Dillafata and Niamey involving 15 households of 11 men and 4 women aged 18 to 100 years old and utilising qualitative and participatory research methods to record using both audio and some video case histories of both migrants and non-migrants related to both personal livelihoods and motivations for settlement in towns (within the past 10 years). Whenever possible, a female interpreter was used for interviews with women participants. The second phase of research took place over a period of two months in 2011 and engaged three female-led and 16 male-led pastoral households in Tillia to understand vulnerabilities to their livelihoods. Secondary data from IOM, expert interviews, and a thorough literature review provided triangulation for the field data as well as guidance for site selection. For migrants, the questionnaire addressed migrants' former and current livelihoods, reasons contributing to their decision to migrate, and observations of environmental change. For non-migrants or current nomadic pastoralists, the questionnaire addressed the difficulties of living in the rural area, observations of environmental change, vulnerabilities to their livelihood, and reasons that others (friends and relatives) in the location had migrated.

In the analysis, several elements were identified related to the participant's decision making process that represent environmental migration or displacement. Analysis served to identify trends and commonalities in responses based upon the research framework. Three types of migrants were identified: economic migrants, environmental migrants, and environmental displacees (Table 3.1).

Migration Decisions of Niger's Pastoralists

Profiles of Movers and Stayers

Despite the high rates of sedentarization in rural villages and towns in the pastoral zone, there are strong cultural aversions to a strictly sedentary life. As stalwart pastoralists, Tuareg, WoDaaBe, and Fulani pastoralists find

Table 3.1 Typology of migrants

Type	Definitions
Economic Migrant	A person who travels from their place of residence to another city or country in order to improve his or her standard of living (proactive).
Environmental Migrant	(Dun et al. 2007) primarily due to environmental concerns or reasons, people who have decided voluntarily to move from their usual place of residence. (proactive)
Environmental Displacee	(Dun et al. 2007) due to either rapid or slowly deteriorating environmental conditions, such people are forced to leave their usual place of residence because their lives, livelihoods, and welfare have been placed at serious risk (reactive).

meaning through their relationship with nature and their livestock, while disparaging the work and lifestyle of sedentary cultures via their cultural symbols and language. As shown by Loftsdottir (2001), a Wodaabe man sees himself as a slave to his cattle. A Tuareg proverb refers to a house with four walls as a tomb (Clarke 1978). Participants referred to agricultural work of the neighbouring Hausa as 'drudgery' to a Wodaabe or 'slave's work' to a Tuareg, and those who leave the bush and settle in the city are still considered by many to be 'lost' or even, 'dead.'

The majority of Abalak migrants arrived less than five years ago, in the aftermath of the drought of 2004. These typically have never before lived and worked in a town setting and received no schooling outside of rudimentary Koranic lessons led by parents. 'I didn't know anything about the town before coming here . . . Since I was born, I have been behind the animals' (#9)[4]. An old man who settled in Abalak five years ago stated, 'No one [helped me move here]. I trembled the entire way to town' (#14). Such migrants also exhibit nostalgia, referring to the way of life in the pastoral zone as the true 'luxury,' defined as the ability to drink the milk of one's animals. The pastoral zone in Niger lacks health centres, schools, roads, markets, and abundant or reliable water sources. In many places, there are not any water resources, despite an abundance of pasture. However, it was difficult to find evidence of migrants seeking access to school, health, water, or markets can be perceived as the primary reasons for migration. Rather, it seems as though most possessed an aversion to staying in town, despite the availability of services. 'There is not a single reason to come into town except that our animals are all dead and nomadic life has changed . . . Here in town there are many people who would like to return to the bush if the environmental situation changes' (#15). They often buy animals with their first earnings in town and send them to non-migrant relatives, contributing

---

4 Participants in the study are represented numerically in the text.

to feed, water and other items to sustain and reconstitute the herd. 'When I lived in the pastoral zone, I never had the intention of coming into town. For me, life is the bush, *la brousse*. There is nothing better than it' (#10). 'Now, if I found animals, I would not even spend the night here. I would leave directly for the bush' (#10).

Niamey migrants on the contrary favoured instead the benefits of development that the city provides such as access to schools and jobs, international markets (for artisan's crafts), social connections, and overall better conditions. Several participants (#19, #20) stated that they chose to come to Niamey because of relatives or friends moving to or already living in the city. The female participant mentioned that she came to Niamey following her familial relations (#18). Moreover, Niamey participants find sufficient opportunities in the city, and thus few spoke of wanting to return to pastoralism. Families of former pastoralists in Niamey are typically larger than those of their counterparts in the other research sites, with particularly greater numbers of children in school. These participants typically find work as guardians or artisans or are unemployed. While the majority of participants expressed nostalgia for *ehare* (having animals), several, especially young people, easily disdained the rural life as too difficult. Instead, they prefer the ease and facility of the city. As one participant stated:

> I'm going to tell you something. You can't compare ease to difficulty. For example, here, my children all have access to schooling. . . . And, thanks to God, each morning, I am able to give them something with which they can buy their needs (money). All this would not be possible in the bush. (#17)

One female participant lived on an undeveloped plot in Niamey. Having grown up beneath the *ehan* (tent) of the Azawak, she expressed deep nostalgia for the bush. 'It's only an obligation that we live within four walls.' Yet, her children had a strong aversion to a difficult life in the pastoral zone.

Non-migrants are not experiencing the 'luxury' spoken about by nostalgic migrants; rather they are finding that pastoralism cannot fulfill their household demands as in years past. Wodaabe women typically produce cheese from the milk of the animals, but find that now milk shortages have pushed them to seek out other activities. During the dry season, women travel on temporary migration to Nigeria and other countries to sell traditional medicine and handicrafts or engage in prostitution. Many more men are finding that 'the bush has refused them' (#7), and leave their livestock with a single shepherd in order to seek seasonal work in Niamey, Nigeria, Ghana, and other southern countries to work as labourers, security guards, shepherding or carving out calabash bowls. '[Those who left] had problems here . . . The reason they leave is because there isn't any food. If there's no food, cows, or animals, they have to go and find something for their children' (#6). Conditions reported back from Nigeria are also not favourable.

Participants reported being harassed, beaten or thrown in jail during their time abroad, 'but they go because they have to' (#5). Risk is also incurred when leaving behind one's family and animals, the latter of which are often neglected by the remaining shepherds. Those staying to guard the herds often are faced with the most difficult constraints due to limited pastoral resources. 'The cows do not have any food. I don't have any other work that I know how to do, so I have to walk far to find where the grass is' (#7).

Environmental Services Disappearing

Pastoralism includes the ability to understand the location and abundance of specific pastoral species that maintain the health and nutrition of the herd. Participants collectively confirmed 33 different species of trees and grasses that are no longer found in the rural area since about 20 years. Women pastoralists noted that specific medicinal herbs used to treat family ailments are disappearing due to desiccation, drought and overgrazing. Reasons for these environmental changes were mainly cited as due to climate. 'Rain, wind, heat has killed the trees' (#7).

> The changing weather is clear. Everyone is aware of it. Because, before, there was lots of pasture and lots of rain. And, when there is a lot of rain we can have what is called ibinkar in the dry season. This means that even the small wells give water all throughout the dry season. And now, since there is no more rain, there is no ibinkar ... the rainfall diminishes every year. (#15)

Concurrently, the reduction in species abundance impacts animal health. Six out of seven participants indicated that diminishing supplies of milk had impacted their household eating habits. 'We used to have an abundance of milk, then there was less and less' (#9). The number of cows necessary to produce enough milk to sustain the family has increased from one or two to seven cows over the past 20 years. Households now purchase cereals (rice, millet, sauce-making ingredients) to supplement the milk that is missing from their diet.

Institutions Supporting the Decline

Governmental institutions and legislation have not supported management of scarce resources in the pastoral zone. Population growth in the south is significantly higher than in pastoral households, due in part to the cultural and livelihood demands of farming households, which have an average of 7.4 children per woman. The natural resources in the pastoral zone are seen as the last frontier for individuals seeking to cultivate land. Local pastoralists observe illegal cultivation (based on the 1961 pastoral zone decree), wood or pasture extraction (#9, #13) and the penetration by large herds owned by southern land-holders (Woodke 2008; Snorek et al. 2014). Southern herds have been using the northern pasture since as early as 1940 (Marty 1989), but the influx of livestock has greatly increased in the last 10 years (Woodke 2005).

Non-migrants in Dillafata expressed exasperation at the changing norms of management. 'When the Wodaabe say "No, you can't do that" to the Hausa people [cutting grass], then that brings fights' (#7). Conflict, sometimes violent, over access to and control of water sources, pasture, and seasonal lakes were widely reported by almost all non-migrants.

> Pastoralists are afraid of the years. They are afraid of what is happening in these years . . . because there is no grain, no water . . . they don't know if there's going to be those things in the future. I've seen someone hit someone until the head bleeds because of grass. I've seen someone kill another person over water . . . [Yet] they want to stay with the cows because that is their life. (#7)

Self-Sufficiency through Adaptation?

Pastoralists are generally perceived as less vulnerable to fluctuations in rainfall due to their mobility (Henry et al. 2004; McLeman and Smit 2006; Pei and Zhang 2014). Yet changes to rainfall coupled with increasing land use pressures, limited pastoral mobility, and conflict over resource access produce a dire future for pastoralists (Pei and Zhang 2014; Snorek et al. 2014). As a result, the pastoralists of the Sahel who have for centuries adapted to great environmental extremes are struggling to adapt.

This is most apparent during the *soudure* or hungry season (May–July, typically). Finding pasture becomes especially challenging for herders due to multiple hydrological and social pressures. While many pastoralists have a traditional territory to which they make the yearly migration, laws prevent the limitation of access to pasture and water in the pastoral zone. These laws sometimes work to benefit the shepherded livestock of southern farmers, who thereby garner tenure in northern and southern zones. Lacking entitlements in the southern agricultural zone, pastoralists are limited in their mobility and thus highly vulnerable during the *soudure*.

Lacking pasture to sustain their animals, participants mentioned two alternative methods of feeding their herds (Table 3.2): buying hay or fodder in towns or cutting pasture. At the peak of the *soudure*, the livestock market price is highly unfavourable to struggling herders. During the drought in 2009, a sack of animal fodder cost the same price as a healthy, female goat. The increasing market price of fodder further exacerbates vulnerability in the pastoral zone.

When some of the herd has been weakened by hunger, the household labor is divided. Young men change livestock itineraries, taking those that are stronger wide distances in search of pasture and water, and the

Table 3.2 Coping and adaptation strategies for pastoral households, based on data collected from Tillia non-migrants

Coping or Adaptation Strategy	% (number) of Households
Purchase fodder	63 % (10)
Transhumance: change routes or itineraries	63 % (10)
Economic migration and remittances	56 % (9)
Cut and store pasture	56 % (9)
Payment for water	50 % (8)
Transport water to pasture-rich areas	44 % (7)
Settlement of pastoralists (cultivation)	38 % (6)
Shepherding for livestock owners	13 % (2)

remaining weaker animals are left in a single camp near a water source and fed purchased supplemental fodder. During drought events, pastoral families have been known to be left without a single animal, forcing them to leave the pastoral system. When asked how their animals died, all of the participants stated reasons related to lack of pasture in the rural area (or starvation, lack of vitamin-rich grasses). Others mentioned lack of rainfall, sickness, and God's will as contributing factors to animal loss. As a result, the concurrent insufficient production is forcing pastoralists to live near towns where they have access to markets to purchase feed and household supplies (Woodke 2005).

Aid programs often respond after major losses of cattle (capital) have already occurred, enhancing a tendency for chronic vulnerability of pastoralists (IRIN 2010). Of those interviewed, only one participant (#14) stated that he had received any aid from the government or non-governmental projects. Two responded indignantly that one must help oneself ('each man with his elbows') since the government does not support their needs.

Thus, many pastoralists feel abandoned in their attempts to face climate events and insufficient environmental resources. Every migrant in Abalak stated that their primary reason for migrating was due to persistent drought and slow-onset environmental change and losses to their herds. As stated by an Abalak migrant, 'If I am living in the bush without animals, what will I do to survive?' (#9). To pay for the various complements to sustain a pastoralist's herd, remittances are often the greatest source of support. Based on a report spanning the pastoral zone performed by Tearfund, 94% of pastoralist households in Niger mentioned sending someone abroad as a method of household economic diversification (Woodke 2005).

Pastoral groups have also used political means to counter their marginalisation. In 1992, the Tuareg Rebellion began as an ideological response to the government's inaction during the 1984 drought. Pastoralists suffered huge losses in 1984 and 1985, resulting in large-scale migrations to city centres, with many heading north to Libya, following Al-Ghaddafi's offers of work visas to Tuareg migrants. The Nigerien and French governments convened a National Conference at the close of the rebellion, which provided the first formal recognition of the suffering and social upheaval experienced by the pastoralists due to the drought in 1984. Pastoralists perceive, however that neglect by the Nigerien government and international aid community continues unrelenting, prompting out-migration, social disintegration, and continued rebellion amongst pastoral groups. With the increasing conflict and insecurity in the wider Sahel/Sahara and Mediterranean Region, migrants now have greater access to weapons, a factor that has promoted some participants to mention that theft and banditry is becoming uncontrollable.

Discussion and Conclusions

This chapter examines a case study of migrants and non-migrants originating in rural, pastoral societies south of the Mediterranean Region in the country of Niger. The changing social and ecological conditions in this highly arid pastoral zone, along with increasing trends of rainfall variability throughout the Sahel resulting from climate change are pushing mainly rural people to seek alternative livelihoods. While the desire for greater access to schools, employment, and government facilities is often presumed to motivate migrants (economic migrants), we found this to be true only of migrants living in large urban areas (Niamey). Rural-based migrants living in smaller towns left the rural areas due to changes in the broader social ecological system, namely drought or losses from drought. After their displacement, a great deal of respondents expressed fear, nostalgia and, most often, a desire to return. As one herder stated, 'What business does a herder have in town?'

The degradation of the pastoral system in Niger has been an ongoing process since colonisation. France established arbitrary national borders,[5] blocked pastoral movement and changed the social structure of pastoral societies (eliminating tribute and slavery), which suppressed pastoral modes of adaptation to drought. After Niger's independence, policies and terms of trade continued to limit pastoral activities, favoring an expansion of agricultural production into pastoral areas. Development policies also promoted pastoral settlement and integration into a market system by commercializing both livestock and the pasture they consume and establishing

---

5 During colonisation, French military leaders imposed penalties on nomads illegally crossing national borders. The borders, while a political tool for the French were arbitrary to the pastoralists, who were now cut off from their traditional migratory routes.

commodity markets that exploit small holders, all of which are contributing to a decline of pastoral life in Niger.

Based on climate change outlooks (Bruggeman 2010) rainfall variability in Niger is likely to increase. As shown by Krätli (2013), pastoral livelihoods have the potential to be more resilient in light of climate variability. They have long-standing experience with the changes that are now understood across the world as occurring due to anthropogenic climate change. As stated in an address by Saoudata Aboubacrine, envoy to the UN Permanent Forum for Indigenous Peoples, 'The communities of Sahelian pastoralists were not waiting for the first alarm bells to sound before reacting, because they were already the direct victims of this phenomenon [climate change]. They adapt because their lives depend upon it' (2008). Yet, these adaptations, highlighted in this chapter, are not leading to a more resilient and sustainable pastoral system. Quite the contrary.

While Niger's government has made attempts to support development in the pastoral zone, most pastoralists have not witnessed these benefits. Niger's economic viability and human security demands a stronger pastoral system, given especially that Niger's second largest export is livestock (the first is uranium). Yet, the social and institutional frameworks do not empower and include sufficiently the local pastoralists' voices and ideas in the region's development. Pastoral policies and development should be enhanced to reinforce resilience and also support transitions to alternative economic activities that do not further degrade the environment.

The environmental migrants and displacees presented in this study possess intricate knowledge of their changing environment. The loss of numerous woody and grass species in the past 10 years highlights an urgent need to curb the non-climate causes of degradation including: overexploitation by commercial herding and wood and pasture cutting for commercial purposes. While the latter practices are illegal by law, non-migrant respondents were exasperated by the impunity of the abusers and the lack of a broader institutional framework. Furthermore, the increasing numbers of livestock in the region are seen to belong to opportunists as opposed to those local, subsistence pastoralists. These changes to the social ecological system promote feelings of hopelessness and a general distrust of government, especially during drought shocks. Many pastoralists expressed doubt that their children would continue in the livelihood, and encouraged their migration into the Mediterranean Region.

The pastures of the Sahel are supplying West Africa with multiple livestock products. Yet despite the economic and social impetus to bring climate-smart development to the pastoral zones, such action and policy is lacking. The management problems in the pastoral system promoting social transitions such as migration demand institutional transformation. To begin, the focus must shift from providing economic and governance capacities primarily to rain-fed agricultural societies to the enhancement of a localised, pastoralist-managed development of a resilient pastoral system. Current laws protecting pastoral resources need to be enforced, and drought early warning and crisis prevention systems need to establish greater and cheaper availability of fodder within the pastoral zone and respond early and efficiently during a drought or flood shock. Finally, local pastoralists need to understand and be empowered by the government's written laws and enforcement thereof. Without the innate contributions of the pastoralist communities in development policies, the sustainability of the former and latter actions will not be lasting.

The perspectives of migrants and non-migrants presented in this chapter have provided insight into what is dysfunctional in the ecology of rural societies of Niger and highlighted the intrinsic link between social and ecological resilience. Indeed, the utter lack of attention to a resilient, inclusive development in these communities contributes to the large exodus of pastoralists to more economically viable countries. What remains to be seen is how the national government and international community will respond and collaborate with pastoralists of the Sahel, before pastoralism as it is known also departs from this zone.

References

Barnett, Jon, and Michael Webber (2009) 'Accommodating migration to promote adaptation to climate change', policy brief prepared for the Secretariat of the Swedish Commission on Climate Change and Development and the World Bank World Development Report 2010 team, The Commission on Climate Change and Development, Stockholm.

Barrios, Salvador, Luisito Bertinelli and Eric Strobl (2006) 'Climate change and rural-urban migration: The case of Sub-Saharan Africa', *Journal of Urban Economics* 60/3 357–71.

Black, Richard, Stephen Bennett, Sandy Thomas and John Beddington (2011a) 'Climate change: migration as adaptation', *Nature* 478 447–9.

Black, Richard, W Neil Adger, Nigel Arnell, Stefan Dercon, Andrew Geddes and David Thomas (2011b) 'The effect of environmental change on human migration', *Global Environmental Change* 21S S3–S11.

Boano, Camillo, Roger Zetter and Tim Morris (2008) 'Environmentally displaced people: understanding the linkages between environment change, livelihoods and forced migration', Forced Migration Policy Briefing Refugee Studies Centre, University of Oxford.

Brooks, Nick (2004) 'Drought in the African Sahel: Long term perspectives and future prospects', Tyndall Center for Climate Change Research Working Paper, 61.

Clarke, Thurston (1978) *The Last Caravan*, G.P. Putnam's Sons, New York.

Colin de Verdière, P (1995) *Etude comparée des trois systèmes agropastoraux dans la région de Filingué, Niger. Les conséquences de la sédentarisation de l'élevage pastoral au Sahel*. Thèse présentée pour l'obtention du titre de Docteur de l'Institut National Agronomique Paris-Grignon, Paris.

D'Amato, N and T Lebel (1998) 'On the characteristics of the rainfall events in the Sahel with a view to the analysis of climatic variability', *International Journal of Climatology* 18 955–97.

De Moraes Farias, Paulo Fernando (2003) 'Bentyia (Kukyia): a Songhay–Mande meeting point, and a "missing link" in the archaeology of the West African diasporas of traders, warriors, praise-singers, and clerics', *Afriques* http://afriques.revues.org/1174?lang=en#bodyftn97 [20/09/2014].

Desanker, Paul and Christopher Magadza (2001) 'Africa', *IPCC Working Group II*. Chapter 10, 489–525, http://www.grida.no/climate/ipcc_tar/wg2/pdf/wg2TARchap10.pdf [12/06/2012].

Dun, Olivia, François Gemenne and Robert Stojanov (2007) 'Environmentally displaced persons: Working definitions for the EACH-FOR project', http://www.each-for.eu/documents/Environmentally_Displaced_Persons_-_Working_Definitions.pdf [29/04/2010].

FEWSNET (2011) *Niger food security outlook update*. USAID November 2012.

Foresight: Migration and Global Environmental Change (2011) Final Project Report. The Government Office for Science, London.

Giannini, Alessandra, Seyni Salack, Tiganadaba Loudoun, Abdou Ali, Amadou Gaye and Ousmane Ndiaye (2013) 'A unifying view of climate change in the Sahel linking intra-seasonal, interannual and longer time scales' *Environmental Research Letters* 8(024010).

Guichaoua, Yvan, Ferdaous Bouhlel-Hardy and Abdoulaye Tamboura (2008) 'Tuareg Crises in Niger and Mali', Seminar on the 27th November, 2007, IFRI Sub-Saharan Africa Program.

Guterres, António (2008b) 'Climate Change, natural disasters and human displacement: a UNHCR perspective', United Nations High Commissioner for Refugees, Geneva, http://www.unhcr.org/refworld/type,RESEARCH,UNHCR,,492bb6b92,0.html.

Hengsdijk, H and H van Kuelen (2002) 'The effect of temporal variation on inputs and outputs of future-oriented land use systems in West Africa', *Agriculture, Ecosystems and Environment* 91, 245–59.

Henry, Sabine, Bruno Schoumaker and Cris Beauchemin (2004) 'The impact of rainfall on the first out-migration: A multi-level event-history analysis in Burkina Faso', *Population and Environment* 25/5 423–60.

Hulme, Mike (1996) 'Recent Climatic Change in the World's Drylands', *Geophysical Research Letters* 23/1 61–4.

IOM (1996) *Migration and Environment*, IOM, RPG, Geneva, Washington D.C.

IOM (2011) 'Résultat de l'Analyse des Enregistrements et Profils socio-économiques des Migrants Nigériens retournés suite à la Crise Libyenne'. International Organization for Migration Report February to August 2011. Niamey.

IOM (2014) 'Niger, carrefour des migrations en Afrique de l'Ouest', Bulletin d'information trimestriel N°5 April – June 2014, International Organisation for Migration.

IOM (2015) 'Number of migrants landing in Europe in 2015 passes 100,000', International Organization for Migration press release from June 9, 2015, https://www.iom.int/news/number-migrants-landing-europe-2015-passes-100000 [06/09/2015].

IPCC (2013) Summary for Policymakers. In: *Climate Change 2013: The Physical Science Basis*. Contribution of Working Group to the 5th Assessment Report of the Intergovernmental Panel on Climate Change [Stocker, T.F., D. Qin, G.-K. Plattner, M. Tignor, S. K. Allen, J. Boschung, A. Nauels, Y. Xia, V. Bex and P.M. Midgley (eds)]. Cambridge University Press, Cambridge and New York.

IPCC (2007) Summary for policymakers, In: *Climate Change 2007: Impacts, Adaptation, and Vulnerability*. Contribution of working group II to the 4th Assessment Report of the UPCC, M.L. Parry; O.F. Canziani; J.P. Palertikof; P.J. van der Linden and C.E. Hansen, eds, Cambridge University Press, Cambridge, 7–22.

IRIN (2010) 'Niger: Chasing after pastoralists with truckloads of aid', IRIN Humanitarian News and Analysis, 5 August, 2010.

IUCN (International Union for Conservation of Nature) (2012) *Supporting sustainable pastoral livelihoods: A global perspective on minimum standards and good practice* 2nd Edition. IUCN ESARO Office, Nairobi.

Krätli, Saverio, Christian Huelsebusch, Sally Brooks and Brigitte Kaufmann (2013) 'Pastoralism: A critical asset for food security under global climate change', *Animal Frontiers* 3/1 42–50.

Lewis, David (2014) 'Special Report: Despite deaths, crackdown, Sahara migrant trail thrives', 15 May 2014, Reuters Online, http://www.reuters.com/article/2014/05/15/us-europe-immigration-niger-specialrepor-idUSBREA4E08W20140515 [01/08/2014].

Loftsdottir, Kristín (2001) 'Birds of the Bush: Wodaabe Distinctions of Society and Nature', *Nordic Journal of African Studies* 10/3 280–98.

MA (Millennium Ecosystem Assessment) (2005a) *Ecosystems and Human Well-Being: Synthesis*, Island Press, Washington, DC.

Marty, A and B Bonnet (1989) 'Etude Socio Economique Rapport de Synthèse République du Niger, Programme Spécial National- Niger-FIDA volet pastoral', Institut de Recherches et d'Applications des Méthodes de Développement.

McLeman, Robert and Barry Smit (2006) 'Migration as an Adaptation to Climate Change', *Climatic Change* 76/1 31–53.

MINUSMA United Nations (2013) *MINUSMA: United Nations Multidimensional Integrated Stabilization Mission in Mali*, http://www.un.org/en/peacekeeping/missions/minusma/background.shtml [31/07/2014].

Nicholson, Sharon E and Ian M Palao (1993) 'A re-evaluation of rainfall variability in the Sahel', *International Journal Climatology* 13 371–89.

Nicholaisen, Johannes (1962) *Ecology and culture of the pastoral Tuareg: with particular reference to the Tuareg of the Air and the Ahaggar*. Copenhagen, National Museum of Copenhagen.

OCHA (2013) Apercu humanitaire provisoire sur les inondations (au 17 Septembre 2013) *OCHA Snapshot of Flood*, http://reliefweb.int/sites/reliefweb.int/files/resources/Snapshot_Inondations%2017%2009%202013.pdf, [07/11/2013].

Parnell, Susan and Ruwani Walawege (2011) 'Sub-Saharan African urbanization and global environmental change', *Global Environmental Change* 21S S12–S20.

Pei, Qing and David D Zhang (2014) 'Long-term relationship between climate change and nomadic migration in historical China', *Ecology and Society* 19/2 68.

Rathgeber, T (2008) 'Climate change, poverty and migration Human rights challenges to the UN human rights system', Global Challenges: Climate Change Social Forum. Forum Human Rights Berlin / University of Kassel, Germany.

REFORM (2009) 'Plan de developpement communal de la commune rurale de Tillia, 2009–2012', May 2009, National Reporting for the Commune Rurale de Tillia by ONG Reform.

Renaud, Fabrice, Janos J Bogardi, Olivia Dun and Koko Warner (2007) 'Control, adapt or flee: how to face environmental migration', *InterSecTions*, 5. Bonn, UNU-EHS.

Renaud, Fabrice G, Olivia Dun, Koko Warner and Janos Bogardi (2011) 'A Decision Framework for Environmentally Induced Migration', *International Migration* 49 e5–e29.

République du Niger (2011) *Initiative '3N' pour la Sécurité Alimentaire et le Développement Agricole Durable 'Les Nigeriens Nourrissent les Nigeriens'*, République du Niger, Presidence de la République, Haut Commissariat à l'Initiative 3N, Niamey.

Richmond, A (1993) 'The environment and refugees: theoretical and policy issues', Revised version of a paper presented at the meetings of the International Union for the Scientific Study of Population, Montreal, August 1993.

Snorek, Julie, Fabrice G Renaud and Julia Kloos (2014) 'Divergent adaptation to climate variability: A case study of pastoral and agro-pastoral societies in Niger', *Global Environmental Change* DOI: 10.1016/j.gloenvcha.2014.06.014.

Snorek, Julie, Fabrice G Renaud and L Moser (unpublished) 'The production of contested landscapes: perceptions of changes to ecosystem services in Niger', Chapter 2 of a PhD Thesis of the Autonomous University of Barcelona.

Trolldalen, Jon Martin, Nina Birkeland, J Borgen and P T Scott (1992) 'Environmental Refugees: a Discussion Paper', Oslo: World Foundation for Environment and Development and Norwegian Refugee Council.

UNEP United Nations Environment Programme (1992) *World Atlas of Desertification*. Edward Arnold, London.

UNHCR (2013) 'New Malian refugee influx into northern Niger', Briefing Notes, 5 April 2013, UNHCR, http://www.unhcr.org/515eadb49.html [31/07/2014].

UNDP (2014). Human Development Index Reports. United Nations Development Programme http://hdr.undp.org/en/composite/HDI [20/12/2015].

UNICEF (2012) 'Statistics: En Bref: Niger' UNICEF, http://www.unicef.org/french/infobycountry/niger_statistics.html [02/08/2014].

Warner, Koko, Tamar Afifi, Olivia Dun, Marc Stal and Sophia Schmidl (2008) *Report: Human Security, Climate Change, and Environmentally Induced Migration*, United Nations University – Institute for Environment and Human Security.

Warner, Koko (2009) 'Global environmental change and migration: Governance challenges', *Global Environmental Change* 20 402–13.

Warren, Andrew, Simon Batterbury and Henny Osbahr (2001) 'Soil erosion in the West African Sahel: a review and an application of a 'local political ecology' approach in South West Niger', *Global Environmental Change* 11 79–95.

Woodke, Jeff (2008) 'Water and climate linkages among pastoralists in Niger: Informing climate change adaptation and water resources management policies', *Tearfund*, June 2008.

Woodke, Jeff (2005) 'Tear Fund Progress Report: PROJECT Amidinine Famine Relief', Jeunesse En Mission Entraide et Développement (JEMED). Reference Number: NGR 00015-2/3. (unpublished internal report).

World Bank (2014). Niger Country Data (population and world development indicators), The World Bank, http://data.worldbank.org/country/niger [20/12/2015].

4 Autonomy in Times of War? The Impact of the Libyan Crisis on Migratory Decisions

Delf Rothe and Mariam Salehi

Introduction

This chapter explores the complex question of how and why an initially peaceful political upheaval could lead to the mass migration of Sub-Saharan Africans from Libya to Europe. We ask why these people left or had to leave Libya and risked their lives to enter the European Union. Peter Seeberg noticed in 2013 that a direct link between the growing number of asylum seekers and the so-called 'Arab Spring' could not be proven statistically because it was 'hardly documented' (Seeberg 2013a 158). As we show in the chapter, this link is also hard to establish empirically without falling into the trap of oversimplification, because there is not a single causal logic that would lead from the onset of violent protests in Libya to a mass migration to Europe. Based on interviews with migrants, we show that there are quite different avenues that link the Libyan upheavals and the resulting civil war with individual decisions to emigrate. We reveal the complexity of cascading events initiated by the Arab upheavals and the impact on migrant workers in Libya. Most importantly, we let the migrants speak and start from their perspectives on their situation under Gaddafi, the Libyan civil war and subsequent NATO intervention. Our first, empirical, aim is hence to prove that a macro-perspective and quantitative research alone does not do justice to the complexity of migration decisions. By putting the migrants' views first, we are able to show that these decisions were based on the interplay of different factors, including racism, physical threats, lack of economic prospects and the unwillingness to become involved in the civil war.

Our second, theoretical, aim is to develop a perspective to theorize migratory decisions in response to the Libyan civil war in a way that understands migrants as purposeful social actors rather than helpless victims, and in a way that accounts for the complexities of events and factors that impact upon any migration project. Taking seriously Ann McNevin's argument of grounding 'theory production in concrete migrant struggle' (McNevin 2013: 198), we firstly outline the perspective of Autonomy of Migration (AoM) and discuss it against the case of migrant workers that had to leave Libya in the aftermath of the upheavals. We combine this approach with the notion of complexity and emergent causality as outlined by William E Connolly (2004, 2005) to break with existing linear, simplifying models of migration.

Theorizing Migratory Decisions

It comes as a truism that the events summarized under the label 'Arab Spring' have triggered a major change in trans-Mediterranean migratory movements (see e.g. Fargues and Fandrich 2012). In this contribution, we seek to challenge this dominant narrative – not by questioning the empirical claim about changing patterns of migration, which is hard to deny given the magnitude of the so-called 'migration crisis' in the region. Instead, we seek to approach this empirical reality through an alternative theoretical lens. As a starting point it is important to outline briefly what we mean by the dominant narrative. According to this reading, the revolts and upheavals in different countries of the Middle East and North Africa (MENA) region are understood as *triggering events* that either directly forced people to leave their countries or fundamentally altered the structural conditions (the push and pull factors) that underlie migratory decisions. From a European perspective especially, political disorder and instability in the southern Mediterranean appear worrisome as they might work as a pull factor attracting Sub-Saharan migrants to seize this opportunity to get on a boat to Europe. This perspective is supported by migration research, which conceptualizes migration decisions as the outcome of push and pull factors (see Chapter 1 in this volume for more detail). This outcome can be understood as the cumulative result of structural factors and events that push people out of their country as well as the structural conditions attracting persons to the target country (Lee 1966). We hold this perspective, which underlies both mainstream media and academic discourse, to be problematic for two reasons: first, as it comes along with an objectification of migration; second, because it rests upon linear, mechanistic causal models that do not account for complexity and non-linearity, including, e.g. feedback loops and cascading events.

To start with the first point of critique, we argue that the terminology of *triggers*, *pushes* and *pulls* is problematic, as it renders the social phenomenon of (e)migration[1] in purely technical, mechanical ways. Migrants appear as mere objects, which are being pushed around, and not as political subjects seeking to realize their own agendas and interests. Drawing on constructivist ontology and the conviction that language, including the use of metaphors (Lakoff and Johnson 1998), shapes our social reality, we claim

---

1 The perspective we promote here transcends the distinction between emigration and immigration as it accounts for both structural factors in target countries as well as personal factors of the migrants. Whether the migratory project is labelled as emigration or immigration (just like the distinction between regular and irregular) is contingent and depends on the perspective of the articulating speaker/author.

that this discursive construction of migration is not trivial but crucial for the perception and treatment of trans-Mediterranean migrants. To develop an alternative perspective we draw on the AoM approach, which stresses the subjective dimension of migration and understands it as the (realization of) social projects based on an incalculable amount of individual decisions (see Papadopoulos and Tsianos 2013; Scheel 2013). To stress the autonomy of migrants as political agents, however, does not mean to neglect the structural forces that affect decisions to migrate or to deny the politics of border control and migration management seeking to prevent an uncontrolled, unregulated movement of people. Rather, proponents of the AoM thesis argue that there is always a moment of autonomy in migration projects, which cannot be captured by attempts to control movement.[2] With the AoM approach, the focus is shifted to the migrants themselves. Their practices are grasped through the notion of *imperceptible politics*, referring to all those mundane and often ignored tactics and practices of migrants with which they manage problematic and dangerous situations, successfully evade control and confront structural barriers.

However, to us the AoM perspective is not without problems. First and foremost, there is a danger of romanticizing migration. As Stephan Scheel remarks, the AoM approach takes the migrant as a unified political subject and thereby fails to account for the lived experiences of actual migrants, just as it fails to account for the varying degrees of autonomy between them (Scheel 2013: 586). In the words of Anne McNevin, AoM proponents 'attribute specific meaning to human mobility and underemphasize its haphazard, short-term and dislocated dimensions' (McNevin 2013: 193). Both Scheel and McNevin stress the need for a more careful conceptualization of autonomy. In this chapter we follow these authors to sketch out a relational concept of autonomy accounting for the actual circumstances under which a migration project is realized as well as for the fact that 'experience is always embodied' (Scheel 2013: 587). This implies that migration decisions can be studied only on the basis of individual cases; accounting for the relational autonomy of the concrete migrant depending on his or her socio-economic position (including material, cultural and symbolic forms of capital), and on the individual's mindset in relation to the structural context of the migration project.

A second problem of recent research on post-'Arab Spring' migration is the linearity undergirding models of migration decisions. The latter are taken as the cumulative result of structural factors as well as external events. A good example is environmentally induced migration (see Chapter 3 in this volume), which is taken as a function of vulnerability, i.e. the exposure to environmental changes or extreme weather events and the adaptive

---

2 While for example the control of the European external border has become ever more technologized this did so far not reduce the number of people that entered the EU to seek refuge.

capacity – including economic performance, social structure, education – of a region. Unlike Chapter 3 in this volume, previous work on environmental migration often drew on macro-studies and a mechanistic notion of causality resembling the billiard ball paradigm (Glynos and Howarth 2007: 92). Such models take causality as a cause-effect sequence in mechanistic terms of pushes and pulls, triggers and effects. So, just as in the case of billiards, you have an initial cause (the shot in the billiards case/the political upheavals in the MENA region) which meets with additional factors – wind, or the condition of the table in a billiards match; the destruction of people's livelihoods and human insecurities in the case of Libya – which in total explain a final result – the ball is driven into a pocket; the migrant leaves towards Europe. The problem is that this model follows a logic of summation (e.g. the migration decision as the result of political unrest+poverty+missing perspectives+the attractiveness of Europe) which hardly matches the reality of complex social systems. What the model misses is the complex interplay between single factors, feedback loops, and resulting chaotic, non-linear change that characterizes social and political phenomena.

As an alternative, we suggest drawing on a notion of *emergent causality*, which seeks 'to challenge the sufficiency of both efficient models of causality in social science and acausal images of mutual constitution in interpretive theory' (Connolly 2004: 342). It distances itself from the idea of a cause-effect sequence and draws on the metaphors of resonance and spiral movement to make sense of causal relations in a world of complexity. Understood as resonance, causality morphs into 'energized complexities of mutual imbrication and interinvolvement, in which heretofore unconnected or loosely associated elements fold, bend, blend, emulsify, and dissolve into each other' (Connolly 2005: 870). This approach does not define social structures, political or natural events as independent (push) factors but stresses their interdependencies and mutual imbrication. For the case under investigation here, this means that the autonomy of migrants is relational as these are embedded in complex social, economic or environmental contexts. Yet, neither do these structural factors determine individual decisions, nor are these structures fixed or given – they are themselves a complex of emerging and changing processes.

An approach of relational autonomy needs to consider this embeddedness of migratory projects within broader complex processes of social and natural change. We try to grasp this notion of a 'context in flux' by drawing on recent concepts from complexity literature: *cascades, feedback loops* and *emergence*. From our perspective, there are no exhaustive push or pull factors but only complex and changing assemblages of *structural forces, events,* and *attraction factors*. These factors make up the relational autonomy of migratory projects. To stress that the latter are not determined by such contexts, we differentiate between two different ways in which migrants engage with this environment. A first way is *migration as adaptation*. Migration here can be seen as a successful adaptation of subjects to a complex and changing environment – for example due to natural disasters, a (perceived) lack of opportunities, or a situation of vulnerability. A second way is *migration as transformation*. The notion of migration as transformation pays tribute to the understanding that migrants are not passive victims to developments beyond their control. Rather, they are actively able to shape and transform the situations they face. Hence, this means that migratory decisions are neither solely determined by external forces, nor completely self-determined.

Take the example of the boat tragedy in October 2013, which cost the lives of 366 migrants that tried to reach Lampedusa on a crowded, unseaworthy boat. A common perspective on this incident is to portray the dead migrants as tragic victims: victims of profit-seeking human traffickers, or of the European migration regime. And while it is certainly true that the EU system of border control and the absence of any legal routes for asylum seekers to reach EU territory prompt people to take ever-bigger risks, this is not the whole story. A perspective of migration as transformation would see the people on the boat as political actors, decidedly risking their lives to pursue a particular goal. And their tragic death produced a massive transformative force, challenging European discourses and regulations with yet unforeseeable implications. Given their transformative potential to challenge established discourses and norms of sovereignty, citizenship, human rights, or international justice, migrants can be considered political actors per se (Nyers 2006: 49). In this chapter, we show how migratory projects that started as a successful adaptation to a complex situation of war and risk subsequently turned into a transformative, political project. We show that the moments of coercion and autonomy in migration stories do not exist independently. Rather, in the case of Sub-Saharan migrants who fled the Libyan civil war, it was exactly the forceful moments within the migrants' experiences which were later used as the basis for political mobilization and argumentation.

Case Study

Setting and Access to the Field

This chapter is based empirically on 15 in-depth, narrative interviews with Sub-Saharan migrants, which we conducted between July and October 2013 in Hamburg and Berlin, Germany. The interviewees can be considered a coherent group in that all of them originally stem from different Sub-Saharan African countries. All of them arrived in Libya before the start of the civil war to find work. They reached Lampedusa, Italy by boat. With one exception, all of our interviewees left Libya in early 2011 because of the uprisings and events in its aftermath, including the NATO campaign. From Lampedusa, they were distributed to different places in Italy where they mostly stayed for about two years in refugee camps until the end of 2012 or beginning of 2013. They reached Germany using different means of transportation, usually by train or plane.

In Hamburg, during the winter of 2013, the refugees[3], who received their stay permits in Italy before they left for Germany, mainly stayed in homeless shelters. When the homeless shelters closed for spring, they found themselves living on the street and, hence, became more 'visible' for the general public. When more and more people with a common migratory history from Libya arrived in Hamburg they managed to organize politically under the label *Lampedusa in Hamburg*. This step was crucial, as it constituted the different migrants as a collective political actor with a unitary identity and increased their public visibility and recognition from local politicians as well as other political actors including unions, NGOs and churches. The group kept track of those staying in their vicinity and people could register to be included on their list. Possibility of 'membership' in the *Lampedusa in Hamburg* group was restricted to those who fled during the 2011 Libyan crisis:

> Our people (.) yes (.) who are from Libya situation (.) to be precise. Not for those that came before we. Just 2011 during Libya crisis. . . . (.) we select (.) we know them according to our arrival in Italy. So, we register if you need to join our group (.) ok. That's the way we take to build our group.[4]

To select our interviewees in Hamburg, we first contacted the speakers of the group, whose contact details could be found on the group's website, and made an appointment at their 'Info-Tent', a tent near Hamburg main station where the group gathered and offered information about their situation to the public. There, we were referred to further interviewees who agreed to speak to us.

Further interviews in Hamburg were conducted at the 'St. Pauli Kirche', the church, which offered places to sleep for about 80 migrants. There, we approached our interviewees and asked for a talk without prior contact. Two other appointments in Hamburg were made by phone after the initial contact.

In Berlin, the setting was different. The group of Lampedusa refugees gathered at 'Oranienplatz', a place where migrants from different groups and situations had already established a 'protest camp' to protest against German immigration and asylum policies. However, the *Lampedusa in Berlin* group was spatially separated from the other migrants, clearly recognizable by a flag.

---

3 The interviewees are referred to as refugees although not all (but many) of them received humanitarian asylum in Italy. All the interviewees applied for asylum in Italy, where they first entered the EU, and were provided with papers and a Schengen visa by the Italian government. As a result they could travel within the Schengen space but could not apply for asylum in Germany, since the Dublin II regulation requires that asylum procedures are carried out by the respective entry-country.

4 Interview with Affo T., Hamburg, July 2013.

In Berlin, one author went to the information tent prior to the day we were planning to come to conduct interviews and made an initial appointment with one of the speakers of the group. We received a phone number and called our contact at the agreed day and time and conducted the interview. Afterwards, he referred us to one further interviewee and we approached others independently. Two further interviews were conducted on a different day without establishing prior contact, but instead by approaching the interviewees independently. All interviewees, in Hamburg as well as in Berlin, were male, as the migrants at both camps were also only male. We asked about women and were told that there were no women who stayed in the camps or lived on the street. We were told that those few women who were part of the *Lampedusa* group were usually there with their family and hosted in houses.

All interviewees were asked for consent regarding the recording of the interview and were offered anonymity as well as the possibility to choose a pseudonym. Two interviewees preferred not to be recorded. Interviews were semi-structured and conducted in either English or French. However, though the interviews were guided by pre-prepared questions, we chose a narrative start to the interview and offered our interviewees the opportunity to determine its initial direction. By asking each interviewee to tell us 'his story' first, we aimed also to capture relevant aspects in migratory decisions we may not have considered in the preparation of our interview guide.

In our analysis, we identified dialectics of coercive measures with moments of autonomy in migratory decisions within the Libyan crisis. Drawing on qualitative data analysis software MAXQDA we identified those factors influencing the decisions of migrants in different stages of their 'journey'. We coded the material along the lines of the categories developed in the theory part of this chapter: 1. the emerging structural context of migratory decision including structural forces, attracting factors, as well as cascading events; 2. the different migration projects based on the subjective interpretation of these context factors as well as the relational autonomy of different migrants.

Structural Forces and Adaptation

The migratory stories of our interviewees did not begin with the onset of the Libyan civil war. All of them started as purposeful individual projects as demonstrated in the following quote of Hamed from Ghana:

> Yeah. My name is Hamed. I am a Ghanaian. I was born in Ghana. Until about (.) when I was about 26 years old I decided to leave Ghana to Libya to do some work.[5]

---

5 Interview Hamed, Hamburg, Summer 2013.

Or the reason to leave their country of origin was related to conflict or 'problems' the migrants had in their home countries, as was the case for Andreas, who is also from Ghana:

> I left Ghana to Italy (.) ehm to Libya (.) because I was (.) I was having a little bit of trouble. Because there was a conflict between my tribe and another tribe. And because of that conflict I lost my family and (.) my life was also threatened together with my brother. People wanted to take our life. Because we belonged to a particular tribe. And because of that we escaped from Ghana to Libya.[6]

In both cases, we can see how migration functions as successful adaptation to (perceived) grievances or vulnerabilities, since our interviewees managed to successfully adapt to adverse situations in their country of origin. It is important to stress the high degree of relative autonomy at this initial stage of the migration journeys: as we know from research on economic migration, it is not the poorest that migrate, because the latter simply lack the resources for such an endeavour (de Haas 2007: 10). The most important factor attracting migrants to Libya was the possibility of working there and of being welcomed as migrant workers. Affo Tchassei, one of the speakers of *Lampedusa in Hamburg* states:

> ... we immigrants – as Africans, Sub-Saharans – living there (.) we were working (.) you know (.) we are millions of us there, with opportunities to work (.) to be educated. Because Libyans really like us to work (.) because the country is so rich. And the government offered them easy possibilities. So, we felt as we were welcome to work (.) to build our lives. That's why you see so many Africans living there for several years. And we tried to build our life there. You know (.) helping our families.[7]

Up to 2011, our interviewees perceived their lives in Libya as having been very positive: 'And we were living there. Working. Everything was ok. Until 2011.'[8] Viktor from Nigeria, for example, came to Libya at the age of 14 and spent a decade in the country, experiencing his whole adulthood and professional development there:

> I'm Viktor. I was born in 1986 in ... in Nigeria. When I was very young, because of the oil conflict in Nigeria in my state, I fled to Libya. ... we went to Libya 2000, doing well, working well. I made good experience of working. I had two jobs. I have two experiences now. Doing well from 2000 to 2011. Before the war broke out.[9]

---

6 Interview Andreas, Hamburg, Summer 2013.
7 Interview with Affo Tchassei, Hamburg, July 2013.
8 Interview with Andreas, Hamburg, Summer 2013.
9 Interview with Viktor, Berlin, Summer 2013.

They worked in different professions, in different parts of the country:

> So, in Libya I found myself well. It was good years (.) with opportunities to work. I worked for the embassy (.) like a chief security for one of the African embassies.[10]

Some of them, like Andreas from Ghana, were not able to work in the profession they previously had in their country of origin: 'In Libya I couldn't use my profession in the marketing sector. I decided to do building construction.'[11] Particularly important for our interviewees was the capability to make a living on their own and being able to support their families via remittances:

> Then I have been in Libya for a couple of ten years. So, I have been there (.) working (.) earning my living (.) supporting my brothers and sisters (.) back in Nigeria.[12]

However, these accomplishments faded in the wake of the war: '(. . .) but when the war started, we lost everything.'[13] From these experiences, one can see that migration was not only a means to adapt to the adverse conditions in their countries of origin, but also a means for transformation. Our interviewees transformed a necessary decision into an opportunity: they did not only leave problems in their home countries behind, but also actively sought to make themselves a good living abroad. They were not only able to accumulate economic capital but were also able to support their families and home communities via remittances and thus gained social capital in the form of reputation and social credit.

All of our interviewees stressed that they did not have any intention to leave Libya prior to the outbreak of political violence in 2011. The reasons for leaving Libya were, with one exception, adaptation strategies directly related to the Libyan crisis of 2011: 'My life went well until this 17 February 2011 when suddenly everything changed in the country. And, we were to run away to the outside.'[14]

But if one takes a closer look at the experiences of our interviewees one can notice that the perception of the civil war as a single push-factor driving people on the boats to Lampedusa falls short of the complex reality in the country. First, it is important to note that those people not based in Tripoli before the crisis initially adapted to the situation by moving *internally* within the country. They migrated from different places in the country and for

---

10 Interview with Affo Tchassei, Hamburg, July 2013.
11 Interview with Andreas, Hamburg, Summer 2013.
12 Interview with Anthony Nwoye, Hamburg, July 2013.
13 Interview with a Lampedusa in Berlin member, Berlin, Summer 2013; own translation.
14 Interview with Affo Tchassei, Hamburg, July 2013.

different reasons to the capital. One of our interviewees, originally from Ghana, was based in Benghazi, where the violence escalated at first in 2011:

> The Libya conflict was in the strait (.) in the middle of the strait of Benghazi (.) in the middle. That's where the conflict started. No place to (.) they closed the barriers. So, we decided to go to Tripoli. There is no place. We tried many times. So, we went there (.)[15]

Hamed, also from Ghana, was based in a small village between the cities of Benghazi and Sirte. There, the reason he decided to leave was a shortage of food: 'Because we were short of food. Where we were there was no supermarket that was opened. So everything was closed.'[16]

Second, the decisive factors for the concrete (e)migration decision from Libya and to Europe differed between the individual projects. Three main clusters of reasons why migrants entered a boat to Lampedusa could be identified. A first cluster comprises concrete and direct threats to their physical well-being as expressed in the following example: 'This war started and our life also became endangered. And there was nowhere you could go back to our country and we had to escape to the sea.'[17] A second cluster comprises political reasons, i.e. the different strategies through which the initially neutral group of working migrants became dragged into the conflict by the Gaddafi forces. Anthony Nwoye from Nigeria, for example, states 'we have two options. One: you join the Gaddafi troops. Or: you face through the water.'[18] Affo Tchassei reported that Gaddafi used migrants as a kind of human weapon against the NATO bombardments and reacted to every attack by deporting people to Europe:

> Because in other way (.) many of us were caught by Gaddafi regime (.) ahm militaries and sending us to go. So they said (.) one missile 1000 people, two missiles 2000 people. They have to send as much as possible going to Western.[19]

A third cluster refers to different forms of racial discrimination people were facing from Libyan rebels. The rebels took the whole black population to be mercenaries of Gaddafi's troops:

> we saw the boys, Libyan people, coming to the house. When they came, they started beating us. . . . You see, many people fighting Mohammed [sic] Gaddafi (.) he was using blacks to fight them.[20]

15 Interview, Anonymous, Hamburg, Summer 2013.
16 Interview with Hamed, Hamburg, Summer.
17 Interview Andreas, Hamburg, Summer 2013.
18 Interview Anthony Nwoye, Hamburg, July 2013.
19 Interview with Affo Tchassei, Hamburg, July 2013.
20 Interview Ymafada Kuaku Gzile, Hamburg, July 2013.

This perception lead to a downright hunt for black people living in Libya: 'They said they would hunt all the blacks down there in Tripoli.'[21]

Third, as indicated in the first statement of the above paragraph, it needs to be emphasized that going to Europe was often not the migrants' primary choice. Bibi from Mali, for example, described the route over the sea as the only solution to leave the country, because the frontiers to Egypt and Tunisia were closed: 'La seule solution était la mer.'[22] There was also no possibility for the migrants to fly out of Libya to their countries of origin. Two of our interviewees reported that they planned to fly back to their home country, which in both cases is Ghana, when they ran out of food: 'see, we don't have any food. So now we want to go back to our countries.'[23]. This however, was not possible because of the no-fly zone NATO enforced over Libya[24]: 'When we reached the airport there was a no-fly-zone. So, we were not able to fly.'[25] Afterwards, Libyan soldiers brought them to the port where the boat to Lampedusa was situated and threatened their lives:

> They took us to a seaport. Took us to a small boat like this [indicates size of the boat]. They told us we should go and not come back. If we come back, they will kill us.[26]

In some cases, the Libyan soldiers seem to have made sure that the boats really were on their way toward Europe: 'Then they escorted us about some kilometres and came back and said we shouldn't come back.'[27]

To sum up, we can notice that the relative autonomy of (e)migrants in their decision to leave Libya towards Europe in the face of the civil war was extremely low. They were literally driven out of the country. At the same time, the different drivers at play have been much more complex than suggested by news media reports warning against the flood of migrants produced by the events of the 'Arab Spring'.[28]

---

21 Interview, Anonymus, Berlin, Summer 2013; own translation.
22 Interview with Bibi, Berlin, Summer 2013; English translation: 'The only solution was the sea.'
23 Interview with Hamed, Hamburg, Summer 2013; see also Interview, Anonymous, Hamburg, Summer 2013.
24 The term 'no-fly zone' describes an area where aircraft are not allowed to fly, often introduced for military purposes and if necessary militarily enforced. In Libya, the no-fly zone formed part of 'Operation UNIFIED PROTECTOR', NATO's 'response to United Nations Security Resolution (UNSCR) 1973.' (http://www.nato.int/nato_static/assets/pdf/pdf_2011_03/20110325_110325-unified-protector-no-fly-zone.pdf, [05/09/2014]).
25 Interview with Hamed, Hamburg, Summer 2013; see also Interview, Anonymus, Hamburg, Summer 2013.
26 Interview, Anonymus, Hamburg, Summer 2013.
27 Interview with Hamed, Hamburg, Summer 2013.
28 For accounts in the German press using the terminology of 'flood' or 'wave' see examples here: http://www.stern.de/politik/ausland/migrantenflut-in-italien-tunesier-fliehen-zu-tausen-

All of our interviewees reached Lampedusa by boat. Afterwards, leaving Lampedusa was predetermined and the migrants were distributed to different cities in Italy:

> Then we stayed at Lampedusa for one week. From one way, they say that the place was not a place at which we can stay. They have to transfer us to another place. I didn't know any place in Italy. So any place they would take me (.) there is no problem. And they took me from Lampedusa to another city.[29]

Though it might have been possible, none of our interviewees decided against the relocation to the different places all over Italy. There, they lived in camps provided by the Italian government.

At a certain point of time at the end of 2012, the Italian government closed down the camps, forcing the migrants to leave these places:

> And when I came to Italy, they put us in camps. We spent about two years in camps. After the two years the government decided to close down the camp.[30]

The camps were shut down, according to officials because money from international donors stopped coming and, therefore, Italy could not afford to keep the camps open. In many cases, the migrants received stay permits only at this stage.

Due to the economic crisis, prospects for work in Italy were poor. Our interviewees were not able to find work and this was a decisive factor in their desire to leave the country (Similar concerns are also discussed in Chapters 6 and 9 of this volume). Migration, therefore, functioned as adaptation to the complex situation of closed camps combined with a lack of prospects in Italy to transform the situation: 'I decided to come to Germany because of the economic crisis. There is no work in Italy'.[31]

For our interviewees, the economic crisis in Italy and the subsequent shutdown of the camps produced a paradoxical state of (unwanted)

---

den-nach-lampedusa-1653605.html, http://www.welt.de/debatte/die-welt-in-worten/article13449930/Im-Zweifel-macht-Europa-seine-Grenzen-lieber-zu.html, http://www.dw.de/die-fl%C3%BCchtlinge-des-arabischen-fr%C3%BChlings/a-15914785-0. For some examples in the English speaking media, see media in the US (http://usatoday30.usatoday.com/news/world/story/2012-06-01/European-Union-migration-Arab-uprisings/55327422/1), the UK (http://www.dailymail.co.uk/news/article-2003537/2-500-illegal-immigrants-week-North-Africa-flooding-Europe-Italy.html), or Canada (http://www.theglobeandmail.com/news/world/how-the-arab-spring-put-lampedusa-in-the-path-of-a-torrent-of-illegal-immigration/article14678375/) [all 11/10/2014].

29 Interview Ymafada Kuaku Gzile, Hamburg, July 2013.
30 Interview Andreas, Hamburg, Summer 2013.
31 Interview Kennedy, Berlin, October 2013.

autonomy through abandonment. They were freed from the repressive forces of encampment and even provided with basic rights, for example freedom of movement within the Schengen space. At the same time, their relational autonomy was restricted by visa regulations and monetary concerns. As mentioned above, they had received stay permits in Italy; hence, at that point their status in Germany was regular but insecure. Our interviewees were well aware that this situation would be aggravated when their Schengen visa and stay permits expired, because this would make them possible subjects of deportation. In general, the 'legal status of migrant workers who are subsequently displaced is uncertain' (Koser 2012). Refugee status is usually tied to the situation in the respective countries of origin – and not those of habitual residence – and the UN Migrant Workers Convention, which is also not widely ratified, does not deal with the issue of subsequent displacement. Since, in absolute numbers, the largest group of people who were forced to leave their homes during the first year of the 'Arab Spring' were migrant workers, this does not only reveal a significant protection gap in the international regime to protect refugees and forced migrants (ibid.), it also hints at the complexity of the situation and the subsequent uncertainty the migrants have to deal with.

From Adaptation to Transformation

While coercive factors indeed play a role regarding the trajectories of our interviewees, we identified moments of autonomy in the individual migratory decisions at all stages of their routes to Germany. Though the structural factors we identified above were 'nudging' people to move, to adapt to adverse conditions, the actual decisions to move or where to go were taken in autonomy relational to the structural factors, using the migratory decision's transformative power. Though the migrants decided to leave their home countries in the first place because of economic reasons or conflicts, the decision to travel to Libya was taken autonomously, taking economic prospects and practicalities into account. Anthony Nwoye from Nigeria, for example, emphasised that before the crisis he deliberately decided to stay on the African continent and against crossing the Mediterranean to Europe:

> Yeah, ok. I lived in Libya for a couple of ten years. I have been there (.) working. I know the time when people liked crossing Europe through the Mediterranean Sea. But it doesn't come to my mind. It doesn't come to my . . . to come to Europe. I'm living very well in Africa over there. I have my handwork (.) working. Earning a nice living. Inviting my friends on a visit.[32]

---

32 Interview Anthony Nwoye, Hamburg, July 2013.

The decision to go on the boat, chosen over the option to join Gaddafi's forces, is also an autonomous one; however, it is relative to the external circumstances. Furthermore, as mentioned above, the decision to travel to Germany was an informed decision, taking the external circumstances like the economic situation, visa regulations and feasibility into account.

All in all, the migrant journey from Libya to Hamburg is best described as a process of on-going adaptation to a complexity of often violent forces and events. This situation changed, however, when the migrants decided at some point to stay in Germany and rejected being pushed around from one country to the other. They decided to fight for their right to stay and started organizing politically:

> And we found ourselves here in Hamburg. And we cannot be touring from one country to another. That's not happening.
>
> The kind of people that come here used their initiatives (.) used their wisdom to organise people. . . . I said no. I cannot be doing (.) I mean (.) been pushed from one country to another. It doesn't work that way.[33]

They looked for partners to realise their project and managed to secure support from powerful societal actors such as the church and the trade union, which they joined.

> If you talk about some institutions in Germany or in Hamburg, you mention churches, you mention trade unions, you mention universities. And these are the strong institutions here, which we have gained (.) ah (.) their permission to be part of us and we are part of them. And our fight has now become their fight. When it comes to the political situation, when it comes to what they call (.) ehm (.) the individual (.) I mean (.) social and humanitarian situation they have become a partner of us.[34]

This reveals a transformation and re-politicisation of the initial moment of forced migration. This initial moment is transformed into an opportunity, a means of identity-building and resistance. Pointing to the forces of war that made migration as adaptation to the situation in Libya necessary, and the NATO intervention, a decisive part of the conflict (Seeberg 2013a: 168), makes it possible to construct the common political subjectivity of *Lampedusa in Hamburg/Berlin*. The interviewees emphasise European participation in the NATO campaign and frame their migration to Europe, and to Germany, as a consequence of the former, which 'destroyed many

---

33 Interview Asuqu Udo, Hamburg, Summer 2013.
34 Interview Asuqu Udo, Hamburg, Summer 2013.

things'[35] for them: 'They cause trouble far away but the troubles come to them now.'[36] The latter quote is fascinating for two reasons. First, it is a perfect expression of the complexity of international relations in which a political action in one place can have unforeseen consequences in other places. And second, it shows that the group is well aware of their political power, which rests in the possibility to make visible that which is otherwise blurred and bring close that which is usually far away. The political identity, which revolves around the common experience of forced migration and the feedback to the NATO intervention, offers discursive means to resist the situation brought about by external factors and functions as a basis for formulating migration as transformation. One can see that migratory decisions are not only influenced by structural forces, but that there are also moments of autonomous decision-making throughout the journey from the migrants' Sub-Saharan countries of origin, through the Mediterranean to Germany, which they decided to make their final destination. However, their autonomy is always relational as they are embedded in particular contexts, which shows that there is a constant interplay between structural factors and individual agency in migratory decision-making, as well as between adaptation and transformation.

Complexity and the Contradictions of the EU Migration System

Individual migratory decisions were influenced by the complex interplay between individual and structural conditions. Global or regional events like the Arab uprisings, the economic crisis in Europe and the war in Mali are interwoven with personal situations each migrant is facing. In this chapter, we would like to highlight the need to look at the micro-perspective to understand how complex macro-level events impact upon the individual, which then, in a kind of feedback loop, result again in a macro-phenomenon. Those kinds of developments are unforeseeable, which shows that causality of migratory decisions is non-linear and emergent. For example, interviewees who originally came from Mali but had been working in Libya for years until being forced to come to Europe by the Libyan civil war, did not receive asylum in Italy before the Northern Mali conflict broke out in 2012. Furthermore, they received a longer stay permit than other interviewees who were from other Sub-Saharan countries:

> After a year and eight months [in Italy], the war in Mali started. Well, and they gave us the protection. For a stay of three years, three years, yes.[37]

---

35 Interview Anthony Nwoye, Hamburg, July 2013.
36 Interview Affo Tchassei, Hamburg, July 2013.
37 Interview Bibi, Berlin, Summer 2013 (own translation).

This quote points to the abovementioned legal problem that migrant workers who are displaced from the country they were working in do not have a clear legal status or a right to protection according to the Refugee Convention. Their legal status is only dependent on the situation in their country of origin, contradicting the fact that their personal situation is tied to the events in the place of habitual residence.

Another example of emergent causality would be how the economic crisis and large number of refugees following the war in Libya not only affect Italy, but other European countries as well. The events in the Mediterranean have lead to 'more complex preconditions for European decision making' (Seeberg 2013b: 72), a situation the EU is hardly able to adapt to. In addition to the fact that there are no clear rules for the legal status of subsequently displaced migrant workers, the current European migration system also does not accommodate for unforeseeable events. The cases of our interviewees prove that the European migration and asylum system, which is fragile and still in the making, was simply overwhelmed by the interplay of two complex crises: the upheavals and the resulting violence in North Africa and the Middle East as well as the global economic crisis and resulting Euro crisis. Both developments culminated in Italy in unforeseen ways and led to a situation in which tens of thousands of migrants were systematically abandoned.

Though the EU launched 'A New Response to a Changing Neighbourhood' to review the European Neighbourhood Policy already in May 2011 as well as a renewed migration strategy, actual policy response and implementation of foreseen measures were not apparent (Seeberg 2013a: 167). There is no flexibility in existing rules to offer a possibility to react quickly to complex global situations. Moreover, the initial steps of the EU regarding migration from the Southern Mediterranean after the outbreak of the Arab uprisings show that there is no political will from the side of the EU to rethink migration and refugee policies. As Seeberg (ibid.: 157) states, 'it seems apparent that the EU has not been able to develop adequate new approaches regarding migration.' Before the Arab Spring, the European Union strived to externalize border control, so that Gaddafi acted as a European 'coastguard', who hindered migrants who tried to reach Europe by boat (e.g. Hamood 2008). After Gaddafi's fall, in the direct aftermath of the war, the Italian government attempted to convince Libya's provisional government to abide by bilateral agreements on migration control (Horst et al. 2013: 3). This shows that the European states continue to pursue a policy of closure and the practice of externalizing borders, though consequences of these practices cannot be foreseen.

Furthermore, not only did it try to keep up existing agreements after the outbreak of the Arab uprisings, but the European Union even enhanced efforts with regard to externalizing migration policy, 'by setting up "mutually beneficial" partnerships with third countries in North Africa' (Carrera et al. 2013: 2). Carrera at al. (2013) note here a 'business-as-usual' approach to migration, building on assumptions of insecurity and focusing on surveillance and control. This goes along with requirements for third countries to embrace European security policy and adopt the corresponding instruments to facilitate surveillance and border management. This lack of flexibility (in existing rules, as well as in European 'thinking' about migration) again has consequences for the individual migrants who have to cope not only with those events that provide the initial reasons to move, but also with rules that are not made for unexpected situations. This chapter has shown, however, that throughout our research we noted an ability among our interviewees not only to adapt to these adverse situations, complex events and rules, but also to use migration as a means for transformation and political change on the micro as well as on the macro level.

Conclusion

We draw four concluding points from our theoretical considerations and the analysis of empirical material we have obtained through field research in Hamburg and Berlin in 2013. The case study on Sub-Saharan migrants travelling to Europe through the Mediterranean points out that, first, migratory decisions depend upon a complex interplay between subjective and structural factors. We were able to show that migrants are not simply pushed or pulled from one place to another, but that there are moments of autonomy in every stage of the journey. Second, autonomy is relational, depending on actual circumstances and the abovementioned interplay between structural factors and individual agency. Therefore, we account for the importance of structural factors – thereby avoiding romanticising the migration process – but still acknowledge the migrants' individual agency. Third, events that develop into decisive factors for migratory decisions are often unpredictable. Hence, causality is not linear but emergent. And fourth, both, emergent causality and moments of autonomy can be traced through qualitative investigation. By taking a closer look at the individual's trajectories, the interplay of macro-level events, personal preferences and relational autonomy on the micro-level, as well as feedback loops again impacting the macro-level can be observed. In 2015, these observations are more relevant than ever. Regarding ever more refugees entering Europe and heated public debates about assumed 'asylum abuse' and the non-functioning of the 'Dublin system', one should keep in mind that simplified explanations do not do justice to any migration project. Furthermore, the failure of EU members to speak with one voice and to agree on a common asylum and migration policy once more illustrates the inability of the EU multi-level system to deal with complex problems. Despite all the misery some hope rests in the transformative potential that undergirds migratory projects themselves. Hence, the multiple political projects of migrants reaching the EU, their increased visibility in mainstream media and increased presence in core EU member states, may feed back to the macro level and hence, could lead to urgently needed reforms of EU migration policies.

References

Carrera, Sergio, Joanna Parkin and Leonhard den Hertog (2013) *EU Migration Policy After the Arab Spring: The Pitfalls of Home Affairs Diplomacy*, Notre Europe – Jacques Delors Institute, Policy Paper 74, Paris, http://www.notre-europe.eu/media/arabspringmigration-carreradenhertogparkin-ne-jdi-feb13.pdf?pdf=ok [30/09/2014].

Connolly, William E (2004) 'Method, Problem, Faith', in Ian Shapiro, Rogers M Smith and Tarek E Masoud (eds) (2004) *Problems and Methods in the Study of Politics*, Cambridge University Press, Cambridge, 332–9.

Connolly, William E (2005) 'The Evangelical-Capitalist Resonance Machine', *Political Theory* 33/6, 869–86.

de Haas, Hein (2007) *Remittances, Migration and Social Development: A Conceptual Review of the Literature*, Social Policy and Development Programme Paper Number 34. Geneva: United Nations Research Institute for Social Development.

Fargues, Phillipe and Christine Fandrich (2012) *Migration after the Arab Spring*, MPC Research Report 2012, San Domenico di Fiesol: European University Institute, Robert Schuman Centre for Advanced Studies, http://www.migrationpolicycentre.eu/docs/MPC%202012%20EN%2009.pdf [30/09/2014].

Hamood, Sara (2008) 'EU–Libya Cooperation on Migration: A Raw Deal for Refugees and Migrants?', *Journal of Refugee Studies*, 21/1 19–42.

Horst, Jakob, Annette Jünemann and Delf Rothe (2013) 'Logics of Action in the Euro-Mediterranean Political Space: An Introduction to the Analytical Framework', in Jakob Horst, Annette Jünemann and Delf Rothe (eds) (2013) *Euro-Mediterranean relations after the Arab Spring: Persistence in times of change*, Ashgate, Farnham, 1–20.

Glynos, Jason and David R Howarth (2007) *Logics of Critical Explanation in Social and Political Theory*, Routledge, London.

Koser, Khalid (2012) 'Migration, Displacement and the Arab Spring: Lessons to Learn', Brookings Opinion, http://www.brookings.edu/research/opinions/2012/03/22-arab-spring-migration-koser [30/09/2014].

Lakoff, George and Mark Johnson (1998) *Metaphors We Live By*, University of Chicago Press, Chicago.

Lee, Everett S (1966) 'A Theory of Migration' *Demography* 5/1 47–57.

McNevin, Anne (2013) 'Ambivalence and Citizenship: Theorizing the Political Claims of Irregular Migrants', *Millennium: Journal of International Studies* 41/2 182–200.

North Atlantic Treaty Organization Fact Sheet (2011) *NATO No-Fly Zone over Libya Operation UNIFIED PROTECTOR*, http://www.nato.int/nato_static/assets/pdf/pdf_2011_03/20110325_110325-unified-protector-no-fly-zone.pdf [05/09/2014].

Nyers, Peter (2006) 'Taking Rights, Mediating Wrongs: Disagreements over the Political Agency of Non-Status Refugees', in Jef Huysmans, Andrew Dobson and Raia Prokhovnik (eds) (2006) *The Politics of Protection: Sites of Insecurity and Political Agency*, Routledge, London, 48–67.

Papadopoulos, Dimitris and Vassilis Tsianos (2013) 'After citizenship: autonomy of migration, organisational ontology and mobile commons', *Citizenship Studies* 17/2 178–96.

Scheel, Stephan (2013) 'Autonomy of Migration Despite its Securitization? Facing the Terms and Conditions of Biometric Rebordering', *Millennium: Journal of International Studies* 41/3 575–600.

Seeberg, Peter (2013a) 'The Arab Uprisings and the EU's Migration Policies—The Cases of Egypt, Libya, and Syria', *Democracy and Security* 9/1–2 157–76.

Seeberg, Peter (2013b) 'Learning to Cope: The Development of European Immigration Policies Concerning the Mediterranean Caught between National and Supra-National Narratives', in Jakob Horst, Annette Jünemann and Delf Rothe (eds) (2013) *Euro-Mediterranean Relations after the Arab Spring: Persistence in Times of Change*, Ashgate, Farnham, 59–78.

5 Privatised Migration Management in the Mediterranean Region and Sub-Saharan Migration Decision-Making*

Tendayi Bloom

Introduction

Privatised migration management in the Mediterranean Region puts migration decision-making increasingly out of the hands of migrants and states and into those of private actors, obscuring policy implications and making responsibility difficult to locate. In the Mediterranean Region, measures taken to curb migration make this particularly relevant. In 2012, the Mediterranean Sea was purportedly one of the busiest and most surveilled stretches of water globally and yet also the one with the highest number of migrant deaths (UN News Centre 2012; see also charts at Brian and Laczko 2014: 18, 20). The concern voiced about the treatment of Sub-Saharan and other migrants in the Mediterranean often ignores the role of non-state actors and the private sector, or focusses only on one side of this – trafficking. This chapter argues that privatisation is a key factor in extraterratorialisation and securitisation of border management in the region. It opens with an overview of privatised Mediterranean migration management and provides an analysis of selected delegated practices across the region. How this may impact upon Sub-Saharan migration decisions is then presented, followed by an analysis of normative-legal implications of this delegation. This chapter argues that delegation leads to an obfuscation of policy and to a relocation of motivations for enforcement which make migration more hazardous and can hamper usual rights protections. This chapter draws heavily upon existing global literature in this area, to look specifically at implications for the Mediterranean Region. The analysis that this makes possible is limited by availability of information and space in these pages, demonstrating the need for much more empirical research in this area.

Privatised Migration Management in the Mediterranean

The Mediterranean context of privatised migration management is important to study, and is becoming more so as the Mediterranean region

---

* This chapter was first submitted in October 2014 and subsequent revisions have been light. I want to thank (in alphabetical order) Megha Amrith, Belachew Gebrewold and Susan Williams, for their thorough comments on earlier drafts of this chapter, and Amy Thomas and Tamsin Ballard for their formatting work. Thanks also go to participants at the UNU-GCM conference on Statelessness and Transcontinental Migration in 2014 for their generous feedback on a presentation on this chapter's themes. All remaining errors are, of course, mine.

becomes increasingly dangerous for migrants. Also important is the global significance of the region itself and its concentration of migration controls (e.g. see Crépeau 2013). As with migration management more generally, measures can be privatised in various ways, which are referred to as: *explicit / implicit* and *direct / indirect*. Explicit privatisation refers to a situation when, for example, a commercial contract is tendered to a private actor. Implicit privatisation, then, involves pressing private entities to undertake migration management activities to avoid sanction or gain award. Sometimes, these functions are delegated directly. On other occasions, the delegation is indirect, for example made by a state to one actor which then re-delegates to another. This taxonomy of privatisation drives the discussion in this chapter.[1]

The Mediterranean Sea has provided crucial maritime connections between Africa, Asia, Europe and the Middle East since the times of the Silk Route which some date to over 2,000 years ago (e.g. Jinyuan 1984; modern perspective in Pliez 2012). It has long been a lively crossing point for trade, ideas and people and still represents a crucial stretch of water. Indeed, of the 35 countries with the world's largest commercial fleets, six have a Mediterranean coastline, representing 15% of the total global number of commercial vessels (UNCTAD 2013: 43). In recent years there has also been an increase in the numbers of military ships in the Mediterranean Sea. For example, NATO counter-terrorism operation Active Endeavour was expanded to cover the whole Mediterranean in March 2004, with collaboration to improve 'Maritime Situational Awareness' approved in 2010,[2] at which time it proclaimed to monitor daily the activity of 'over 8,000 vessels passing through the Mediterranean' (NATO 2010). Meanwhile, the increased tensions in the Southern and Eastern Mediterranean, particularly now in Syria, have drawn still more vessels from outside the region, for example from America (e.g. Shalal-Esa 2013) and Russia (Heritage 2013).

The regions intersecting in the Mediterranean have different levels and types of power. The EU, as a key regional power, has led a process of European-driven Mediterranean engagement since its inception (e.g. Jones 2011). Frontex, the EU's border management agency, is therefore crucial to understanding the Mediterranean migration management context, starting its major sea operations with Operation HERA in 2006 (Andersson 2012: 7). Then Frontex Executive Director Ilkka Laitinen presents this within a 'four-tier access control model' (Laitinen 2007: 129) involving: measures in third countries; cooperation with neighbouring countries; border control; and control measures within the area of free movement, including return.

---

1 For now-classic contemporary analyses of non-state actors, particularly the private sector, in migration control, see, for example: Gammeltoft-Hansen 2011; essays in Gammeltoft-Hansen and Nyberg Sorensen 2013; Kritzman-Amir 2011; Lahav 2003; Lahav 2004; Menz 2009; Salt 2001.
2 www.nato.int/cps/en/natolive/topics_7932.htm [18/07/2014].

This chapter demonstrates that, though not mentioned by Laitinen, private actors are crucial to all four tiers (though much work is also carried out by Frontex and member state staff – e.g. Fischer-Lescano et al. 2009). Privatised migration management in the Mediterranean Region can be difficult to classify. For example, consider Eubam Libya ('the EU Border Assistance Mission'), set up by Frontex in 2013 with an initial annual budget of €30 million for training and developing a border management strategy (Rettman 2013). While the creation of Eubam relocated measures away from Frontex, private actors were then hired within the Eubam framework. For example, in 2013, Eubam Libya contracted the Canadian company GardaWorld (GardaWorld 2014: 38), which also connected with other missions in Niger and Mali.[3] Alongside this, individual States have developed their own frameworks involving non-State entities in migration control.

For this chapter, a detailed analysis was carried out on key instantiations of migration management delegation in legislation. Following the framework set by Gallya Lahav, key scholar in this area (2003 224), Mediterranean states were examined for their use of: sanctions against transport companies carrying persons without documents; punishment for irregular entry or stay of migrants; and sanctions against members of civil society for helping irregular migrants. Figures 5.1, 5.2 and 5.3 demonstrate that most Mediterranean states which have competence and clear policy in this area are imposing sanctions on irregular migration. What becomes clear from the detail, however, is that this is driven by developments in the wider regions intersecting the Mediterranean. For example, some of these sanctions have been introduced, or their punishments made more severe, as part of the EU integration packages for some former Yugoslav Republics, and as part of European Neighbourhood Policy frameworks in North Africa. Figures 5.1 and 5.3 establish the prevalence of some implicit delegation measures. Figure 5.2 exposes the wider context of criminalising irregular entry and stay that supports the delegated measures, and indeed which seems in direct conflict with the 1951 Refugee Convention Article 31 (against penalising refugees for unlawful entry or presence). It is important to recognise that changes imposed in 2015 have not been included, so that in some ways this can now be used as a historical analysis within which to understand subsequent developments.

There is a danger, however, of over-simplification. In several countries, there are ethnic or familial exceptions to sanctions, such as in Malta's 1970 Immigration Act Article 32, which makes an exception to civil society sanction if the person is helping a 'descendent, ascendant, spouse, brother or

---

3 www.eeas.europa.eu/csdp/missions_operations/eubam-libya/eubam_factsheet_en.pdf [13/08/2014].

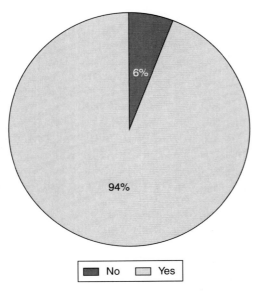

Figure 5.1 Proportion of Mediterranean states imposing carrier sanctions

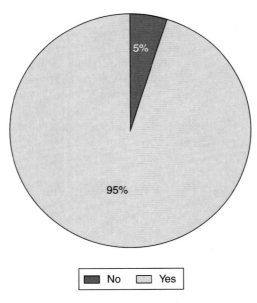

Figure 5.2 Proportion of Mediterranean states imposing punishments on migrants for irregular entry or stay

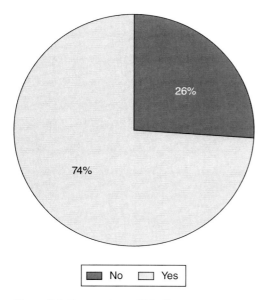

Figure 5.3 Proportion of Mediterranean states imposing sanctions on civil society assistance of irregular immigrants

sister',[4] and Greece's Law 3386/2005(2009), which waives the sanctions on what it construes as illegal entry for persons of Greek descent.[5] In Bosnia and Herzegovina, the civil society sanction is stated indirectly, such that the 2008 Immigration and Asylum Law entitles civil society members to provide irregular migrants with accommodation, but they must also check and report upon their status. The sanction is imposed on failure to declare that an irregular immigrant is residing in your home. This indirect sanction is facilitated by the view that irregular stay is itself considered to be a serious misdemeanour. Two types of privatised migration management in the Mediterranean Region will now be considered: explicit delegation to security companies and implicit privatisation to transporters. Third state delegation will then be introduced, as a mode of indirect privatisation. These discussions can only touch upon key aspects for consideration. See Table 5.1 for a summary of ways in which migration management is privatised in the Mediterranean region.

4 English language version of 1970 Immigration Act with 2009 amendment: http://www.justiceservices.gov.mt/DownloadDocument.aspx?app=lom&itemid=8722&l=1 [October 2014].
5 English language version of 2005 Law 3386 amended in 2009: http://www.mfa.gr/images/docs/ethnikes_theoriseis/codification_of_legislation_en.pdf [October 2014].

Table 5.1 Some ways migration management is privatised in the Mediterranean Region[6]

	Transport Companies and assistance (sanctions)	Immigrants (punishment for irregular entry or stay)	Civil society (sanctions for helping irregular immigrants)
Albania	Yes	Yes	No
Algeria	Yes	Yes	Yes
Bosnia and Herzegovina	Yes	Yes	Yes
Croatia	Yes	Yes	Yes
Cyprus	No	Yes	Yes
Egypt	Yes	Yes	Yes
France	Yes	Yes	Yes
Greece	Yes	Yes	Yes
Israel	Yes	Yes	Yes
Italy	Yes	Yes	Yes
Lebanon	Yes	Yes	Unclear
Libya	Unclear	Yes	Yes
Malta	Yes	No.	Yes
Monaco	n.a.	n.a.	n.a.
Montenegro	Yes	Yes	Yes
Morocco	Yes	Yes	No
Palestinian Territories	n.a.	n.a.	n.a.
Slovenia	Yes	Yes	Yes
Spain	Yes	Yes	No
Syria	Yes	Yes	No
Turkey	Unclear	Yes	Yes
Tunisia	Yes	Yes	Yes

6 This table's structure is based upon that of Gallya Lahav in 2003 (224) and all efforts were made to ensure accuracy according to each country's legal framework as of September 2014.

Explicit Privatisation: Security Companies

The role of the private security industry in migration management in the Mediterranean region is complex. Private actors supply 'border control technologies' and ground-staff as well as providing high-level expertise and engaging in lobbying (e.g. Lemberg-Pedersen 2013: 153; Andersson 2012: 10). This section examines two levels of private security company engagement that are particularly relevant to the discussion in this book of Sub-Saharan migrants in the Mediterranean. The first is at the level of policy-making. The second is in the running of detention facilities. Security companies, individually and cooperatively, both advise on policy and supply the security tools needed to respond to the advice (e.g. Leander 2005). Migration has arisen as a security issue in the Mediterranean region for a complex constellation of reasons (e.g. see Huysmans 2000). While the private security sector in migration control helped to respond to an already developing tendency to connect migration and security issues from 2001 onwards, it seems subsequently to have used its role to contribute to an escalation in these security concerns. Gallya Lahav, who has worked extensively on the role of the private sector in migration, notes:

> The involvement of migrants, foreign networks, and ethnic minorities in terrorist attacks across the United States and Europe consummated the link between security and mobility (Lahav 2013: 148).

She describes a developing sense of 'migration as a security issue' largely from the start of the twenty-first century (Lahav 2004: 31). States were left unsure how to meet border security needs, and private companies responded by supplying expertise and manpower. This can be seen in legal mechanisms put in place to allow this relocation of powers. For example, in 2012 Greece added an article to allow the Minister of Citizens Protection to transfer responsibility to private firms.[7]

Where possible documents were read in the original. Otherwise, official translations or unofficial translations produced by NGOs or law offices were used. In three cases electronic language tools were used alongside secondary literature. The work was greatly assisted by the support of staff at the Institute of Advanced Legal Studies in London. Limits of space have precluded explanations of each datum with explicit references. This information is available upon request. Four assumptions were made. First, expulsion has been counted as a punishment if and only if it was characterised as such in the relevant documents. Second, an instance of carrier sanctions was only recorded where transport companies were fined even if they unintentionally carried people across a border. Third, a sanction is recorded even if it has wide-ranging caveats and exclusions. Fourth, housing irregular migrants has been counted as an instance of 'helping' in the second column, while enabling border crossing has not. 'Unclear' indicates that it was difficult to assign a value, based on the assumptions above. Where there is not jurisdiction over policy in the area in question, the value given is 'n.a.'.

7 Document pdf: www.ohchr.org/Documents/Issues/Mercenaries/WG/Law/Greece.pdf [13/08/2014].

Having begun, the process of privatisation in the migration sectors seems to have increased rapidly, so that:

> ... the migration control industry has not only come to encompass almost every aspect of migration management, it also seems to have substantially transformed the way that migration control is being carried out. Privatization first of all feeds into more general trends, such as security logistics and the externalization of control. (Gammeltoft-Hansen 2013: 135)

A number of forums and collaborative entities developed, bringing together European, state and private actors in this area (e.g. see Lemberg-Pedersen 2013: 153). The private sector-led European Organization for Security (EOS) High-level Security Roundtables provides one example of the role of the private security lobby in Mediterranean migration management. EOS describes itself as representing: '41 Members involved in Security providing technology Solutions and Services from 13 different countries of the European Economic Area'[8]. The Roundtables occurred at a time of heightened European fears about cross-Mediterranean migration. Six days after the 2011 Roundtable Italy requested Frontex support securing its southern islands (including, famously, Lampedusa) against elevated migration pressures from North Africa, eventually leading to the HERMES operation.[9] At this 2011 meeting, then Commissioner for Home Affairs Cecilia Malmström declared support for EOS and reaffirmed border control as one of five key objectives in the European Internal Security Strategy that had been adopted in 2010 (EOS 2011: 3), reaffirming migration specifically as a security concern.

A blurring between government and private sector roles can be observed in the institution of the EOS itself and in wider developments around the security lobby. The EOS is a private sector entity, with state and EU actors participating in the Roundtables. Other theorists observe other examples of blurring in this area, in forums like the European Security Research Advisory Board (ESRAB) and the European Research and Innovation Forum (ESRIF), which 'have been granted a large influence on the formulation of the European Union's (EU) priorities on security research' (Lemberg-Pedersen 2013: 153). Indeed, the strong voice of the private sector in EOS Roundtables is clear from Figure 5.4.[10]

Immigration detention is also commonly privatised, often to those private companies also engaged in delegated criminal detention.

---

8 www.eos-eu.com/?Page=whatiseos&tID=1 [15/07/2014].
9 http://frontex.europa.eu/news/hermes-2011-starts-tomorrow-in-lampedusa-X4XZcr [15/07/2014].
10 Data based upon official attendance lists for the events in question.

The Global Detention Project[11] observes an increasing delegation of immigration detention facilities since its inception, including in the Mediterranean, to both private and not-for-profit organisations (Flynn and Cannon 2009: 4). Some detention may also occur outside the borders of the State that seeks the detention, such as in the third-state-run EU-funded detention 'removal centres' in Turkey (e.g. OHCHR 2013b: 11) and the notorious Italian/EU-funded immigrant detention centres in Libya (e.g. HRW 2014). Away from the Spanish mainland, private companies operate in temporary stay centres known as CETIs (Centros de Estancia Temporal de Inmigrantes), founded in 2000 and 1999 in Ceuta and Melilla respectively, the contested (e.g. Gold 2000) Spanish enclaves in Morocco.[12] Eulen Seguridad S.A. was contracted in 2005 for half a million euros for services in Ceuta[13] and in 2013 in both Ceuta and Melilla for €2.9 million.[14] 2013 also saw Serramar Vigilancia y Seguridad S.L. contracted for €2.3 million in the territories.

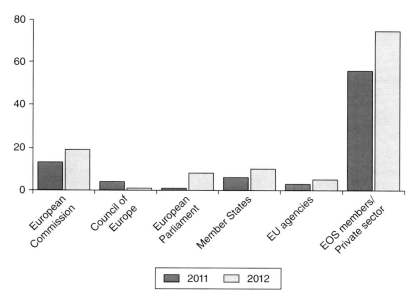

Figure 5.4 Number of attendees from each sector at the EOS High Level Roundtables in 2011 and 2012 (EOS 2011 1, 2; EOS 2012 24–26)

11 The Global Detention Project is an independent research initiative maintaining up-to-date information on migration-related detention globally since 2005. Its funding comes from several philanthropic organisations.
12 Spanish Government website: http://www.empleo.gob.es/es/Guia/texto/guia_15/contenidos/guia_15_37_3.htm [13/05/2014].
13 Official Announcement: www.boe.es/diario_boe/txt.php?id=BOE-B-2005-41031 [13/08/2014].
14 www.boe.es/diario_boe/txt.php?id=BOE-B-2013-19267 [13/08/2014].

Evidence from 2014 suggested that the detained demographic in the CETIs were primarily from Sub-Saharan countries (CoR 2014) and press coverage reinforced the sense that the migration management measures in the Mediterranean at the time were largely seen as directed towards Sub-Saharan migrants.[15] While Sub-Saharans made up a large proportion of this migration phenomenon, Table 5.2 demonstrates that other populations were also migrating through these routes. In 2015, this is further diversified. Private security company activity in the Mediterranean Region, both at level of policy advice and lobbying and in running detention centres, seems based in the region's particular complexity of borderscapes and contributes to, and evolves from, its historical and political peculiarities.

Table 5.2 Frontex detection of irregular[16] border crossing at the external sea borders, by top ten nationalities (Frontex 2012: 47)[17]

	2008	2009	2010	2011	% of Total
Tunisia	7602	1643	711	28013	39
Not Specified	1926	503	288	9153	13
Nigeria	6966	1749	196	6380	9.0
Ghana	2406	351	207	2734	3.8
Afghanistan	18060	12129	3074	2598	3.7
Mali	2334	723	23	2484	3.5
Egypt	2667	544	713	1948	2.7
Côte d'Ivoire	1809	500	142	1734	2.4
Pakistan	517	264	203	1594	2.2
Morocco	3589	973	640	1544	2.2
Others	37856	27779	8063	12990	18
Total for Sea Borders	85732	47159	14260	71172	

Implicit Privatisation: Transporters

As Figure 5.1, above, demonstrates, more than 90% of Mediterranean states impose some form of carrier sanction. Dating back at least 300 years,

---

15 E.g. http://politica.elpais.com/politica/2014/03/17/actualidad/1395088108_855266.html [17/07/2014]; www.nytimes.com/2014/02/28/world/europe/africans-battered-and-broke-surge-to-europes-door.html?_r=0 [13/08/2014].
16 The data source for this uses the Frontex terminology of illegality rather than irregularity.
17 Note that this includes only those who have been caught and includes nationality only as Frontex has managed to establish.

'carrier sanctions' include fines and loss of landing privileges imposed on private companies bringing passengers to a state without required paperwork. Seen as a useful measure against smuggling and trafficking, various instruments oblige states to impose carrier sanctions of some form (see discussion in Rodenhäuser 2014: s2) Contemporary forms of carrier sanctions, as found in the European Council Directive 2004/82/EC, can assume the travel to be by air.[18] This subsection focuses on *maritime* carrier sanctions which have particular relevance to the Mediterranean and lead to specific difficulties. First, like those imposed on air carriers, maritime carrier sanctions can make migration policy *de facto* more restrictive. Second, they can also deter private vessels from rescuing persons in distress at sea, making travel by such routes more dangerous.

Private carrier companies are commercial enterprises. Several commentators have demonstrated, particularly with regard to land and air transport, that in the interests of profit, sanctions demotivate companies from providing humanitarian passage to persons where there is a risk of rejection by the receiving state (eg. Kritzman-Amir 2011; Gammeltoft-Hansen 2013; FRA 2014: 2). The same economic considerations hold for shipping. Erika Feller, who became Assistant High Commissioner (Protection) of UNHCR in 2006, already explained the difficulty in the 1980s:

> A high risk-taking and profit-oriented transport carrier cannot reasonably be expected to make humanitarian decisions based only on a possibility that sanctions will later be waived [if the person's case *is* found to be humanitarian], particularly where the burden of proof is on the carrier. (Feller 1989 57)

Researcher Tally Kritzman-Amir has more recently presented the implications:

> While carriers are threatened with sanctions if they err and allow entry to undocumented migrants, they are not subject to any sanction if they effectively deny entry and admission of asylum seekers. (Kritzman-Amir 2011 203)

That is, to avoid sanction, carriers may be more restrictive than officially required by policy in passenger selection. This makes the safer option of travelling on a passenger ship without relevant documentation more difficult. When migrants plan to claim asylum on arrival, this could be seen as being in tension with the 1951 Refugee Convention Article 33 (against refoulement) (e.g. analysis in Rodenhäuser 2014; see also wider analysis of implications for non-refoulement of external border controls in Fischer-Lescano et al. 2009).

---

18 Indeed, the primary international agreement regarding modern carrier sanctions is the 1944 Chicago Convention (Articles 13 and 29).

The implications of this in the Mediterranean Sea are tragic. Unable to board commercial ships, migrants from Sub-Saharan Africa and elsewhere are often driven to travel in unsafe, overcrowded boats. Indeed, UNHCR has estimated that around 15,500 Sub-Saharan migrants took unsafe crossings in 2012 alone.[19] That number has risen considerably since. The sanctions on carriers impose a further impediment at this stage. If migrants in unseaworthy vessels experience difficulties, commercial vessels may risk sanction if they respond – especially given that rescue of people at sea may already have associated costs relating to deviation and delayed cargo (e.g. Bailout 2003: 749). Indeed, this was one of the conditions blamed for the loss of 63 passengers on the so-called 'left-to-die' boat in March 2011 which was the subject of several investigations (e.g. Strik 2012: 3) and explains the UNHCR decision to give an award to the captain and crew of the ship, *Tampa*, in 2010, which altered course to save migrants in distress at sea.[20] This concern was also raised by the OHCHR Special Rapporteur:

> . . . as the Mediterranean is a busy sea, private vessels could potentially provide invaluable assistance to migrants in distress at sea. Border guards mentioned to the Special Rapporteur that boats in distress are often sighted by private vessels prior to getting into danger. However, the criminalization of migration has contributed to the reluctance of private vessels in assisting migrants in distress. (Crépeau 2013 12)

This has also been recently highlighted by other international organisations, such as UNHCR[21] and UNODC[22], who suggest ways to avoid any deterrence from the obligation to rescue those in distress at sea.

Sanctions placed on maritime carriers are problematic, then, at two levels. First, the resulting restrictions on movement are greater than those explicitly stated in policy and, second, migrants thereby travelling irregularly on unseaworthy vessels are at heightened risk if they experience difficulties.

---

19 http://www.un.org/apps/nes/story.asp?NewsID=45346&Cr=asylum&Cr1#.U8zXLrSD6S4 [15/07/2014], though figures are difficult to confirm and estimates differ between agencies.
20 http://www.unhcr.org/3c975a254.html; Bailliet 2003 gives a useful description of the *Tampa* case and issues that it raises.
21 E.g. in Volker Türk's 2014 statement to the High Level Panel discussion on human rights mainstreaming http://www.unhcr.org/5315b27c9.pdf
22 E.g. 3(3) at p60 in the Model Law against the Smuggling of Migrants, https://www.unodc.org/documents/human-trafficking/Model_Law_Smuggling_of_Migrants_10-52715_Ebook.pdf

Delegating to Third States

Third-state delegation of migration management in the Mediterranean is central to what is known as the 'extraterritorialization' of EU border control, whereby migration management measures are enacted outside the European territories (e.g. see Gammeltoft-Hanson 2011b: 129; more general definition in Milanovic 2011: 8). This is a vast and complex topic that has been carefully examined by leading scholars (e.g. see essays in Ryan and Mitsilegas 2010; also classic discussion in Guild 2001). This section intends only to indicate the context insofar as it is relevant to the discussion here. The importance of the Mediterranean to the EU migration strategy is demonstrated by the Mediterranean focus in the European Neighbourhood Policy (ENP). Of the 16 ENP member states, over half have a Mediterranean coastline. It is also clear from the strong European role in the Union for the Mediterranean (UfM), which has 43 member states (including all EU member states and 15 MENA states). There is an emphasis on tackling what is referred to as illegal or irregular migration to Europe in the Strategy Papers and Action Plans for each of the ENP Mediterranean countries.[23] In the period 2007–2013 nearly €12 billion in grants were provided to the ENP. This remained a priority in 2014. In the early days of the UfM, when it was still the Barcelona Process, migration featured prominently, though this has decreased more recently (e.g. see Solier i Lecha and García 2009).

This third-state delegation alters power dynamics. This is illustrated by the public threat reportedly made by former Libyan President Muammar Al-Gaddafi that 'millions of blacks' could travel to Europe if he were overthrown (Reuters, quoted in Lucht 2013: 174). Whether he actually made this comment or not, it is part of a context in which Al-Gaddafi (accurately) considered Libya's role in curtailing Sub-Saharan migration to Europe as a strong bargaining chip. This arose in the context of substantial EU-Libyan cooperation, as well as cooperation between Libya and individual European states, over migration management since the early 2000s, including the lifting, in 2004, of a 20-year arms embargo (Lutterbeck 2009: 171). This enabled the sale by European private companies of equipment needed to control migration (Lemberg-Pedersen 2013: 158). Directly after the arms embargo on Libya was lifted, Martin Lemberg-Pedersen has found that private security companies from France, UK, Germany, Malta and Russia obtained large contracts with Al-Gaddafi and the European Credit Agencies provided loans for the purchases.

In 2008, the 'friendship pact' committed Italy and Libya to 'cooperation in fighting terrorism, organized crime, drug trafficking, and illegal immigration' (Yaghmaian 2011). This deal included US$5 billion

---

23 Find Strategy Papers at http://eeas.europa.eu/enp/documents/strategy-papers/index_en.htm and Action Plans at http://eeas.europa.eu/enp/documents/action-plans/index_en.htm [13/08/2014].

of Italian investment in Libya and six patrol boats. In 2010 European JHA Commissioner Malmström (who was later to be present at the EOS Roundtables discussed above) signed a €60 million agreement with the Libyan Regime, including the establishment of 'an integrated surveillance system along the Libyan land borders, with a focus on the areas prone to irregular migration flows' (Lemberg-Pedersen 2013: 158). In 2013, the Eubam Libya project (discussed above) was launched, a large portion of which has been allocated to equipment and infrastructure. The private sector has been crucial to this engagement, supplying equipment, expertise, and even financial services. For example, consider the 2006 joint venture between Augusta Westland (subsidiary of Finmeccanica), Italy and Libya, to create LIATEC (Libyan Italian Advanced Technology Company), which received a helicopters contract worth €80 million (Lemberg-Pedersen 2013: 159). LIATEC continued to operate during the Libyan uprisings, but references to it seem to stop after 2010. As the Al-Gaddafi regime fell, the difficulties for Sub-Saharan migrants in the country changed, as they suffered reprisals based on accusations of having had a mercenary role in supporting Al-Gaddafi (see discussions in other chapters in this book).

Bilateral 'pushback' agreements have existed between a number of European and other Mediterranean countries, for example, between Italy and Libya, Italy and Morocco, France and Morocco and Greece and Turkey (e.g. HRW 2014b), such that the receiving partner is given money and equipment in exchange for controlling the flow of migrants and receiving return migrants from their Mediterranean coastal borders.[24] Bilateral agreements or cooperation on migration management are, then, central both to power struggles and to the wider delegated and private migration management infrastructure in the Mediterranean Region. This is also evidenced through the relationship of North African states with the ENP Action Plans, for example. Delegating to Third States, then, alters political power distribution in the Region, not only through the States directly involved but also relating to private interests that are engaged, and in turn changes the migration decision-making context, both for States and for migrants.

Circumventing Regulation

This chapter has indicated some ways in which delegated and privatised migration management, a largely unregulated industry, in the Mediterranean Region, may fall outside the purview of international conventions and agreements. This is because such agreements are made by states primarily in order to regulate the actions of states. Consequently, when migration management activities are privatised, this can seem to obscure the line of responsibility for specific actions undertaken and decisions made. Substantial work has

---

24 Severely criticised in Hirsi Jamaa and Others v Italy, 23/02/2012 ECHRts, leading to Italy's formal cessation of 'pushbacks'.

been done in specific areas to present how state responsibility can be traced (e.g. Rodenhäuser 2014; Pugh 2004; Moreno-Lax 2011). There is, however, a relatively young area of agreement-making, specifically relating to private actors. Three processes will be touched upon here, relating to international corporate social responsibility (e.g. see OHCHR 2013 25):

1   International Code of Conduct for Private Security Providers (ICOC-PSP) (process started 2006, current instantiation since 2013);
2   United Nations Global Compact (since 1990s); and
3   Guiding Principles on Business and Human Rights (2011).

None of these mentions migration management of the delegated form discussed here per se, and certainly not in the role of private actors in the migration industry. ICOC-PSP Article 33 refers to detention in its broadest sense and Article 39 to trafficking. Of the three instruments, the Guiding Principles is perhaps the most direct in addressing migration, referring in II.A.14 to the International Convention on the Protection of the Rights of All Migrant Workers and Members of their Families.

All three make extensive reference to human rights. The discussion of this in the Guiding Principles is particularly interesting, providing three key considerations (also see HRC 2011; OHCHR 2011):

a   States' existing obligations to respect, protect and fulfill human rights and fundamental freedoms;
b   The role of business enterprises as specialized organs of society performing specialized functions, required to comply with all applicable laws and to respect human rights;
c   The need for rights and obligations to be matched to appropriate and effective remedies when breached.

Indeed, the document continues:

> States individually are the primary duty-bearers under international human rights law, and collectively they are the trustees of the international human rights regime. (OHCHR 2011: 7)

However, (b) suggests that private companies do have a responsibility to *respect* human rights. This might extend to refraining from activities contravening this responsibility even when contracted by States (Bloom 2014: 30). Indeed, this notion finds itself in national law. For example, Bosnia and Herzegovina's 2008 Immigration and Asylum Law explicitly prohibits non-refoulement, without specifying who is forbidden from performing it. This is not unique. Indeed, the non-refoulement provision itself shows a recognition of responsibility for what may or may not happen elsewhere (e.g. see Milanovic's 2011 analysis of Soering v UK).

The Articles on the Responsibility of States for Internationally Wrongful Acts 2001 provides a useful idea of how state responsibility may arise (e.g. discussed in Gammeltoft-Hansen 2011: 180): when private actors are empowered to exercise government authority (Article 5); or when States authorise, direct or control private conduct (Article 8). Applying this, however, particularly to implicit measures like carrier sanctions, is not trivial. For example, it is difficult to locate those wrongly prevented from leaving dangerous situations as a result of sanctions in the first place. A combination of bilateral agreements and privatisation, then, allows a new approach to migration management, within a protection framework that is not yet equipped to respond. Although instruments are already in place to allocate responsibility for some of the situations described, this chapter argues that further development is crucial to the continued sovereignty discussions of States, their accountability to their citizens, and to the nature of the relationship between states and noncitizens; and primarily, for the continued protection of the rights of migrants. Moreover, the conditions for, and preventable deaths of, Sub-Saharan and other migrants in the Mediterranean Region make this a particularly pressing concern.

Circumventing Barriers (Smuggling and Trafficking)

Barriers to regular migration options for Sub-Saharan and other migrants to or through the Mediterranean Region lead to an increase in irregular migration, and to new forms of migration. That is:

> Efforts to prevent unauthorized entry and deflect and deter migration not only force sojourners to use facilitators (who now charge migrants higher fees), but also give rise to 'bastard' industries of extortion, trafficking and kidnapping of migrants. (Hernández-León 2013 31)[25]

Evidence suggests that as both legally sanctioned and irregular migration routes become increasingly difficult to access, private enterprises specialising in evading migration restrictions gain in importance (e.g. Lucht 2013: 186). And Aderanti Adepoju, a key scholar of migration in the Sub-Saharan Region, notes that while trafficking was rare in the twentieth century, by 2001 its prevalence was already increasing, as she puts it, 'as young people become involved in daredevil ventures to gain entry to Europe' (Adepoju 2001: 65). However, this also corresponds with the increased securitisation of migration discussed above.

The grey- and black-market migration industry is broader than simply a series of irregular travel agents (e.g. Lucht 2013). It includes the same sectors as those that are involved in privatised state migration management (e.g. see list in UNODC 2013: 11, 18). Evidence suggests that as migration

---

25 Note that Hernández-Léon's focus is upon the US-Mexico border.

management methods become increasingly advanced, the tools of smugglers and traffickers also advance (e.g. Gammeltoft-Hansen and Nyberg Sorensen).

The privatised migration management measures discussed in this chapter are sometimes defended as measures against trafficking and smuggling.[26] This is problematic in two ways. First, as shown, it is not evidentially corroborated that such measures are effective at stopping trafficking. Second, if such measures *can* stop trafficking, they cannot avoid also stopping smuggling, thereby removing what may be the only means of travel for persons in desperate situations.

Before continuing, it is important to note that trafficking and smuggling are distinct, though they can sometimes be conflated, especially in calls for them to be combatted (e.g. UNODC 2014). This ignores the fact that smuggling may often be the only available means of travel for individuals who need to travel (UNODC 2013: 6). Their similarity makes it difficult to combat trafficking without also impeding smuggling and other irregular channels. In the case of smuggling, the middleman performs a service for a fee, enabling the paying migrant to cross the relevant borders and arrive to a particular destination avoiding state detection. This may be dangerous and include unforeseen difficulties, but essentially it is a service that the migrant has decided to pay for, risks and all. Trafficking resembles smuggling, and the line between them can be difficult to draw. However, in cases of trafficking, the migrant undergoes further coercion from the traffickers. This may include having his or her travel documents removed and withheld, or being forced to perform work or services that were not part of the initial agreement and not related to the migration itself. Both the smuggling and trafficking industries benefit from increasingly restrictive border controls, since their services become increasingly necessary. This puts already vulnerable persons at increased risk as they become more dependent upon private migration facilitators.

Increased migration control measures therefore lead to a disempowerment of individuals:

> . . . as the trafficking business expands, the smugglers, rather than the migrants and asylum seekers, make more decisions regarding where their customers go. (Kolowski 2000: 581, discussion on Salt and Stern's classic piece on this topic)

The privatised migration governance in the Mediterranean described in this chapter is, then, expensive, not only for the states who spend large amounts of euros to implement the barriers, but also for the sub-Saharan and other migrants who individually or as households spend thousands of US dollars

---

26 E.g. recommended in Article 11(3) of Protocol replacing the UN Convention Against Transnational Organised Crime (Bloom and Risse 2014).

to circumvent them (e.g. see first-hand account in Chapter 10 of this volume). It also leads to a situation of decreased security, both for states and for migrants. State security decreases as more people are forced to migrate in an irregular and increasingly secretive way, pushing states to turn to private companies for advice and expertise in an ever more specialist industry. The human security of migrants is compromised as they are forced to take greater risks and are, like the states, required to entrust their well-being to the market-driven private actors of the migration management industry. Crucially, though, it relocates decision-making competences away from States and away from migrants.

Conclusion: Changed Relationships and Altered Protections

John Salt, arguably one of the first writers characterising migration as a business, saw the whole of migration, including the role of state actors as behaving within a business-like structure (Salt 2001). He argued that '[t]o understand why migration occurs means studying the operation of institutions which manage and control movement within these businesses' (ibid.: 90). This chapter has argued that the system of protection for vulnerable migrants is designed as if there were only public sector entities involved in these activities. Yet, as many have argued, the migration management infrastructure has become an important and lucrative business for a range of sectors (e.g. Andersson 2012: 7), not least in the Mediterranean Region.

The privatised migration management described in this chapter makes it increasingly difficult and unsafe for Sub-Saharans and others to migrate to or through the Mediterranean Region, either regularly or irregularly. This chapter has presented four types of delegated migration management in the Mediterranean. It has shown the prevalence of explicit delegation to private security companies in a range of contexts and problematised their role, particularly in driving an increasingly security-focused discourse. It then presented the implicit delegation of migration management through carrier sanctions, a measure adopted by more than 90% of Mediterranean states with competence and clear policy in this area. It has argued that maritime carrier sanctions in the Mediterranean are particularly problematic, increasing the danger to migrants in two dimensions.

The chapter also presented indirect privatisation through third states, raising concern that this and the other measures could lead to a circumvention of regulations intended to protect migrants primarily from the actions of states. Moreover, other forms of migration management delegation, smuggling and trafficking, it was argued, are driven by this narrowing of options. For, as barriers to migration are made increasingly complex, increasing layers of (private sector) experts are needed in order both to cross them and to enforce them. This moves migration decision-making away from migrants and states and instead into the hands of smugglers, traffickers, carrier company employees, security companies and migration management experts. Privatised migration management in the Mediterranean, then, needs to be examined carefully in terms of international state obligations and, crucially, sub-Saharan migration decision-making.

References

Adepoju, Aderanti (2001) 'Regional Integration, Continuity and Changing Patterns of Intra-Regional Migration in Sub-Saharan Africa', in M.A.B. Siddique (ed) (2001) *International Migration into the 21st Century: Essays in honour of Reginald Appleyard*, Edward Elgar, Cheltenham, 50–73.

Andersson, Ruben (2012) 'A game of risk: Boat migration and the business of bordering Europe', *Anthropology Today* 28/6 7–11.

Bailliet, Cecilia (2003) 'The Tampa Case and its Impact on Burden Sharing at Sea', *Human Rights Quarterly* 25(3) 741–74.

Bialasiewicz, Luiza (ed) (2011) *Europe in the World*, Ashgate.

Bloom, Tendayi (2014) 'The Business of Migration Management: Delegating Migration Control Functions to Private Actors', *Global Policy*.

Bloom, Tendayi and Verena Risse (2014) 'Hidden Coercion at State Borders: Why Carrier Sanctions Cannot be Justified', *Ethics and Global Politics* 7/2, 65–82.

Brian, Tara and Frank Laczko (2014) *Fatal Journeys: Tracking Lives Lost during Migration*, International Organization for Migration, Geneva.

Cook, Maria Lorena (2008) *Unauthorized Migration and Border "Control"*, Cornell University, School of Industrial and Labor Relations, Ithaca, NY.

CoR (2014) 'In Ceuta and Melilla', Committee of the Regions, European Union, http://cor.europa.eu/en/news/Pages/in-ceuta-and-melilla-cor-president-urges-europe-to-come-up-with-a-common-repsonse-to-immigration.aspx [13/08/2014].

Crépeau, François (2013) 'Management of the external borders of the European Union and its impact on the human rights of migrants' Report of the Special Rapporteur on the human rights of migrants, François Crépeau, Human Rights Council, UNGA, A/HRC/23/46.

Di Bartolomeo, Anna, Thibaut Jaulin and Delphine Perrin (2011) *Palestine: (CARIM) Migration Profile*, Robert Schuman Centre for Advanced Studies, European University Institute, July 2011.

EOS (2012) *A vision for security*, Report of the second High Level Security Round Table, 21 March 2012 Under the high patronage of EC Vice-President A Tajani and EU Commissioner C Malmström.

EOS (2011) *High Level Security Roundtable*, Berlaymont 09 February 2011, Organised by the European Organisation for Security, Under the high patronage of DG HOME Commissioner C. Malmström.

Feller, Erika (1989) 'Carrier Sanctions and International Law', *International Journal of Refugee Law* 1/1 48–66.

Flynn, Michael and Cecilia Cannon (2009) *The Privatization of Immigration Detention*, Global Detention Project Working Paper, GDP, Geneva.

FRA (2014) *Criminalisation of migrants in an irregular situation and of persons engaging with them*, European Union Agency for Fundamental Rights, Vienna.

Frontex (2012) *Annual Risk Analysis*, Frontex, Warsaw.

Gammeltoft-Hansen, Thomas (2013) 'The rise of the private border guard', 128–51 in (Gammeltoft-Hansen and Nyberg Sorensen 2013).

Gammeltoft-Hansen, Thomas (2011) *Access to Asylum*, Cambridge University Press, Cambridge.
Gammeltoft-Hansen, Thomas (2011b) 'Outsourcing Asylum: The Advent of Protection Lite', 129–52 in (Bialasiewicz 2011).
Gammeltoft-Hansen, Thomas and Ninna Nyberg Sorensen (eds) (2013) *The Migration Industry and the Commercialization of International Migration*, Routledge, Abingdon.
GardaWorld (2014) *International Protective Services Brochure*, GardaWorld, Dubai.
Gold, Peter (2000) *Europe or Africa?*, Liverpool University Press, Liverpool.
Guild, Elspeth (2001) *Moving the Borders of Europe*, Inaugural Lecture, University of Nijmegen, 30 May 2001.
Fischer-Lescano, Andreas, Tillmann Löhr and Timo Tohidipur (2009) 'Border Controls at Sea: Requirements under International Human Rights and Refugee Law', *International Journal of Refugee Law* 21/2 256–96.
Heritage, Timothy (2013) 'Russia sends warships to Mediterranean as Syria tensions rise', Reuters, Moscow, 29 August 2013.
Hernández-León, Rubén (2013) 'Conceptualizing the migration industry', in Gammeltoft-Hansen and Nyberg Sorensen 2013, 24–44.
HRW (2014) 'Libya: Whipped, Beaten, and Hung from Trees, Detained Migrants, Asylum Seekers Describe Torture, Other Abuse in Detention', Human Rights Watch, June 22 2014.
HRW (2014b) 'Greece: Investigate Pushbacks, Summary Expulsions', Human Rights Watch, 30 January 2014.
Hilal, Leila and Shahira Samy (2008) Asylum and Migration in the Mashrek, Asylum and Migration Country Fact Sheet, Egypt, Euro-Mediterranean Human Rights Network, Copenhagen.
Huysmans, Jef (2000) 'The European Union and the Securitization of Migration', *Journal of Common Market Studies* 38/5 751–77.
Jones, Alun (2011) 'Making Regions for EU Action: The EU and the Mediterranean', in Bialasiewcz 2011, 41–58.
Jinyuan, Gao (1984) 'China and Africa', *African Affairs* 83/331, 241–50.
Kritzman-Amir, Tally (2011) 'Privatization and Delegation of State Authority in Asylum Systems', *Law and Ethics of Human Rights* 5 193–215.
Lahav, Gallya (2013) 'Mobilizing Against Mobility', in Ola Soderstrom, Didier Ruedin, Shalini Randeria, Gianni D'Amato and Francesco Panese (eds) (2013) *Critical Mobilities*, Routledge, 147–75.
Lahav, Gallya (2004) *Immigration and Politics in the New Europe*, Cambridge University Press, Cambridge.
Lahav, Gallya (2003) 'The Rise of Nonstate Actors in Migration Regulation in the United States and Europe', in Nancy Foner, Rubén Rumbaut and Steven Gold (eds) (2003) *Immigration Research for a New Century*, Russell Sage, 215–41.
Laitinen, Ilkka (2007) 'Frontex and African Illegal Migration to Europe', in Belachew Gebrewold (ed) (2007) *Africa and Fortress Europe: Threats and Opportunities*, Ashgate 127–38.
Leander, Anna (2005) 'The Market for Force and Public Security' in *Journal of Peace Research* 42/5.
Lemberg-Pedersen, Martin (2013) 'Private security companies and the European borderscapes', in Gammeltoft-Hansen and Nyberg Sorensen 2013, 152–72.
Lucht, Hans (2013) 'Pusher stories', in Gammeltoft-Hansen and Nyberg Sorensen 2013, 173–89.

Lutterbeck, Derek (2009) 'Migrants, weapons and oil: Europe and Libya after the sanctions', *The Journal of North African Studies* 14/2 169–84.
Menz, Georg (2009) *The Political Economy of Managed Migration: Nonstate Actors, Europeanization, and the Politics of Designing Migration Policies*, Oxford University Press, Oxford.
Milanovic, Marko (2011) *Extraterritorial Application of Human Rights Treaties*, Oxford University Press, Oxford.
Moreno-Lax, Violeta (2011) 'Seeking Asylum in the Mediterranean: Against a Fragmentary Reading of EU Member States' Obligations Accruing at Sea', *International Journal of Refugee Law* 23/2 1–47.
NATO (2010) 'The God's eye view', Operation Active Endeavour, www.nato.int/docu/review/2010/Maritime_Security/Active-Endeavour/EN/index.htm [13/08/2014].
Pliez, Olivier (2012) 'Following the New Silk Road Between Yiwu and Cairo', 19–35 in Mathews, Gordon, Gustavo Lins Ribero and Carlos Alba Vega (eds) (2012) *Globalization from Below*, Routledge, London.
Pugh, Michael (2004) 'Drowning not Waving: Boat People and Humanitarianism at Sea', *Journal of Refugee Studies* 17/1 50–69.
Rettman, Andrew (2013) 'EU 'mentors' helping Libya stop unwanted migrants', in *EU Observer* 14 October 2013.
Rodenhäuser, Tilman (2014) 'Another Brick in the Wall: Carrier Sanctions and the Privatization of Immigration Control', *International Journal of Refugee Law* 26(2).
Ryan, Bernard and Valsamis Mitsilegas (eds) (2010) *Extraterritorial Immigration Control: Legal Challenges*, Martinus Nijhoff Publishers, Leiden.
Salt, John (2001) 'The Business of International Migration', in M.A.B. Siddique (ed) (2001) *International Migration into the 21st Century*, Edward Elgar, Cheltenham, 86–108.
Shalal-Esa, Andrea (2013) 'Sixth U.S. ship now in eastern Mediterranean "as precaution"', Reuters, Washington, 30 August 2013.
Solier i Lecha, Eduard and Irene García (2009) 'The Union for the Mediterranean', INEX Policy Brief 4/Dec2009, Centre for European Policy Studies.
OHCHR (2013) *Who will be Accountable? Human Rights and the Post-2015 Development Agenda*. OHCHR, Geneva and New York.
OHCHR (2013b) *Report by the Special Rapporteur on the human rights of migrants, François Crépeau, Addendum Mission to Turkey (25–29 June 2012)*, United Nations General Assembly A/HRC/23/46/Add.2.
OHCHR (2011) *Guiding Principles on Business and Human Rights, Implementing the United Nations 'Protect, Respect and Remedy' Framework*. Office of the High Commissioner for Human Rights, UN, New York and Geneva.
UN News Centre (2012) 'Mediterranean the deadliest sea for refugees and migrants, says UN agency' 31 January 2012, www.un.org/apps/news/story.asp?NewsID=41084&#.U8UJ67SD6S4 [15/07/2014].
UNCTAD (2013) *Review of Maritime Transport 2013*, United Nations Conference on Trade and Development. United Nations. Geneva.
UNODC (2014) document supplied for the 12th Coordination Meeting on International Migration, 20–21 Feb 2014, www.un.org/esa/population/meetings/twelftcoord2014/documents/papers/07_UNODC.pdf [13/08/2014].
UNODC (2013) *Corruption and the Smuggling of Migrants*, United Nations Office on Drugs and Crime Issue Paper, United Nations, Vienna.
Yaghmaian, Behzad (2011) 'EU Immigration Policy and the North African Uprising', *Foreign Affairs*, 11/03/2011.

6 Navigating the Eastern Mediterranean

The Diversification of Sub-Saharan African Migration Patterns in Turkey and Greece

Marieke Wissink and Orçun Ulusoy

Introduction

> Boubakar flew from Senegal to Turkey, from where he travelled to Greece in a small boat. After a few months in Greece, his parents suggested that he would come back to Senegal, as he had not yet found a job in Greece. Instead Boubakar returned to Turkey. Not just because there were better job opportunities, but also because he wanted to escape the racism he was violently confronted with in Greece.

> Filemon, from Eritrea, was recognised as a refugee by the UNHCR in Turkey. Years passed by as he was waiting to be resettled to a third country. His girlfriend, who had been working as a housekeeper in Dubai, joined him in Turkey in 2011. A year later their baby was born. In 2013, when resettlement was still not in sight, Filemon re-established contact with former classmates who now lived in Europe. Together they started an import-export business. With the money they earn he plans to apply for a visa to go to Canada.

In common representations of migration from Africa, Europe is considered the intended destination and its neighbouring countries as 'transit zones'. These representations are nourished by images in the media of overcrowded boats and political rhetoric of 'influxes' of migrants, which foster the idea that migrants are heading *en masse* for Europe. The stories of Boubakar and Filemon illustrate that migration processes of African migrants in the Mediterranean Region do not necessarily develop along straightforward lines following the decision to migrate (cf. Wissink et al. 2013). Neither is Europe always the intended final destination. Moreover, their experiences indicate that decisions on migrating to and through the Mediterranean are not only taken at the beginning of the journey; migration is a process which involves various moments of decision-making (see Chapters 4, 9 and 10).

Numerous persons have migrated from sub-Saharan Africa to and through the Mediterranean with the aim of travelling onward to Europe. This chapter portrays a variety of African migration patterns that has emerged in the region during the past few years. Boubakar's return from

Greece to Turkey and Filemon's on-going residence in Turkey to become an entrepreneur instead of awaiting resettlement are two examples of such patterns. They show that migration processes develop in various directions both geographically as well as socially, and challenge common distinctions between categories of migrants that guide policy and research, such as asylum-seekers, labour migrants and irregular migrants, which only capture a snapshot of the migration process as statuses and migration strategies can change day by day (Wissink et al. 2013).

The aim of this chapter is twofold: first it describes how a diversification of African migration patterns has emerged in the Aegean region (i.e. Turkey and Greece) during the past decade in terms of the geographic direction in which the migration process develops. Secondly, it argues how this diversification can be understood in relation to three societal trends. The first is a reverse economic development in Turkey and Greece. While Turkey's economy was growing, Greece experienced a severe financial crisis. The second concerns an increase in xenophobic sentiments in Greece, which is expressed in violent public attacks on migrants. The third is a securitisation of migration that is visible in migration policies. A securitisation of migration entails migration being framed and debated as an existential threat and a security problem (Huysmans 2006). Consequently, migration policies are externalised, which entails states dealing with migration as much as possible outside of the territory to which it is perceived as a threat.

Earlier studies have discussed whether and how securitised migration policy measures have impacted on migration processes, in particular with respect to the effect of border controls on migration flows (Spijkerboer 2007; Baldwin-Edwards 2006; Carling 2007; Pugh 2004; Kiza 2008). These studies have shown that these policies do not deter migration but, in fact, lead migrants to choose other, more dangerous routes. In this chapter, we do not merely assess whether migration has been reduced as a consequence of policies, or whether there are any adverse effects. Instead, we assess how a securitisation of migration has contributed to an environment in which a diversity of migration patterns has emerged.

In our analysis we draw from two main sources. The first is the PhD project of Marieke Wissink at Maastricht University, for which she followed the migration processes of 40 African migrants in Turkey and Greece over a period between one and four years. The aim of the project is to explore the association between changes in migrants' migration trajectories and changes in their personal social networks. The second is the project entitled 'Border Policies and Sovereignty. Human rights and the right to life of irregular migrants', a research project headed by Prof. Thomas Spijkerboer at VU University Amsterdam and coordinated by Orçun Ulusoy. This project aims to analyse the link between border control policies and migrant fatalities at the border. We further draw from shared working experience at the Association for Solidarity with Refugees (Multeci-Der) in Izmir (Turkey), and from our membership in *Kayiki* – a network of professionals, activists and academics with the aim of raising awareness and sharing information on migration on both sides of the Aegean.

The chapter is organised as follows. The next section introduces the migration context in Turkey and Greece to and through which migrants from Sub-Saharan Africa have migrated historically. This is followed by a description of empirical case studies illustrating the diversity of Sub-Saharan African migration patterns in the region. The subsequent sections describe the societal trends, in which we will later situate the diversification of migration patterns.

African Migration in the Aegean

With frequently changing borders and demographics, Turkey and Greece have witnessed internal and international human movement throughout history (İçduygu 2000). Cross-border migration in this part of Europe is therefore not a recent phenomenon that has reached unprecedented levels, as political rhetoric and some media images suggest (De Haas 2008). In the same vein, African migration to and through the Aegean Region is not new. Documented historical relations and human movement between sub-Saharan Africa and the Aegean Region date back to the Ottoman Empire. Several sub-Saharan African countries, including Sudan, Ethiopia, Eritrea and Nigeria were colonised or befriended by the Ottoman Empire and Greece, fostering migration corridors between the regions (Özkan and Akgün 2010; Wheeler 2011).

The number of people clandestinely crossing Europe's southern borders to seek asylum or move onward to other European countries has grown since the 1990s (Düvell and Vollmer 2009). This rise is commonly being associated with more restrictive migration policies that were adopted in the European Union at that time, which made it harder to travel to Europe (Içduygu 2000; Joly 1998; De Haas 2008; Düvell and Vollmer 2009). It has been argued that migrants from sub-Saharan Africa who migrated to seek better living conditions, therefore, engaged in alternative migration strategies, such as travelling by small fishing boats, or by hiding in trucks (De Haas 2008; Carling 2007). At first, this notably happened in the Western and Central Mediterranean, but when border controls intensified, it shifted towards the Eastern Mediterranean (Brewer and Yükseker 2009; Düvell and Vollmer 2009; İçduygu and Yükseker 2012).

In the little scholarly work that is available on African migrants in Turkey and Greece, it is indeed a common presumption that migrants intend to move on to Northern and Western Europe. Brewer & Yükseker (2009) argue based on their 2005–2006 study that most African migrants aspire to reach Western Europe. Referring to migrants from Asia and Africa, the International Organisation for Migration (IOM) (2003: 8) reported that: 'the overwhelming majority of migrants intended to stay in Turkey only temporarily before moving on to western and northern European countries.'

Similarly, Suter (2013: 12) notes that most studies on Africans in Turkey depart from 'an understanding of a temporarily limited stay' but refers to some recent studies that mention settlement of sub-Saharan African nationals (DeClerck 2013; Fait 2013; Suter 2012; Wissink et al. 2013). Part of the explanation for the finding that African migrants in the Aegean intend to migrate to Europe can be found in the widely reported malfunctioning asylum systems, limited possibilities to regularise, and failure to offer protection in both countries on which we will elaborate later.

While migrants indeed continue to take enormous risks to cross Europe's southern borders, field observations and recent studies give at the same time another image of changing migration strategies of African migrants in this region. For many, Europe is no longer the intended destination, and business opportunities incite prolonged stay in Turkey, or a total change of direction, for example to Dubai or China (DeClerck, 2015; Schapendonk 2013; Şaul 2014). These various patterns are presented in the next section.

A Diversification of Migration Patterns

We distinguish between migration patterns based on the geographic direction in which migration processes unfold, in order to nuance the common presumptions that migration is commonly directed at Europe. Indeed, migrants continue to aspire to migrate to Europe and numerous migrants take risks to do so. Yet, with these patterns we will show that there is a diversification of directions in which migration processes evolve. The patterns are exemplified based on individual cases that were encountered during fieldwork and working experience, and which are not in any way exhaustive.

Pattern 1: From Wanting to Leave Turkey to Wanting to Stay

Mohamed travelled from Guinea to Turkey with the idea of moving onwards to Greece, and from there to Western Europe. Once in Turkey, he realised that in order to travel to Greece, he needed more money than anticipated. Furthermore, from others who already travelled from Turkey to Greece, he understood that he would need to save money in Turkey before coming to Greece, because in Greece it would be very difficult. Based on this, Mohamed decided to explore possibilities to make a living in Turkey instead. In May 2013, a year after Wissink's first meeting with Mohamed, he no longer aspired to go to Greece. Instead, he was in the process of starting his own successful business by assisting business people who had come from West Africa or Europe to Turkey to purchase goods. For now he was content to stay in Turkey. His dream for the future is to live in Guinea and become like some of the traders he assists: living in Guinea and only coming to Turkey to purchase goods and resell them at home.

Mekdes, from Ethiopia, made the choice to stay in Turkey only after she had already tried several times to leave Turkey clandestinely for Greece. Before coming to Turkey, she had been living in Syria for a few years where she worked as a domestic worker. At the end of her contract she developed the plan of going to Europe via Turkey, as she believed the chances of finding a job would be higher in Europe than in Ethiopia. Twice she was arrested at the Turkish-Greek border. When she became pregnant she decided to stay in Turkey. Her partner then successfully started a cargo business in Turkey, and Mekdes no longer saw the need to take the risk of crossing the border to Greece with a child. Occasionally she works in a restaurant and does not struggle much to make ends meet. She does, however, aspire to leave Turkey if opportunities to regularise her son are not forthcoming.

Pattern 2: Reorienting Away from Europe and Turkey

The example of Filemon in the introduction illustrates that migrants are seeking alternative strategies to leave Turkey when resettlement is not in sight. He believed it would be easier to obtain a visa for Canada than for a European country. 'Europe? That is definitely over', said Moussa, from Senegal, as well, while sitting in a living room in Istanbul that was stuffed with merchandise such as bags, shoes, perfumes, watches and jewellery. When we met he was on his way from Senegal to Dubai from where he would continue to China. He only stopped by in Istanbul to meet some of his old friends from the time when he used to live there. He had returned to Senegal to start a trading business. Senegal was his base, but for many months he was on the road looking for trading opportunities. In his opinion it is no longer possible to do business in Europe because they do not grant visas. He alleged that it is much easier in Dubai and China. During his stay in Istanbul he encouraged his friends to do the same.

Not only China, but also other countries are becoming new (intended) destinations for migrants in Turkey. Maryam, from Senegal, intends to go to Morocco. She explained that an acquaintance of hers lives there and sells goods in public spaces without being troubled by the police. Maryam was also selling in Turkey, but her goods were regularly taken by the *zabıta*, the city surveillance which controls whether street vendors have a license. This happened at least once a week. Maryam has family in Spain: two uncles and their children. She does not initiate contact with them, but when they call she always answers. During our first meetings in 2012 her family in Spain encouraged her to join them. Maryam did not consider this option as she believed it would be easier to sell in public spaces in countries such as Turkey and Morocco. Indeed, the *zabıta* constitutes a big problem for her, but in Europe it would not even be possible to try, she reckoned. A year later, she said her family now understood she is really not interested in going to Spain, or any European country anymore.

Pattern 3: Returning from Greece to Turkey

Boubakar's story in the introduction is not an isolated case. In 2012, and even more in 2013, groups of returnees from Greece would arrive in Istanbul on a daily basis. Abdu, from Senegal, arrived in Greece in 2007 after having only spent one day in Turkey. After three months in Greece, he found a job in an electronics company where he worked for about 1.5 years but was fired when the crisis started. He explained that:

> After the crisis, life in Greece became harder. Before the crisis, the police and the original Greeks were ok. But after the crisis, they caused many problems, and they became racists. Sometimes, the racist people organise themselves. They go inside our community and they shoot. My friend was killed by them. They don't come every time, but you just don't know when they come. (Abdu, Istanbul, June 2012)

Like Boubakar, Abdu heard from fellow migrants in Istanbul that conditions were better there, both economically as well as in terms of safety, and he decided to return.

Safiye, from Somalia, returned from Greece to Turkey as well. She applied for asylum in Turkey in 2008. She wished to be resettled in Norway where her son lived and from whom she was separated about 15 years before, but the Norwegian Embassy rejected her application. Upon this, Safiye decided to travel to Norway by herself. With financial help from her son, she crossed the land border and spent a few months in Greece, where she contacted the Norwegian Embassy, as well. Also the Embassy in Greece could not help her. Next, Safiye tried leaving Greece several times with fake documents but was arrested each time. One day she reckoned her only chance would be to go back to Turkey, try to reopen her file at the UNHCR that had been closed, and wait for resettlement elsewhere. Safiye took a train to the land border with Turkey and crossed the Evros River which forms the border by foot. She walked through a forest for days and survived by eating wild fruits. Once in Turkey, the *jandarma* (the Turkish military police) found her and put her in detention. Two weeks later she was released, and travelled to the city where she used to live, and moved back to her old house. She reported herself to the UNHCR who ultimately reopened her case.

Pattern 4: Leaving Greece through the Balkans

Common ways by which migrants try to leave Greece are by plane and boat. Ilyaas from Somalia attempted to leave Athens by plane several times. Almost each time, he was violently confronted by the police, who escorted him to a basement where he claims to have been punched in his face, a claim that was made by various interviewees. One day, Mohamed decided that he would not want to try and leave Greece again by this means. Instead, he started walking from Greece to Macedonia, Serbia and Hungary. Patrick, from Senegal, travelled the same route and described his journey as follows: 'I thought I had seen it all when I was beaten at the airport. But that is nothing compared to the mafia you meet in Macedonia. When I was in the woods, I wished I had stayed in Greece.'

Osman from Eritrea had tried leaving Greece by climbing under trucks that would be loaded on ships to Italy. He lived in a forest nearby the harbour so that he could try regularly to climb under a truck. He said during an interview in May 2012: 'when I lived in the forest, I felt like a free man. I did not need to worry about paying the rent, or being attacked by someone. Most importantly, when I lived in the forest I still had hopes that one day it would be better'. One day, he broke his arm and had to return to Athens. A year later, he started walking, as Ilyaas and Mohamed did: through Macedonia, Serbia and Hungary.

This chapter will argue that these new patterns are embedded in three societal trends, which are first described in the following two sections.

Reverse Economic Developments and Xenophobia in the Aegean

The economic power balance in the Aegean region has taken a remarkable turn during the past decade. Whereas Greece has suffered from one of its severest economic crises since WWII, Turkey has witnessed its largest economic growth. In this section, we describe the parallel developments in both countries and relate this to increased xenophobic violence in Greece.

In 2009, a large budget deficit marked the onset of Greece's economic crisis. Since then, Greece has implemented strict austerity measures to be able to qualify for loans. Despite these measures, Greece' debts continued to increase while unemployment rates went up (Kentikelenis et al. 2011; Matsaganis 2011). The Migration Policy Institute (2012) argues that the harshened labour conditions have in particular had negative implications for the immigrant population, although Triandafyllidou and Lazarescu (2009) note that, in Greece, migrants' labour conditions have always been harsh. When the Greek court acquitted farmers who shot 28 Bangladeshi strawberry pickers in July 2014 (Smith 2014), anti-racist groups saw this as another sign of the degrading conditions migrants are kept in in the country.

The economic crisis paved the way for the electorate to turn away from mainstream parties towards the far-right anti-system and anti-immigrant party the Golden Dawn (cf. Ellinas 2013). The Golden Dawn aims to radically transform the Greek State by excluding non-Greeks to form a democracy which they define as '[the] state of the demos, that is of the People, made up of individuals of common descent' (Golden Dawn 2012). Until the late 2000s, the nationalist ideology was not very popular in Greece. Yet, when mainstream political parties lost their legitimacy and Greece faced challenges with managing migration, the anti-systemic profile of the Golden Dawn attracted a relatively large part of the electorate (Ellinas 2013); it received 0.29% of the votes in 2009 and nearly 7% in 2012.

Doxianis and Matsaganis (2012) argue that by 2012, xenophobic nationalism had become the mainstream ideology in Greece. Interviews and observations in the field showed what this meant for the everyday realities of migrants in Greece. Ibrahim, from Eritrea, for example explained:

> When they arrest us on the street, first they ask what we are doing here, and they ask for papers. . . . Then they ask for our belongings, we have to give them everything we have, our money. Then they handcuff us. Also people with pink card [asylum documents]. They beat and kick us, and then we are put in a bus. It is awful. When they do that, I feel like I killed someone, or that I am a terrorist. But I didn't do anything; they just catch people when they are sitting in a park, or in the internet cafe, or when are walking on the street. (Ibrahim, Athens, 5 May 2012)

By 2012, migrants did not only increasingly face xenophobic and aggressive behaviour by state officials; the HRW (2012) reported various accounts of violence against immigrants where groups of people used bare feet or bottles as weapons in public attacks. The HRW further found that the police failed to effectively protect victims and bring the perpetrators to justice (Human Rights Watch 2012).

Unlike Greece, Turkey has experienced strong economic growth during the past decade. This is expressed in a nearly doubling of the GDP since 2002, and a steep decline in unemployment figures (Commission on Growth and Development 2010). Moreover, Turkey has drawn the attention of international investors, expressed in Turkey's first investment-grade credit rating in two decades (Peker 2014). The growing economy and expanding investment climate in Turkey has gone hand in hand with an expanding informal economy, mainly in the trade, textile and cargo sectors. Working opportunities in trade and petty jobs for migrants have risen as a consequence (Şaul 2014; Schapendonk 2013). An increase of 68% in the granting of working permits to third country nationals further points to improved employment opportunities in Turkey (Toksöz et al 2012).

Seen from an economic perspective the developments in Turkey seem positive. Yet, from a human rights perspective there is much to be desired. Working conditions in informal petty jobs are challenging, and migrants are prone to exploitation (Toksöz et al. 2012). Furthermore, the expansion of the informal labour market mostly concerns Istanbul, and to a lesser extent Ankara and Izmir. Asylum-seekers and refugees residing in satellite cities continue to have much fewer opportunities to benefit from economic development.

The Securitisation of Migration in the EU, Turkey and Greece

Marcelino, Ferreira and Mazzaglia argue in Chapter 2 of this volume that a 'securitarian narrative to migration' characterises European public policies, a widely accepted view in scholarly literature on migration and asylum in the EU (see Léonard 2010; Buonfino 2004; Huysmans 2006; van Munster 2009) although critical views are put forward, too (Boswell 2007). Securitisation means that in political and societal arenas migration is being framed as a threat to security, and it is is expressed in policy measures that are aimed at deterring migration (Van Munster 2009). In this section, we first briefly describe what this entailed in the European Union, and then how this has impacted on the migration systems in the Aegean. We reiterate that the type of migration we are referring to is irregular migration; policies on other forms of migration, such as high-skilled labour migration, are less often regarded from a security perspective (although it could be argued that the distinction between 'wanted' and 'unwanted' migration is in itself a manifestation of the securitisation discourse).

The Securitisation of Migration in the EU

Notably in the early 2000s, the management of irregular migration in Europe and at its external borders had become a controversial topic in political and societal debates. The securitisation process gained momentum after 9/11 2001 and the Madrid and London bombings on 11 March 2004 and 7 July 2005, respectively, when migration became associated with terrorism and criminality (Neal 2009). Yet, the need for greater legislative action regarding the external borders and the treatment of third-country nationals is also analysed as a consequence of the abolishment of the internal borders within the EU, and the decision to develop an Area of Freedom, Security and Justice (AFSJ) (European Council 1999; Cardwell 2013).

Frontex was established in 2004 to coordinate external border management. Among its activities are the assessments of the 'risk' of migration towards the EU. Marcelino et al. (Chapter 2 in this volume) analyse the framing of migration as a risk as a demonstration of securitisation. This was also concluded by Léonard (2010), who further demonstrated that Frontex constitutes securitising practices by conducting activities that are traditionally used to tackle security issues and extraordinary measures, which further include the training of national border guards, the coordination of joint surveillance and control and joint return operations.

Policies with respect to irregular migration and asylum policies were further securitised in the EU by the establishment of EUROSUR to coordinate surveillance at the maritime borders; the signing of readmission agreements by which undocumented third-nationals can return to neighbouring transit countries and countries of origin; and the creation of mobility partnerships where development funding was exchanged for measures preventing irregular migration (see Chapter 5 about the privatisation of such measures). We will go deeper into the measures taken that impacted on the Aegean migration context below.

The Securitisation of Migration in Turkey and Greece

Our analysis of the securitisation of migration in Turkey and Greece starts from the observation of three shared characteristics of migration systems in both countries, which are based on a national security approach, reactive instead of proactive migration management, and operate in the shadow of the EU. While the first two have been shaping the migration system since the establishment of both countries, the EU has predominantly been leaving its mark on the migration systems in the Aegean for the past 20 years.

The national security approach in both countries can be explained by their history of nation-building (Cizre 2003; Karaosmanoglu 2000). While Greece declared independence from the Ottoman Empire in 1822, the First World War (1914–1918) and the Greco-Turkish War (1919–1922) shaped the borders and international relations of present-day Greece and Turkey. One of the most defining events for the process of nation-building was the population exchange between Turkey and Greece which followed the Convention Concerning the Exchange of Greek and Turkish Populations, signed in Lausanne on 30 January 1923. The exchange involved the expulsion of Anatolian Greeks to Greece, and Greek Muslims to Turkey (Long 2008). Clearly, by the forced population exchange, national security concerns were separated from human rights (Long 2008). Long (2008) argues that because of the 'un-mixing of peoples' key political figures considered the exchange as a contribution towards 'long-term stability of the Aegean through the nationalisation of political power structures and thus the exclusion of difference'. The 'successful' execution of the Treaty of Lausanne thus paved the way for both governments to implement reforms for the nation-building process, without the threat of internal minorities, or external interventions related to their protection (Oran 2007; Pentzopoulos 2002).

Related to the national-security approach is the reactive way in which both countries develop migration policies (Triandafyllidou 2012). For the past two decades, main migration policy was realised only after unanticipated arrivals of migrants. In Greece, the first law on immigration was implemented in 1992 to address the irregular migrant flows from Albania (Triandafyllidou 2012). Almost simultaneously, Turkey faced a humanitarian crisis at the southern borders when hundreds of thousands of Kurds fled from their homes in Iraq to escape Saddam Hussein's threats (Içduygu 2000). Until then, there was an absence of legal instruments and policies on migration, but the sudden political and humanitarian crisis forced Turkey to issue the first regulation on migration and asylum in 1994 (Kirişci 2000).

This chapter argues that the reactive, rather ad-hoc migration policies in Turkey and Greece stem from a political gap that was created on purpose to deregulate migration, in particular irregular migration. As argued above, migration is in both countries closely connected to national security concerns (Oran 2007). Therefore, the management of migration was left to bureaucratic elites and security forces, such as police or coast guards. In the absence of asylum and migration legislation, their responses to the arrival of migrants would not be bound by existing regulations and hence not be held liable. This legal vacuum enabled the prevalence of human security concerns over human rights concerns.

The national security-based and reactive approach in both countries was sustainable until the 2000s. While the irregular migration flow from Africa and Asia to Europe via Turkey and Greece already existed, until then the relatively low numbers meant that the situation was under control. However, with the changes in EU migration policies, the migration system in the Aegean became the subject of international migration policies. As a consequence, migration in the region became regulated following a logic of securitisation.

The logic of securitisation in the Aegean migration system is visible at three levels: EU intervention, Turkish-Greek bilateral relations, and national Turkish and Greek asylum and migration policies. In late 2010, Greece called upon the EU for assistance with protecting its borders. The original Regulation 2004/2007 by which Frontex was established was amended, to be able to employ *rapid border intervention teams* (RABIT). These teams consisted of border guards from all member states which could be rapidly employed to provide operational assistance to member states 'facing a situation of urgent and exceptional migratory pressure' (FRONTEX 2007). The RABIT operation was followed by Operation Poseidon, and Poseidon Sea in 2013, to further '[combat] illegal migration flows from Turkey and North Africa towards Greece' (Frontex 2014a). Border control in the Turkish-Greek border region was further strengthened in 2013 by EUROSUR providing surveillance technology, such as drones and night-vision cameras.

One way in which Turkey and Greece have strengthened cooperation on the bilateral level was by implementing a readmission protocol. This had already been signed in 2001 but was put into effect in 2010 as a response to increasing numbers of migrants crossing the Turkish-Greek border. İçduygu (2011) calculated[1] that between 2002 and 2010, 2,425 migrants were readmitted by Turkey, yet in 2010 both countries agreed that Turkey would take at least 1,000 migrants per year. The first group of 30 migrants was readmitted by Turkey in 2010. At that time both authors

---

1 Based on statistics provided by the Bureau for Foreigners, Borders and Asylum, at the Directorate of General Security of the Ministry of Interior of Turkey.

of this chapter worked for a local NGO[2] in Izmir, to where the readmitted migrants were brought. The planned readmission centre had not yet been established[3]. Furthermore, we received testimonies from this group of migrants claiming that Greece reported them as Syrian, whereas in fact only three were from Syria. Considering that Turkey has a readmission agreement with Syria, a readmission protocol between Turkey and Greece could lead to violations on the non-refoulement principle, where persons in need of international protection are returned to Syria. Turkey has also approached African countries, including Sudan, Ethiopia and Nigeria to sign readmission agreements, which implies that the non-refoulement principle could become at risk in the future for African migrants as well (Dervis et al. 2004).

Besides the readmitted migrants, several NGOs have reported the systematic occurrence of 'push-backs', where persons are being returned to Turkey from Greece without court decisions or formal agreements between Turkey and Greece, and 'without being given the opportunity to request international protection or to challenge their illegal removal' (ProAsyl 2013). These push-backs are often violent, of which the incident in the Greek island of Farmakonisi in January 2014 during which 12 refugees died is a tragic example (ProAsyl 2014).

On the national level, action plans were drafted in both countries to strengthen external borders and asylum systems. For Turkey this was done in the context of the Turkey-EU Twinning project on Integrated Border Management (IBM) which commenced in 2010 (Pierini 2010) and meeting the European *acquis* in admission negotiations. The IBM project distinguished between the challenges of creating "open borders" for people and "secure borders" to diminish crime, and by regarding irregular migration as a common interest to be "tackled" by the EU and Turkey (Pierini 2010).

Turkey has adopted its first law on undocumented migrants and asylum-seekers in 2013, which was put into effect in April 2014. Until then, the migration and asylum system in Turkey was regulated by policy directives which lack legislative power. Although Turkey has ratified the 1951 Geneva Convention on the international protection of refugees, it applies a geographical limitation such that nationals from non-European countries cannot receive refugee status and permanent residence in Turkey. With the adoption of its first asylum law, Turkey does not lift this geographical limitation. As before, the UNHCR will continue to assess the asylum claims of non-European asylum-seekers and request their resettlement to third countries (e.g. the United States and Canada). In reality, only a small percentage will eventually be resettled (Blaser 2014). During the asylum procedure carried out by the UNHCR, asylum-seekers are obliged to reside

---

2 Mültecilerle Dayanışma Derneği; www.multeci.org.tr
3 See also the report of the Special Rapporteur of the Human Rights Council of the UN (Crépeau 2013)

in one of the 50 'satellite cities' – normally rural towns where normally no accommodation is provided and asylum-seekers are not allowed to work.

In June 2012, Turkey offered the opportunity for visa over-stayers to obtain a six-month residence permit after paying a fee and a penalty.[4] Migrants who applied for this claimed to have been instructed by police officers to return to their countries of origin to be able to renew their visas upon return. This seemed to be a widespread belief among migrant communities, although no formal instructions had been communicated by the Turkish authorities. In December 2012, this residence permit turned out not to be renewable, and was therefore perceived by many as a way for the Turkish government to collect money and expel migrants.

Greece implemented several measures aiming to stop irregular migration towards and within Greece, including operation *Aspida* that deployed police officers and equipment to the Evros region, and operation *Xenios Zeus* that focused on 'inland detections of illegal stays and their return' (Frontex 2014b np). The rhetoric used by Frontex to describe this mission points out a highly securitised and criminalised approach towards migrants in Greece. Greece further attempted to protect its borders through the establishment of a 12 km fence along the Evros River. Because this only covers 10% of the border, Tsitselikis (2013) analyses this as a response to a 'xenophobic audience' in Greece, rather than as a measure to curb migration. It nevertheless indicates Greece's inclination to deter irregular migration.

Greece has a legislative framework to assess asylum claims and host non-European refugees in accordance with EU law which is, however, largely dysfunctional. In a court ruling by the European Court of Human Rights, Greece was found to be a country where asylum-seekers face inhuman and degrading treatment.[5] Most member states, therefore, do not return asylum-seekers to Greece despite the Dublin Regulation in which members states agreed to return people to the first country of arrival in the EU. Greece has a backlog of 45,000 asylum applications, whereas it is almost impossible for new asylum-seekers to file an asylum claim (Human Rights Watch 2013). During the time of fieldwork in 2012–2013, it was observed that hundreds of people queue up for days in front of the Immigration Office in Athens, where once a week only about 20 applications are taken. They wait on a road in an industrial area, lacking basic facilities such as sanitation or shelter (see UNCHR 2012).

In conclusion, whereas migration in Turkey and Greece has always been a security issue, their responses towards migration flows had been purposefully left to the discretion of bureaucrats. However, when the Turkish-Greek migration context became an object of European security concern, migration policies, including asylum and border policies,

---

4 Based on a policy circular 37 issued by the Ministry of Interior dated 07/06/2012.
5 M.S.S. vs Belgium and Greece, European Court of Human Rights (ECtHR) Case no: 30696/09 Judgment Date: 21/01/2011.

became regulated. To maintain the valued protection of national security concerns, this regulation followed the logic of securitisation that was already prevalent in the EU.

Navigating Societal Trends in the Eastern Mediterranean

From the reviewed studies and the field work the image emerges that until the late 2000s, most migrants from Africa (and elsewhere) perceived both Turkey and Greece as transit countries on their way to Western and Northern Europe, either through their own arrangements or resettlement programmes. The reversed economic developments, xenophobic violence, and securitised migration policies have reshaped opportunities and constraints for migrants in terms of their geographic mobility in the region. Migrants navigate these opportunities and constraints by rethinking migration goals and strategies. As they do so in various ways, a large variety of migration patterns has emerged in the region.

The reversed economic trends in both countries have incited new preferences and options concerning moving to or staying in Turkey and Greece. In Turkey, the economic growth has, for some, created the opportunity to gain an income with business activities, notably in the cargo and textile business. While some have accordingly adapted their original migration goal of seeking asylum in Europe, for others moving on was no longer necessary to realize the original goal of setting up a business. For some, the growing business opportunities in Turkey provided a reason to return from Greece. As these opportunities were mainly unfolding in Istanbul, migrants residing in satellite cities were also drawn to the city. In particular, prolonged stays in satellite cities without the opportunity to work and no resettlement prospects incite migrants to pull out from the asylum procedure and reside in Istanbul instead. Changing economic opportunities and constraints in Turkey and Greece as such impact on original migratory goals, as well as on available financial resources to pursue desired migration strategies.

Strengthened border controls between Turkey and Greece, and between Greece and its bordering countries have resulted in higher apprehension risks and increased smuggler's fees. For migrants in Turkey, this often implied that more funds had to be mobilised and higher risks to be accepted in order to leave Turkey. As in Greece the economic situation was worse and xenophobia widespread, and for many the incentive to mobilise more funds disappeared. At the same time, a permanent state of limbo in Turkey made the challenges foreseen in Greece acceptable for some, if only because there was still a chance of individual success.

For migrants in Greece, the securitised borders meant that leaving the country by air or boat was increasingly challenging. Nevertheless, nearly all migrants we spoke with aimed to leave Greece, including migrants who had stayed in Greece for up to 20 years until the crisis broke out in 2008. Intended departure from Greece was commonly incited by a perceived inability to maintain a livelihood and find protection in Greece due to economic hardship and xenophobic violence. Two patterns have emerged as such: migration over land via the Balkans and return to Turkey. The Balkan-route is experienced as extremely dangerous: several migrants we spoke with claimed that if they had known the dangers in advance, they would have stayed in Greece and accepted living in fear of violent attacks and remaining undocumented instead. Return to Turkey is a recent phenomenon that to our knowledge has not yet received attention within scholarly literature. It was remarkable that whereas migrants in Istanbul spoke rather critically of the local residents in the neighbourhoods where they lived because of their perceived ignorance of foreign cultures, migrants in Greece remember the residents of the same neighbourhoods as tolerant, welcoming and open-minded.

Concluding Remarks

For the past decade, Turkey and Greece have constituted one of the main entry points of irregular migration to the EU. While today numerous migrants from sub-Saharan Africa and other continents continue to intend and attempt travelling this route, recent societal trends have largely reshaped the context in which African migrants in the Aegean (re-)decide upon their migration processes. The trends we described in this chapter concern a rise in xenophobic violence in Greece, a securitisation of migration policies, and reversed economic trends in Turkey and Greece. These trends bring about opportunities and constraints in shaping migration processes. As migrants respond to these in various ways, a diversification of migration patterns has emerged, where in fact some are returning from Greece to Turkey, some are choosing to reside in Turkey instead of migrating to Europe, and others aim to migrate elsewhere or engage in new routes out of Greece.

This chapter limited itself to analysing the link between migration patterns and regional societal trends, but a diversification of patterns naturally arises in interactions with constraints and opportunities that unfold beyond the Aegean. This is especially so for the observed pattern where migrants in the Aegean reorient from Europe and Turkey, notably to the Middle and Far East. Developments in countries of origin, such as the increasingly widespread awareness of the realities of migration in Europe, also influence the creation of new migration patterns.

Restrictive migration policies are often aimed at discouraging and deterring irregular migration, and evaluations of policy are concerned with the question of whether this is achieved or desired. The diversification of migration patterns shows that migration needs to be conceptualised as a process, rather than as a straightforward movement from one country to another that can be stopped or deterred; decisions are often taken on the spot, where current opportunities and constraints are guiding the continuation of the migration process. It furthermore challenges common distinctions between migrants based on a currently applied migration strategy: irregular versus labour migrants versus refugees and asylum-seekers. While navigating societal trends, migrants can be or become all during the migration process. The conceptualisation of migration as a process will generate new policy and research questions. Instead of asking only why migrants move from one place to another, it raises the question of by what mechanisms and under what circumstances migrants re-decide upon routes, intentions and strategies. This will ultimately yield more in-depth insights in the shaping of migration processes.

References

Baldwin-Edwards, Martin (2006) 'Between a Rock & a Hard Place: North Africa as a Region of Emigration, Immigration and Transit Migration', *Review of African Political Economy* 33/108 311–24.

Blaser (2014, 12 November) 'Turkey's 'other' Refugees Languish in Limbo' [online]. *Aljazeera.* http://www.aljazeera.com/news/middleeast/2014/11/turkey-other-refugees-languish-limbo-2014111083938134850.html

Boswell, Christina (2007) 'Migration Control in Europe After 9/11: Explaining the Absence of Securitisation', *JCMS: Journal of Common Market Studies* 45/3 589–610.

Brewer, Kelly T and Deniz Yükseker (2009) 'A Survey on African Migrants and Asylum Seekers in Istanbul' in Ahmet İçduygu and Kemal Kirişçi (eds) (2009) *Land of Diverse Migrations*, İstanbul Bilgi University Press, İstanbul, 637–723.

Buonfino, Alessandra (2004) 'Between Unity and Plurality: the Politicisation and Securitisation of the Discourse of Immigration in Europe', *New Political Science* 26/1 23–49.

Cardwell, Paul James (2013) 'New Modes of Governance in the External Dimension of EU Migration Policy', *International Migration* 51/6 54–66.

Carling, Jorgen (2007) 'Migration Control and Migrant Fatalities at the Spanish-African Borders', *International Migration Review* 41/2 316–43.

Cizre, Ümit (2003) 'Demythologyzing The National Security Concept: The Case of Turkey', *Middle East Journal* 57/2 213–29.

Commission on Growth and Development (2010) *Post-Crisis Growth in the Developing Countries; A Special Report of the Commission on Growth and Development on the Implications of the 2008 Financial Crisis*, Washington DC: The World Bank.

Crépeau, François (2013) 'Report by the Special Rapporteur on the human rights of migrants, François Crépeau: Addendum – Mission to Turkey' (A/HRC/23/46/Add.2): http://ap.ohchr.org/documents/dpage_e.aspx?si=A/HRC/23/46/Add.2

DeClerck, Helene Marie-Lou (2013) 'Sub-Saharan African Migrants in Turkey. A Case Study on Senegalese Migrants in Istanbul', *Ankara Universitesi SBF Dergisi* 68/1 39–58.

DeClerck, Helene Marie-Lou (2015)., Europe is no longer the only "El Dorado" for sub-Saharan Africans: the case of contemporary Senegalese migration to Turkey', *Migration and Development*, (ahead-of-print), 1–19.

Dervis, Kemal, Michael Emerson, Daniel Gros and Sinan Ülgen (2004) *The European Transformation of Modern Turkey*, CEPS, Brussels.

Doxianis, Aristos and Manos Matsaganis (2012) 'National Populism and Xenophobia in Greece', in Fieschi, Catherine, Marley Morris and Lila Caballero (eds)

(2012) *Populist Fantasies: European Revolts in Contexts*, Counterpoint, L. Creative Commons, UK.

Düvell, Franck and Bastian Vollmer (2009) *Irregular Migration in and from the Neighbourhood of the EU. A Comparison of Morocco, Turkey and Ukraine*, Eliamep, Athens.

Ellinas, Antonis (2013) 'The Rise of Golden Dawn: The New Face of the Far Right in Greece', *South European Society and Politics* 18/4 543–65.

European Council (1999) Tampere European Council 15–16 October 1999, Presidency Conclusions.

Fait, Nicolas (2013) 'African Migration Toward Turkey: Beyond the Stepping Stone', *Ankara Universitesi SBF Dergisi* 68/1 21–38.

FRONTEX (2014a) *Archive of Operations. Poseidon*, http://frontex.europa.eu/operations/archive-of-operations/ZCQzCe [20/09/2014].

FRONTEX (2014b) *Eastern Mediterranean Route*, http://frontex.europa.eu/trends-and-routes/eastern-mediterranean-route [20/09/2014].

Golden Dawn (2012) Θέσεις: Ταυτότητα [Positions: identity], http://www.xryshaygh.com/index.php/kinima [6/10/2014].

De Haas, Hein (2008) 'The Myth of Invasion; Irregular Migration From West Africa to the Maghreb and the European Union', *Third World Quarterly* 29/7 1305–22.

Human Rights Watch (2013) *Unwelcome Guests; Greek Police Abuses of Migrants in Athens*, Human Rights Watch, Washington, DC.

Huysmans, Jef (2006) *The Politics of Insecurity: Fear, Migration and Asylum in the EU* 1st edition, Routledge, New York.

İçduygu, Ahmet (2011) *The Irregular Migration Corridor Between the EU and Turkey: Is it Possible to Block it with a Readmission Agreement?*, EU-US Immigration Systems 2011/14, Robert Schuman Centre for Advanced Studies, European University Intitute, San Domenico di Fiesole.

İçduygu, Ahmet (2000) 'The Politics of International Migratory Regimes: Transit Migration Flows in Turkey', *International Social Science Journal* 52/165 357–67.

İçduygu, Ahmet and Deniz Yükseker (2012) 'Rethinking Transit Migration in Turkey: Reality and Re-presentation in the Creation of a Migratory Phenomenon', *Population, Space and Place* 18/4 441–56.

International Organisation for Migration (2003) *Irregular Migration in Turkey*, IOM Research Paper Series, No. 12. International Organisation for Migration, Geneva.

Joly, Danièle (1998) 'Temporary Protection within the Framework of a New European Asylum Regime', *The International Jounral of Human Rights* 2/3 49–76.

Karaosmanoglu, Ali L (2000) 'The Evolution of the National Security Culture and the Military in Turkey', *Journal of International Affairs* 54/1 199–216.

Kentikelenis, Alexander, Marina Karanikolos, Irene Papanicolas, Sanjay Bascu, Martin McKee and David Stuckler (2011) 'Health Effects of Financial Crisis: Omens of a Greek Tragedy', *Lancet* 378/9801 1457–8.

Kirişci, Kemal (2000) 'Disaggregating Turkish Citisenship and Immigration Practices', *Middle Eastern Studies* 36/3 1–22.

Kiza, Ernesto (2008) *Tödliche Grenzen – Die Fatalen Auswirkungen Europäischer Zuwanderungspolitik*, Lit Verlag, Zürich/Berlin.

Léonard, Sarah (2010) 'EU Border Security and Migration into the European Union: FRONTEX and Securitisation Through Practices', *European Security* 19/2 231–54.

Long, Katy (2008) *State, Nation, Citizen: Rethinking Repatriation*, RSC Working Paper Series, University of Oxford, Oxford.

The Migration Policy Institute (2012) *Greece: Illegal Immigration in the Midst of Crisis*, http://www.migrationpolicy.org/article/greece-illegal-immigration-midst-crisis [14/07/2014].
Matsaganis, Manos (2011) 'The Welfare State and the Crisis: The Case of Greece', *Journal of European Social Policy* 21/5 501–12.
Van Munster, Rens (2009) *Securitizing Immigration: The Politics of Risk in the EU* 1st edition, Palgrave Macmillan, Basingstoke.
Neal, Andrew W (2009) 'Securitisation and Risk at the EU Border: The Origins of FRONTEX', *JCMS: Journal of Common Market Studies* 47/2 333–356.
Oran, Baskin (2007) 'Minority Concept and Rights in Turkey: The Lausanne Peace Treaty and Current Issues', in Zahra F Kabasakal Arat (ed) (2007) *Human Rights in Turkey*, University of Pennsylvania Press, Philadelphia, 35–52.
Özkan, Mehmet and Birol Akgün (2010) 'Turkey's Opening to Africa', *The Journal of Modern African Studies* 48/4 525–46.
Peker, Emre (2014) 'Turkey Exits Junk Status', *The Wall Street Journal*, http://online.wsj.com/news/articles/SB10001424052970204349404578100614003177302 [15/09/2014].
Pentzopoulos, Dimitri (2002) *The Balkan Exchange of Minorities and its Impact on Greece* 2nd edition, Hurst & Company, London.
Pierini, Marc (2010) 'Turkey-EU Twinning project on Integrated Border Management (IBM) Opening Ceremony', 3 June 2010 Speech outline of Ambassador Marc Pierini, Head of the EU Delegation, http://www.avrupa.info.tr/resource-centre/news-archive/news-single-view/article/integrated-border-management-twinning-project-1.html [15/09/2014].
ProAsyl (2014) '12 Refugees Die During Alleged Push-back Operation off Greek island', Press release, http://www.ecre.org/component/content/article/70-weekly-bulletin-articles/574-12-refugees-die-during-alleged-push-back-operation-off-greek-island.html [11/08/2014].
ProAsyl (2013) *Pushed Back; Systematic Push Backs of Refugees in the Aegean Sea, From Greek Islands and at the Greek-Turkish Land Border*, ProAsyl, Frankfurt/Main.
Pugh, Michael (2004) 'Drowning not Waving: Boat People and Humanitarianism at Sea', *Journal of Refugee Studies* 17/1 50–69.
Şaul, Mahir (2014) 'A Different Kargo : Sub-Saharan Migrants In Istanbul And African Commerce', *Urban Anthropology* 43/1, 2, 3 143–203.
Schapendonk, Jan (2013) 'From Transit Migrants to Trading Migrants: Development Opportunities for Nigerians in the Transnational Trade Sector of Istanbul', *Sustainability* 5/7 2856–73.
Spijkerboer, Thomas (2007) 'The Human Costs of Border Control', *European Journal of Migration and Law* 9/1 127–39.
Smith, Helena (2014) 'Greek court acquits farmers who shot 28 Bangladeshi strawberry pickers', *The Guardian*, http://www.theguardian.com/world/2014/jul/31/greek-court-acquits-farmers-shot-strawberry-pickers [15/09/2014].
Suter, Brigitte (2013) *Asylum and Migration in Turkey An Overview of Developments in the Field 1990–2013*, Mim Working paper Series, Univeristy of Malmo, Malmo.
Suter, Brigitte (2012) *Tales of Transit. Sub-Saharan African Migrants' Experiences in Istanbul.* PhD Dissertation in Ethnic and Migration Studies, Linköping and Malmö University, Malmö and Linköping.
Toksöz, Gülay, Seyhan Erdoğdu and Selmin Kaşka (2012) *Irregular Labour Migration in Turkey and the Situation of Migrants Workers in the Labour Market*, Unpublished Research Report.

Triandafyllidou, Anna (2012) *Greece: How a State in Crisis Manages its Migration Crisis?*, IFRI Working Paper, IFRI, Paris.

Triandafyllidou, Anna and Daria Lazarescu (2009) *The Impact of the Recent Global Economic Crisis on Migration. Preliminary Insights from the South Eastern Borders of the EU (Greece)*, CARIM AS 2009/40, Robert Schuman Centre for Advanced Studies, European University Institute, San Domenico di Fiesole.

Tsitselikis, Konstantinos (2013) 'Sticks, Not Carrots: Immigration and Rights in Greece and Turkey', *Southeast European and Black Sea Studies* 13/3 421–34.

UNHCR (2012) *Dozens Queue Every Week to Apply for Asylum* [online], http://www.unhcr.org/4f6c8b6a6.html [14/07/2014].

Wheeler, Ambassador Tom (2011) 'Ankara to Africa: Turkey's Outreach Since 2005', *South African Journal of International Affairs* 18/1 43–62.

Wissink, Marieke, Franck Düvell and Anouka van Eerdewijk (2013) 'Dynamic Migration Intentions and the Impact of Socio-Institutional Environments: A Transit Migration Hub in Turkey', *Journal of Ethnic and Migration Studies* 39/7 1087–1105.

7 Morocco as a Destination for Labour Migrants?
Experiences of Sub-Saharan Migrants in the Call Centre Sector

Silja Weyel

Introduction

When in 2013 Morocco announced the introduction of a new immigration policy and the regularization of many irregular migrants, the authorities also officially recognized that Morocco has become an immigration country. While references were mainly made to the irregular migrant population that now lives in Morocco many of whom probably aim to continue on their way to Europe, Morocco actually hosts a very mixed population of Sub-Saharan origin, reflecting the country's historical and religious relations on the continent as well as its economic and foreign policy ambitions and its geographical position. One of the recent migration movements to the country is that of call centre workers coming from Senegal and heading to Morocco explicitly for work purposes. In Morocco, they integrate in the call centre industry which is, together with the construction sector, probably one of the most important sectors in terms of numbers for labour market integration of the Sub-Saharan population. Senegalese labour migrants in call centres are joined by current and former students of Sub-Saharan origin who are looking for jobs and integrate in call centres more easily than in any other sector. Rather than being linked to recent developments after the uprisings in North Africa or the downturn of southern European countries, it is the changes in the Moroccan economic landscape, the situation in the home country as well as study purposes that primarily shape the migration decisions of those call centre workers. Drawing on interviews in Rabat and Casablanca in 2013, this chapter discusses migration decisions in more detail, together with the question of why they are hardly influenced by the protest movements. To put the call centre worker migration in context, the chapter starts with an overview of different movements of Sub-Saharan migration to Morocco and the illustration of the development of the call centre industry in the country. It closes by showing employment conditions, what legal constraints migrants face and how they try to circumvent these.

Sub-Saharan African Migration to Morocco

Migration from Sub-Saharan countries to Morocco is an old phenomenon which dates back to pre-colonial times when trans-Saharan routes were used for caravan trade and for religious pilgrimage. Commerce through the Sahara had existed for centuries and it enabled exchanges between the north, including Europe, and the regions south of the Sahara. Countries south of Morocco included in the caravan trade were, among others, Mauritania, Mali and Senegal. Caravans not only transported goods like salt, gold, gum Arabic, ivory, green tea or sugar but also enabled the exchange of cultural and religious practices (Lydon 2005).

Gradually, trade between Morocco and Sub-Saharan countries relied more and more on maritime transportation and later on airline connections, which started working in 1956 between Senegal and Morocco. While today the overall trade between the Moroccan kingdom and countries on the continent is not very big in volume (Antil 2010; Jeune Afrique 2014), trade on a small level and with individual traders who are coming either by plane or on the road to Morocco on a monthly or bi-monthly basis is very much alive. This is especially true for Senegalese traders, and specifically for women, who have developed functioning networks and regularly come to Casablanca for their commerce (Marfaing 2005; Pian 2005).

Religious Migration

Apart from trade, it was religious exchanges and pilgrimage that fostered migration from Sub-Saharan Africa to Morocco, and this movement is still very present today. Religious linkages are especially strong between Morocco and Senegal. Muslim brotherhoods entered Senegal through commerce and travellers and played an important role in the islamisation of the country. With continuing islamisation came the need for religious education and religious students of Senegalese marabout families were sent on a regular basis to Moroccan cities like Sousse, Fes and Marrakech for study purposes (Demba Fall 2004). The Tijaniyya brotherhood, especially, to which the majority of Senegalese Muslims belong, fosters religious links between the two countries and a growing number of adherents make pilgrimages to the Moroccan city of Fes each year where they visit the tomb of the brotherhood's founder. Their number has been growing since independence (Lanza 2011). According to some scholars, it is the dream of each Tidjani to pray at least once in their life in Fes (Demba Fall 2004). Currently, pilgrim journeys from Senegal to Fes with a stop in at the Zaouia, the theological centre of a brotherhood, of Rabat are organised every year. The importance of the religious links between the countries can also be seen in the fact that on every political visit between Morocco and Senegal, some representatives of the Tijaniyya accompany the official visit (Lanza 2011).

Student Migration

One important group of migrants in Morocco today are students from an array of countries, most of them from Sub-Saharan Africa. Since the beginning of the 1970s, around a decade and a half after independence, Sub-Saharan students have been attending Morocco's public universities in part because the country started offering scholarships to foreign students. At first, only nationals of a few selected countries were able to participate in this programme but the number of countries participating in the programme continuously rose and today includes numerous countries, mostly from francophone West and Central Africa.

The scholarship programme for Sub-Saharan students is closely linked to Morocco's political and economic goals on the African continent and is implemented by the Moroccan agency for international cooperation, AMCI (Agence Marocaine de Coopération Internationale, 'Moroccan Agency for International Cooperation'). In contrast to its neighbouring Maghreb countries, Morocco pursued an active foreign policy in Africa after independence from France and especially after 1963 when the first agreement with Senegal was signed (Sambe 2010). Cooperation with Sub-Saharan African countries exists in the field of education, technical cooperation, the facilitation of trade relations and in some cases security and religious issues (Berriane 2009). The education of Sub-Saharan students at Moroccan universities is one important part of the country's policy aims to create a moroccophile Sub-Saharan elite, which will be knowledgeable of the Moroccan (educational) system and way of working (Antil 2003). Sub-Saharan students with scholarships of the AMCI can sign up in public universities, but there are also scholarships for 'internships' for civil servants. This, in the long run, is thought to be beneficial for investments and business or institutional relations in African countries. The distribution of scholarships to Sub-Saharan students multiplied from 1986 onwards when AMCI was created and went up from between 200 and 400 per year to 2,000 stipends per year in the early 2000s (Antil 2003).

The number of foreign students in both public and private universities or higher educational institutions is estimated at more than 15,000 today (Meyer and Laouali 2012), the majority of which are of Sub-Saharan origin. The rise in numbers is not only due to the increasing number of scholarships but also to the development of private schools and universities which is very much encouraged by the government since the 2000s. In 2011, the year when large protests occurred in Morocco, there were 198 private institutions for higher education that were accredited by the Ministry for Higher Education, most of them located either in Casablanca or Rabat, while in 1997 their number had been less than 80 (Meyer and Laouali 2012).

Rise of Sub-Saharan African Migration to the Maghreb in the 1990s

Trans-Saharan routes that had been used historically to connect Morocco and countries south of the Sahara were re-activated by migrants intending to use Morocco as a transit country on the way to Europe. The number of Sub-Saharan migrants heading to North Africa and Europe started rising in the 1990s, with Morocco being just one of the countries that migrants went to. Libya, and to a lesser extent Algeria, had been destination countries for Sub-Saharan migrants due to their labour demand and Libya's pan-African policy, when in 2000 Libya drastically changed its policies and started expelling Sub-Saharan workers (de Haas 2008; see also Chapter 3 of this volume). This led migrants to head increasingly towards other North African countries, including Morocco.

These migrants have been presented as adventurers ('aventuriers'), distinct from some other categories of migrants in the sense that their migration project and route is characterised by strong uncertainties and multiple bifurcations, not strictly determined in advance but adapted according to possibilities that open up during the journey (Pian 2009; Collyer 2009). Their migration has also been labelled as stepwise migration ('migration par étape', Bredeloup and Pliez 2005) since it does not necessarily follow a predetermined plan but is reconsidered after each step.

Labour Migration

Since about 2010, Morocco has experienced the arrival of Senegalese migrants who come to the country to work in call centres. This is not a major movement in terms of numbers – official counts do not exist – but it is qualitatively different from most other migration to the country in the sense that migrants arrive with the specific goal to work in Morocco. Labour migration from Sub-Saharan African countries to Morocco so far existed mainly in the arrival of housemaids who would work for families in different cities and the back and forth movement of traders selling their merchandise in Casablanca and other places. Many of the Senegalese call centre workers have worked in the same business before and, in some cases, a kind of chain migration can be observed where workers from one of the biggest call centres in Dakar migrate to Morocco to work in a specific centre in Casablanca after having heard of the possibilities there from friends or former colleagues.

Development of Call Centre Sector in Morocco in the Last 15 Years

Since around 2000, the opening of international call centres in Morocco has presented the possibility of new jobs for many Moroccans and foreigners alike. Since then, the number of call centres has been steadily on the rise and Morocco developed into the main destination for service outsourcing of French companies (ANRT 2004). This development started after the privatisation and liberalisation of the telecommunication sector at the end of the 1990s, and while in 2000 the number of call centres was around two, today there are almost 500 centres, not including the numerous unofficial ones.

The Moroccan government invested, like Senegal and Tunisia, in technology parks, like Casanearshore in Casablanca and Technopolis near Rabat, that are specialised in communication technology to foster innovation and attract foreign investors (Dahmani and Ledjou 2011), and these equally host international call centres. In order to promote the attractiveness of the country to potential investors, the government underlines the low wages of qualified employees, the geographical proximity to Europe and the existence of a good infrastructure in the telecommunication sector (Saad 2010). The offshoring sector is one of the six priority areas of Morocco's industrial strategy programme, the 'plan émergence', and the government's efforts to boost the call centre industry has turned the sector into an interesting field of investment and led the country to be named the '2012 offshoring destination of the year'.

The importance that the government attaches to the insertion of young graduates in the call centre labour market shows in the fact that it finances an educational programme called 'call academy', which prepares graduates during a several months class for the work in call centres. This programme, implemented in cooperation with the state's labour office Anapec and the Moroccan Association of Client Relations (Association Marocaine des Relations Clients, AMRC), is an indicator for the current availability of call centre jobs and the potential that is seen in the sector, but it reveals at the same time an educational lack among those willing to work in call centres. Large parts of the programme consist in French language training. The lack of proficiency in French is also seen as one of the major challenges by the AMRC and might be seen as a result of the Moroccan educational system (Géopolitik 2012) which leaves only specific graduates with fluent French, while the majority follows classes mainly in Arabic. In contrast, many of the Sub-Saharan migrants present in Morocco and with a secondary education speak French with ease. In most West African countries schooling is entirely in French, which gives migrants in Morocco a language advantage for call centre work compared to many Moroccans. However, in 2012 call centres were estimated to employ around 45,000 workers, not including those who work unofficially.

Since the beginning, most call centres have been located in Casablanca, the country's economic centre, followed by Rabat, the political capital. This has not changed today, but other cities like Marrakech, Tangiers and Fes are catching up, showing the country-wide settlement process of the sector. While in 2007 Casablanca and Rabat hosted about 80% of all call centres in Morocco, today it is around 50%.

Migration Motivations

Like staff in call centres worldwide, the majority of Sub-Saharan migrants working in call centres in Morocco are in their 20s and early 30s and include a fair percentage of women (estimates range between 40 and 60%). The

144 *Silja Weyel*

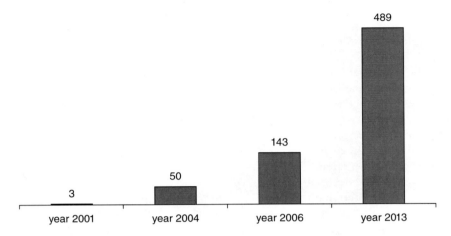

Figure 7.1 Number of official call centres in Morocco 2001–2013

Source: Agence Nationale de Réglementation des Télécommunications (ANRT)

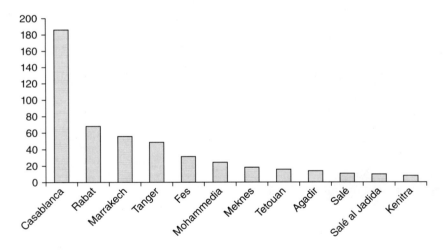

Figure 7.2 Numbers of call centres in Moroccan cities 2013

Source: Agence Nationale de Réglementation des Télécommunications (ANRT)

rather balanced distribution of both sexes contrasts with characteristics of other migrations discussed in this volume which are often either largely male (Chapters 4 and 9) or female (Chapter 8). The majority are Senegalese nationals, but other nationalities frequently represented are Cameroonian, Congolese and Ivorian while other nationals, like Burkinabe, Central African Republic or Rwandans are also present but are less numerous.

With rare exceptions, Senegalese are the only Sub-Saharan African nationals who leave their country for labour migration into Morocco which is, among other factors, linked to their preferential status in the Moroccan labour code that makes it easier for employers to recruit Senegalese than any other Sub-Saharan national and thus leads to more regular employment possibilities. Indeed, it is not just Senegalese migrants that are attracted by Morocco for its job possibilities, and in the years after the economic downturn in Southern European countries there are an increasing number of French and Spanish young people coming to Morocco to find work (Mounir 2012; Roger 2013). While many find qualified jobs, some are also known to start working in call centres in Morocco, a sector that is thus integrating European migrants affected by the economic changes in their origin countries. For Senegalese migrants, typically, the impossibility of finding a job in Senegal despite university education or work experience makes them leave, combined with the knowledge that jobs are available in Morocco and salaries are higher than in Senegal. Official data on Senagalese labour migrants into Morocco is difficult to find and the numbers used here are based on informal estimates from diaspora organisations unless otherwise stated.

One woman from Dakar who had worked as a secretary for several years but was struggling during the last years and could not find a good paying job was especially interested in the salary in Morocco and explained:

> When I left Senegal they had already told me about the call centres here in Morocco ... and the salaries that are not the same as in Senegal. You are paid better here than there. So I said to myself: why not go there. First for vacation. Try my luck. If I succeed to get a job in a call centre, great, if not, I return to Senegal. (Marie, Rabat, July 2013)[1]

She has now been in Morocco for several years and assists with the daily needs of her family in Senegal. Like the majority of migrants she supports her family financially, but due to the difficulties of legally sending money from Morocco to Senegal she buys merchandise in Morocco, sends it to Senegal where friends sell them and, after having taken their part, give the sales revenues to her family.

A young man, also from Dakar, with a background in informatics, describes his decision as rooted in the lack of employment opportunities in Dakar, though his intention is not a permanent relocation to Morocco. He puts it in the following way:

---

1 Names of interviewees are pseudonyms in order to keep anonymity. Interviews were conducted in French and quotations are translated from French to English by the author.

> I have an education as computer scientist. In Dakar I worked for a company called 'Arc Informatique'. It's a well-known company in Dakar but at a certain point in time it went through a crisis and actually disappeared. Even with difficulties I stayed during almost eight months, sometimes without a salary. But it could not last . . . Later we submitted (CVs) everywhere but in Dakar the employment system is a little saturated. There are many graduates, there is an enormous number of graduates. So, not as many places as graduates, the demand is bigger than the offer, so I said to myself perhaps go to Morocco, do something different, find a job and so on. (Babakar, Rabat, April 2013)

He works in a centre in Rabat while planning to go back to Senegal and open a small company with a friend. With his salary he finances online classes that he deems important for his career. In general, next to sending money to their family back home, several migrants also have specific targets like saving money to buy merchandise and open a business in Senegal or financing (future) studies that will enable them to work in a different sector.

In sum, situations of unemployment or low payment, information about recruitment possibilities in Morocco and contacts to other Senegalese persons already in Morocco are a frequent combination of circumstances for migrants when they take the decision to travel. The role of networks also needs to be taken into account. It is very common for Senegalese migrants either to have a family member or friend already staying Morocco who will host and help them find their way after arrival or to be referred to someone Senegalese in Morocco for help. Due to the relatively large community in Morocco, there always seems to be someone to contact and ask for support in the job search and orientation. Migrants typically report how contacts in Morocco tell them about opportunities in the country and encourage them to travel. While most interviewees mentioned that their job situation was playing a role in their motivation to leave, some migrants decided to travel to Morocco after having received pressure from family members who had heard about possibilities to earn large sums of money. Morocco has the reputation of a well-developed country and for some it comes as a surprise when they realise that poverty is regularly present.

In the case of current or former students now working in call centres, motivations to travel to Morocco are different and not linked to job possibilities. The education in Morocco has a good reputation among many Sub-Saharan migrants, specifically in the technical and engineering fields, and for some it represents the possibility to avoid the ill-functioning university system of their home country, as mentioned by several interviewees. Apart from the quality of education, the guarantee that the academic year will run without interruption and strikes is also seen as an advantage. However, for many, the motivation to study in Morocco is the receipt of a scholarship from the Moroccan AMCI rather than Morocco as a first choice for education. Others who opt for payable private education are attracted by the possibility to get bi-national Moroccan European or North American diplomas which are offered by some institutions. The presence of other family members is also a reason to choose Morocco and in some cases, parents chose their children's education to take place in Morocco since they have some connections to the country and it corresponds to what they can afford financially. Few explicitly come with the idea of staying on in Morocco. However, some students stay after finishing their studies and integrate into the labour market to gain some work experience, to finance further studies or because they find themselves with stronger networks in Morocco than in their origin countries. Networks in origin countries are usually regarded as an important requirement for finding a job and some consider it easier to start working in Morocco.

A young migrant who went to a private university in Fes and now works in a call centre in Rabat where he just got promoted to the role of supervisor underlines the positive image of education abroad and the advantages it has when looking for employment in Senegal:

> You can have a master, a PhD, a lot of things, but you find yourself in the street because there are not enough engagements . . . or there are not enough companies that are ready to engage you . . . And there is a myth that says once you have a degree from abroad with some experience abroad, they pay a little more attention to you . . . the administration, the big companies, private and public alike. Once you apply and you say: I went to x university in Europe or Morocco or something like that or you worked for a French company in Morocco, you feel that there clearly is a little more interest in you, in your experience, than in other persons. (Cheikh, Rabat, September 2013)

What is interesting in this interviewee's point of view is that he puts education in Morocco at the same level as education in Europe when it comes to the advantages in the labour market in Senegal. What is more, the possibility of working in French companies (call centres), which are much less present in Senegal than in Morocco, can act as a plus for a CV. In sum, Morocco is chosen as a destination country by migrants because it is thought to offer good education that brings valuable references for future employment and because the call centres are known as an industry that pays reasonable salaries, making it possible to earn for a certain target or to support family back home. The stories of other successful migrants in Morocco and the existence of networks and, in the case of Senegalese nationals, the close links between the countries giving them legal advantages and the possibility of visa-free entry add to the attractiveness of the country.

How were migration plans affected after the uprisings that occurred from late 2010 in Tunisia and later on spread to other countries? Interestingly, none of the interviewees mentioned the uprisings in Morocco in relation to their migration motivations. Some had come before the uprisings started, but in general the economic situation and migrants' job and study possibilities in Morocco seem unaffected by political protests. In Morocco, mass protests started in February 2011, shortly after uprisings had begun in Tunisia, and gave rise to the 20 February movement, which gave a voice to the feeling of many Moroccans of regular harassment and the impossibility of social advancement. However, the events did not lead to major changes as in some other Arab countries since, the King reacted swiftly, announcing important changes to the constitution and a referendum thereof for the same year.

The new constitution was accepted by a large majority of those who went to give their vote in the referendum and was followed by anticipated parliamentary elections in November 2011 bringing into power an Islamic party as in other countries affected by the uprisings. While the new constitution strengthens the role of the Parliament and the Prime Minister, it still keeps vast possibilities of influence for the King and ensures the continuing authoritarian character of the monarchic system (Eibel and Engelcke 2012). The strong role of the King is also seen by migrants as the reason for Morocco being relatively little affected by the uprisings – and thus remaining a destination country. One Senegalese interviewee who had left her daughter in Senegal to work in Morocco underlines the role of the King and how, in her point of view, his presence is the reason for differences between Morocco and other countries with mass protests:

> It did not find me here, I was still in Senegal . . . It does not make you afraid. Was I afraid? *Interviewer:* I don't know, maybe you say to yourself you should not come. *Interviewee:* No, no, because, you know, Morocco and the other Arab countries are not the same . . . I am apolitical, but from what I see the King manages, it is not the same thing. I don't think it will come here. Because they venerate I think. They like the royal family a lot . . . If it should arrive here, it would have arrived a long time ago. But we have seen Egypt, Syria where there are dead people every day so we also saw Egypt, at the moment there are still problems there. We saw Libya, but, alhamdoulilah ['all praise to God' in Arabic], I don't think it will come. (Fatou, Casablanca, August 2013)

Indeed, so far Morocco did not see major unrest similar to other countries in the region. Demonstrations against social injustice are frequent, but only a minority protests against the King or asks for a radical change of his role. Observers see an amplification of requests for social justice, for access to education, health and justice but point to the fact that demonstrations have existed for a long time in Morocco and in contrast to other Arab countries the regime is not 'sclerotic and aging', having undergone some reforms in the last years (Hibou 2012).

Migrants judged everyday situations in Morocco to be safe and, as another Senegalese woman explained, in the question of whether it would be safe to go to Morocco, she had relied on a contact person already in Morocco rather than on advice from family in Europe:

> When I came, my brother was against me coming. Because of that (the uprisings in Morocco). My brother who is in Germany. So there were conflicts, he said it was not safe . . . But the person with whom I had been put in contact (in Morocco) told me: well this is what you hear, but everybody lives normally. So that was also an influence in relation to me coming here. (Aissatou, Rabat, August 2013)

Some migrants believe that Moroccans don't have a reason to protest and complain since they consider life relatively cheap for Moroccans, they are convinced that jobs are available and the King who is seen as the warrantor of stability makes gifts to the people. Others compare the situation to the one in Senegal and the Casemance, the southern province of Senegal where several rebel groups aim for independence and fight the government. They acknowledge the conflict's existence but find it unimportant for their daily lives in Senegal. In the same way, they find the Moroccan uprisings unimportant to their current situation in Rabat or Casablanca.

Call Centre Work – Employment Conditions and Recruitment

Most employees in call centres work in a position called 'téléacteur', i.e. the person talking to clients on the phone, and most are in positions for outbound calls. Two very wide-spread activities are the selling of mobile phone contracts for French phone companies and the promotion of photovoltaic panels in France (used to convert the energy of sunlight to electricity). Other, less frequent activities are the selling of frozen food in France, the promotion of magazine subscriptions in Québec, Canada and technical assistance with internet connection and computer issues. Almost all migrants describe their job as stressful since there is pressure to reach certain sales figures and clients can at times be demanding or harassing. Sub-Saharan migrants share the difficulty of finding jobs other than those in call centres and as a consequence the call centre industry shows a concentration of Sub-Saharan workers. Senegalese call centre employees alone are estimated to be around 10,000, representing more than 20% of the official total number employed in Moroccan call centres and which compares to less than 1% of foreigners in Morocco.

A woman from Burkina Faso who used to work for radio and theatre and arrived recently in Morocco shares her observations on job search:

> I don't know what this is linked to but Sub-Saharans have this problem of finding a real job here. I don't know if it is linked to racism, you need to say it in inverted commas, if it is a racist thing. I don't know, it's possible. But it is actually quite difficult. It is super difficult . . . Most young people who are Sub-Saharans always tell you that their last exit is the call centres. (Ida, Rabat, June 2013)

The difficulties in finding a different job than that in call centres that this Burkinabe migrant describes lead to a situation of segmentation of the labour market, present in many migrant hosting countries worldwide, and call centre work has become a typical migrant job in Morocco. The need for workers – which goes along with a relatively high unemployment rate of young Moroccans – shows in the call centres' numerous advertisements and in their recruitment strategies: some centres use a sponsorship system and offer their staff bonuses of 1,000 dirhams if they successfully recruit a new employee, other centres recruited, until recently, some of their staff via websites and Skype calls directly in Senegal, sometimes even paying for their plane tickets to Morocco. Migrants are convinced that they are recruited for their good level of French and because they are, more than Moroccans, dependent on the job, therefore more reliable in their work attitude and more exploitable. In some centres, Senegalese have the best sales figures among employees and, as a manager pointed out, are thus in demand.

Given the high unemployment rate in the country, specifically among the 'chômeurs diplômés' ('unemployed persons with qualifications'), the Moroccan government wants to keep numbers of foreign workers low and prefers to give jobs to Moroccan nationals in the first place. The labour code stipulates that, with the exception of Algerian, Tunisian and Senegalese persons, foreign nationals can only be recruited if no Moroccan can fill the job. The interest of employers, however, does not necessarily correspond to that of the government and numerous foreigners are recruited anyways – leading to many different ways of employment and of circumventing the law.

Size, trustworthiness and employment conditions of the different call centres vary a lot. Some centres, at times called 'phantom centres', are only set up for a short period of time, do not give any contracts or guarantees to their employees, and suddenly disappear, leaving their staff without prior notice and without payment. On the other end of the spectrum, some big centres are known as good and reliable employers which give contracts, health insurance and social security payments to all employees and provide support with housing, residence permits and contact with insurances. Due to the labour code, among Sub-Saharan migrants, usually only Senegalese nationals will get the kind of contracts that are recognized by the Ministry of Labour which include benefits and social security payments. This, however, does not mean that all Senegalese have valid contracts, especially not in Casablanca. In sum, the practice in employment conditions ranges from not giving contracts at all and paying cash to giving legally recognized contracts with all insurance and social security contributions. The number of employees is not necessarily an indicator of trustworthiness or of how centres deal with administrative procedures and contracts. Among the bigger centres, especially in Rabat, are some that are known for not giving legal contracts to their Sub-Saharan workers (with the exception of Senegalese migrants) and not handing out any copies of their contracts, just making workers sign a payslip at the end of the month without handing out a copy to them. It seems to be the aim of those call centres not to leave any traces of the employment of Sub-Saharan nationals who are, as a consequence, unsure about the kind of contract they signed and if health insurance and taxes are taken from their salary or not.

In other centres, sub-Saharan employees have internship contracts, their salaries are transferred to bank accounts and health insurance and CNSS (caisse nationale de sécurité sociale, 'national social security fund') is paid. Moreover, taxes are taken from their salaries. In sum their situation is a good example of what Kubal (2012) calls semi-legal. With reference to migrants and their relation to the law, semi-legality refers to the many different nuances that exist between the often used simple dichotomy of 'legal/ illegal'. This means, while a migrant might not have the right to work, he or she might still pay taxes, insurance contributions and sign work contracts.

Many centres ask their Sub-Saharan staff to have a valid residence permit. Given that a work contract and a rental agreement are usually required to get a residence permit, this causes a problem to numerous migrants. A common way to go about this is to sign up in private educational institutions to officially be a student and then ask for a student residence permit. However, private educational institutions ask up to 2,000 dirhams (around €180) for inscription, which represents more than half a monthly salary for many. Rental agreements, one of the other prerequisites for a residence permit, can also be bought. Since it is not unusual for Moroccan landlords to avoid legal rental agreements in order to save taxes, some migrants buy a rental agreement to complete their dossier for the residence permit – which increases the sum they have to spend in order to 'legalize' their situation. Ruhs and Anderson define as semi-compliance the 'employment of migrants who are legally resident but working in violation of the employment restrictions attached to their immigration status' (Ruhs and Anderson 2012). Semi-compliance is thought to maximize economic benefits from employment and to minimize the threat for state sanctions due to violation of the immigration law. While semi-compliance is found in the UK and expected to be relevant for many high-income countries (Ruhs and Anderson 2012), the situation of many sub-Saharan call centre workers also seems to reflect it.

Future Perspectives

Most migrants in call centres work as simple 'téléacteurs' and aim at keeping this job or finding a job that suits their educational background better. However, some are actively pursuing a career and climb the ladder in their company or, alternatively, open their own call centre. The first career step in a company is usually to become a supervisor of a group of call centre agents which can be followed by the position of a project manager. In those cases, work experience and contacts may also open possibilities in Europe as one interviewee was convinced who had started in a call centre in Dakar and is now at the management of a call centre in Casablanca:

> ... the most important is, you need to have a certain background. If you have the background, if you have a degree, because now in Europe it's chosen immigration as they say, right ... So if you have some degrees, no need to worry. Because you know how this works in the professional environment, you know the French mentality a little bit, European in general, afterwards the inclusion (into the labour market) can be more quick. And you also have an address book. Because the clients are European and for the most part they are French. So you have some contacts, they come over here also to control the work, see how things work here. So there are opportunities, there are contacts that establish. Later, if you want to go, of course you have much more contacts. Because the contacts that you have, they already know your know-how, they have an idea of the way you work and there are even some who are willing to recommend you to other people. In the end you need to seize the opportunity. (Oumar, Casablanca, August 2013)

Some migrants who wish to go back to their origin country are thinking about opening a call centre there since, apart from in Senegal, there are few call centres in the Sub-Saharan region. In some cases, the know-how they acquired in their job in Morocco opens for them new job possibilities in their origin country. For example, Orange, an internet and phone service provider for which they had counselled clients in Morocco, is introducing some call centre services elsewhere and they have the perfect profile to start working. While for some migrants their working experience in call centres is valuable, for many their job just represents a means to finance their studies or support their families back home and they do not see it as valuable step in their professional development. Some, mainly in Casablanca with its many 'small centres', due to the legal constraints and the way some call centres exploit that situation are only struggling to keep a job to be able to pay their bills.

Conclusion

To many Europeans, Morocco is mainly known as a country of origin of migrants, but, as the movement of call centre workers and students shows, it is equally interesting as a destination country for many migrants from Sub-Saharan Africa (and increasingly so for some Europeans). Specifically Senegalese migrants are attracted to Morocco, and due to the close relations between the two countries, they enjoy several advantages compared to other nationals. Migration motivations of Senegalese labour migrants typically include the difficulties of finding a job in the origin country, the availability of jobs in Morocco and the encouragement or offer of support of someone already present in Morocco. Many others come to Morocco as students since they receive scholarships or are attracted by the offer of private universities. In contrast to what is discussed in many other chapters of this book which focus on different countries, the uprisings have not had much of an effect on the motivations of migrants travelling to Morocco. Dynamics of protests in Morocco were rather different than in other countries and migrants do not consider the social movement in Morocco to have an influence on their daily lives. Due to the strong support he has from the local population, the King is seen as a warrantor of stability and his presence is regarded as one of the major differences between Morocco and other countries in the region.

The daily lives of Sub-Saharan call centre workers is structured by the routine and fatigue of their job, and many experience difficulties in their legal situation since they do not have the right to work in positions in call centres that could be filled by a Moroccan. In consequence, often in cooperation with employers, they find ways to circumvent legal regulations, which can be costly but serves the interest of employers and migrants alike. Future perspectives for call centre workers vary. While some have already started a career in their centre and are part of management or are supervisors, for many the call centre activity just represents a job that serves a certain need or goal, such as financing their current lives, their current studies or, to a certain extent, their families' needs in origin countries. Several migrants, especially in Casablanca, are mainly struggling to find a job where payment is regular and where they do not need to fear they cannot pay bills next month.

To policy makers, the presence of sub-Saharan call centre workers in Morocco can serve as a reminder that much migration is happening within the origin continent of migrants and that economic opportunities are key in these migration decisions.

References

Antil, Alain (2010) *Le Maroc et sa « nouvelle frontière ». Lecture critique du versant économique de la stratégie africaine du Maroc.* Note de l'Ifri. Le Maghreb dans son environnement régional et international. Ifri, programme Afrique subsaharienne, http://www.ifri.org/?page=detail-contribution&id=6120&id_provenance=97 [03/2014].

Antil, Alain (2003) *Le royaume du Maroc et sa politique envers l'Afrique subsaharienne.* Institut français des relations internationales (IFRI), Paris.

ANRT (Agence nationale de réglementation des télécommunications) (2004) *Du développment des centres d'appels . . . à l'émergence du BPO au Maroc,* http://www.anrt.ma/sites/default/files/Etudes_centres_appel_maroc_2004_0.pdf [22/10/2014].

Berriane, Johara (2012) 'La formation des élites subsahariennes au Maroc', in Mansouria Mokhefi and Alain Antil (eds) (2012) *Le Maghreb et son Sud : vers des liens renouvelés,* CNRS Editions, Paris, 155–71.

Berriane, Johara (2009) 'Studierende aus dem subsaharischen Afrika in Marokko. Motive, Alltag und Zukunftspläne einer Bildungsmigration', *Diskussionspapiere* 103, Klaus Schwarz Verlag, Berlin.

Bredeloup, Sylvie and Olivier Pliez (2005) 'Migrations entre les deux rives du Sahara', *Autrepart* 36, 3–20.

Collyer, Michael (2007) 'In-between places: trans-Saharan transit migrants in Morocco and the fragmented journey to Europe', *Antipode* 39/4 668–90.

Dahmani, Ahmed and Jean-Michel Ledjou (2011) 'Le développement des télécommunications dans le Sud. Retour sur une décennie de diffusion des TIC en Afrique de l´Ouest et le Maghreb', *Tic & Société* 5/2–3.

De Haas, Hein (2008) 'Irregular migration from West Africa to the Maghreb and the European Union: an overview and recent trends', *IOM migration research series* 32.

Demba Fall, Papa (2004) 'Les sénégalais au Maroc: histoire et anthropologie d´un espace migratoire', in Laurence Marfaing and Steffen Wippel (eds) (2004) *Les relations transsahariennes à l´époque contemporaine*, Karthala and ZMO, Paris, 277–91.

Eibel, Ferdinand and Dörthe Engelcke (2012) 'Islamisten und der "Arabische Frühling" in Marokko: Der Kontinuität verschrieben?', in Sigrid Faath (ed) (2012) *Islamische Akteure in Nordafrika*, Konrad Adenauer Stiftung, Sankt-Augustin, 111–30.

Géopolitik (2012) 'Maroc, vers un nouvel ordre linguistique. Dossier spécial', *Géopolitik. Le monde vu par l´institut Amadeus*, 2 February 2010, http://www.amadeusonline.org/pdf/GeopolitikLD.pdf [19/10/2014].

Hibou, Béatrice (2012) *Le mouvement du 20 février, le Makhzen et l´antipolitique. L´impensé des réformes au Maroc*, http://www.sciencespo.fr/ceri/sites/sciencespo.fr.ceri/files/art_bh2.pdf [19/10/2014].

Jeune Afrique (2014) 'Orange Tunisie, enquête sur une spoliation', *Jeune Afrique* 2773.

Kubal, Agnieszka (2012) 'Conceptualizing semi-legality in migration research', *Working Papers* 58, International Migration Institute, Oxford.

Lanza, Nazarena (2011) 'Liens et échanges entre le Maroc et l'Afrique subsaharienne: éléments pour une perspective historique', in Michel Peraldi (ed) (2011) *D'une Afrique à l'autre. Migrations subsahariennes au Maroc*, Karthala, Paris, 23–36.

Lydon, Ghislaine (2005) 'Writing trans-saharan history: methods, sources and interpretations across the African divide', *The Journal of North African Studies* 10/3–4 293–324.

Marfaing, Laurence (2004) 'Relations et échanges des commerçants sénégalais vers la Mauritanie et le Maroc au XXe siècle', in Laurence Marfaing and Steffen Wippel (eds) (2004) *Les relations transsahariennes à l´époque contemporaine*, Karthala and ZMO, Paris 251–76.

Meyer, Jean-Baptiste and Souley Mahamadou Laouali (2012) 'Mobilité internationale des étudiants étrangers vers le Maroc: quelles particularités?', *Les Etudes et Essais du Centre Jacques Berque* 10, http://www.cjb.ma/images/stories/publications/Meyer-Souley_EE10.pdf [17/10/2014].

Mounir, Nezha (2012) 'Le Maroc, terre d´asile des travailleurs espagnols et français', *Libération*. 27 August, http://www.ccme.org.ma/images/documents/fr/2012/08/img550.pdf [23/10/2014].

Pian, Anaik (2009) 'Entre « visibilisation » et « invisibilation », les migrations subsahariennes au Maroc', in Ali Bensaad (ed) (2009) *Le Maghreb à l'épreuve des migrations subsahariennes. Immigration sur emigration*, Karthala, Paris, 63–85.

Pian, Anaik (2005) 'Aventuriers et commerçants sénégalais à Casablanca: des parcours entrecroisés', *Autrepart* 36 167–82.

Roger, Benjamin (2013) 'Le monde à l'envers', in *Un autre Maroc?*, Special Report, *Jeune Afrique* 2741.

Ruhs, Martin and Bridget Anderson (2012) 'Semi-compliance and illegality in migrant labour markets: an analysis of migrants, employers and the state in the UK', *Population, Space and Place* 16 195–211.

Saadi, Mohamed Saïd (2010) 'Investissement direct étranger et emploi féminin au Maroc', *Critique économique* 26 43–64.

Sambe, Bakary (2010) *Islam et diplomatie: la politique africaine du Maroc*, Marsam, Rabat.

8 Gendered Differences in Migration and Return
Perspectives from Ethiopia

Sarah Langley

Introduction

The rapid growth of economies in the Middle East has led to an increased need for migrant labor within the region. One main source country is Ethiopia. Ethiopian men and women migrate to the region predominantly for economic purposes, often citing employment opportunities or higher wages as the reason for their journey. While some migrants are undoubtedly successful and secure both economic and social benefits from their migration, others are less fortunate and face challenges as a result of their journey. Many of these issues are encountered abroad, others upon return to Ethiopia. Accordingly, this chapter will analyze migration and returnee experiences in both settings. Specifically, it utilizes results from the IS Academy: Migration and Development Survey, conducted in 2011 in Ethiopia. A total of 1,285 household surveys were completed, including 96 households with return migrants from the Middle East. The survey contains information on the returnees' situation prior to migration, their decision to migrate, their experiences in the country of migration, their decision to return and their experiences upon return. Due to gendered demand for labour within the Middle East and the strongly patriarchal nature of both Middle Eastern and Ethiopian societies, the author examines the challenges faced by Ethiopian migrants through a gender conscious lens by questioning how men and women's experiences differ and agree. Based on the perceptions return migrants have of their time abroad and their return to Ethiopia, it is argued that conditions within both destination and origin countries need to be adapted if migration is to lead to positive development outcomes for all involved.

This chapter begins with a discussion of the role of gender within migration and how it impacts outcomes both abroad and upon return. This is followed by an introduction to the phenomenon of Ethiopian migration to the Middle East, detailing the factors driving Ethiopians to migrate, the demand that exists within the Middle East for such migrants and the working conditions that migrants face upon arrival in their destination country. Next, the results of the IS Academy: Migration and Development Survey will be discussed, with special attention paid to gendered differences in perceptions of the success of migration and return. The chapter will conclude with a discussion section, suggesting positive and productive steps that could be taken in order to protect the rights of Ethiopian migrants and to unearth the positive effects of migration through the inclusion of gender consciousness. It argues that more information is needed, with urgency, about this important topic.

Gender in Migration

This chapter uses the term 'gender' to inform its analysis and findings. Gender has been intentionally selected over the term 'sex', which refers only to a simple binary of biological characteristics. Gender incorporates the social constructions and conceptions that have developed around each of the sexes. Being male or female in different cultures, time settings and geographical locations confers upon a person a different set of expectations and accepted ways of acting. Men and women commonly adopt different roles within the economic and familial spheres and partake in differing forms of social interaction as a result of their constructed gender identity. The influences of gender constructs are apparent not only at the individual and familial level, but also at the national and supranational level, with state and national structures embracing gendered constructions within structures, policies and practices (Pessar and Mahler 2003). It is from this basis that the concept of gender is applied to the phenomenon of migration.

Scholars have noted that past theories of international migration have lacked attention to gender and its impact on the migration experience (Donato et al. 2006; Hondagneu-Sotelo 2000). For example, theories that emphasize the family as the decision maker instead of the individual, such as the New Economics of Labour Migration (NELM), seem to assume that the benefits or detriments of a family member's migration will be shared fairly among all family members, ignoring the reality that sometimes power struggles between men and women and gender discrimination exist within the family unit (Grieco and Boyd 1998). Mahler and Pessar (2006) state that while families may make fair and rational migration decisions with the benefit of all members in mind, these decisions may also be based upon 'hierarchies of power along gender and generational lines' (33).

Network Theory has also been criticized for its lack of gender awareness, focusing on networks that were established and maintained by male migrants (Mahler and Pessar 2006). However, these networks were not necessarily shared with female members of families or social groups. Furthermore, it has been said that more research on female networks is needed, as they can vary significantly from male networks. For example, women going abroad for gendered occupations such as domestic work may establish predominantly female social networks that they use to facilitate better working or living conditions or lower costs of migration (Hondagneu-Sotelo 1994). From these examples, the need for greater attention to gender within international migration theory becomes apparent.

A woman or a man's ability and desire to migrate will likely be affected by a variety of factors, including the health of the labour market, labour laws, government infrastructure, land tenure laws and educational systems (Grieco and Boyd 1998). All of these factors impact men and women differently. Taking Ethiopia as an example, women may have more limited access to educational systems and the labour market than men, impacting upon their desire and ability to migrate. Demand for migrant labour may also be affected by gender. In the Middle East, as will be noted in the background section, the economy has evolved to include a high demand for low-skilled female migrants to take up domestic work. Accordingly, the economic situation, both abroad and in the origin country, impacts upon migration in a gendered fashion.

The role of the state as evidenced through its emigration and immigration policies is also highly gendered. Some countries have enacted gender-conscious emigration policies that can either restrict or encourage certain groups. These policies are often the result of gender roles and stereotypes in that country (Calavita 2006; Grieco and Boyd 1998). For example, in 2013 the Ethiopian government banned the international migration of domestic workers in an effort to stem human trafficking and the exploitation and abuse of female domestic workers in the Middle East (Kuschminder 2014). While this policy clearly seeks to protect women, barring women from migrating internationally may also eliminate a vital channel of upward economic mobility.

After migration has occurred, men and women will also face different circumstances and situations when attempting to establish themselves in their destination countries. For example, the immigration of women and girls has historically been viewed with alarm as they are able to reproduce, leading to a fear of growing immigrant or minority communities within the destination country. Women may also face gender discrimination in their destination country by being classified as 'dependents' and having their legal status tied to that of a man (Castles and Miller 2009). On the other hand, men have been viewed by some countries as a greater security threat and thereby have faced greater degrees of abuse and mistreatment than women (Mahler and Pessar 2006). Men may also face more difficult requirements to gain entry or residence in a destination country as they are traditionally viewed as being family providers and thereby labour market competitors (Mahler and Pessar 2006).

Migrants face gendered elements in their origin countries, in the economic determinants of their migration and in their destination countries, as well as in countless other spheres that could not be covered here. Moreover, gender cannot be analyzed independently, but must be examined in tandem with issues of race, economic status and other differences. This chapter adopts a strong focus on gender in evaluating the differing perceptions of the migration and return process, but also examines how aspects of social and economic status play into the process.

Background

Drivers of Ethiopian migration

Although Ethiopia is a country characterised by relatively low emigration rates, its sizeable population of 82.8 million makes its absolute number of emigrants large, with an estimated 620,000 Ethiopians currently living abroad (World Bank 2011). Ethiopian emigration can historically be classified into four movements. The first "wave" took place prior to 1974 and largely consisted of the emigration and return of elite members of Ethiopian society, usually traveling abroad for educational purposes. From 1974 to 1982, the flow of emigrants shifted to consist predominantly of refugees fleeing the Dergue regime and associated conflict or persecution. From 1982 to 1991, the emigration flow shifted again, this time to include mainly family members of initial refugees that had left the country during the second wave. These individuals normally went abroad on family reunification schemes and therefore intended for their migration to be long-term in nature. The fourth wave is one which is still visible today. This flow is different from its predecessors in that while it does include some individuals fleeing persecution, the majority of emigrants are going abroad to search for economic opportunities and are more varied in their socioeconomic origins in Ethiopia (Kuschminder and Siegel 2010).

The reasons for migration given by current Ethiopian emigrants illustrate the present state of the country. Ethiopia is an extremely poor state with few economic or educational opportunities offered to its population (World Bank 2013a). The country faces food insecurity, environmental challenges, ethnic tension and a volatile political situation, all of which create a complex and challenging situation for its inhabitants (UNICEF 2013). Ethiopia's ever-growing population and changing weather patterns/ desertification place extreme pressure on traditional subsistence farming lifestyles. Furthermore, only 1% of the country's arable land is irrigated, leaving people and the agriculturally based economy extremely vulnerable to drought (World Bank 2013b).

Finding employment in Ethiopia is not easy. Youth unemployment in 2006 stood at 24.9%, with the female population experiencing a rate of 29.4% (Ethiopia Data Series 2014). This unemployment is usually long-term in nature, spanning a number of years. Partly as a result of this, the majority of the population is estimated to work in the informal economic sector, due to the lack of formal opportunities. High unemployment is paired with low school enrollment rates. School life expectancy for Ethiopian children is only 8 years for males and 6 years for females. This has a ripple effect on other aspects of society, with literacy rates standing at 49% for males and

29% for females and 53% of children aged 5–14 being engaged in child labour of some form (Ethiopia Data Series, 2014).

In addition to food security concerns and a lack of opportunities, the country is also divided along ethnic lines. There are over 77 different ethnic groups in the country, with the Oromo, Amhara and Tigray groups making up the majority. As late as 1991, people who identified with the Omoro ethnic group experienced blatant and institutionalized discrimination in favour of the Amhara group and were not allowed to exercise their right to cultural freedom. This pattern, although not overtly institutionalized in the present, still persists today. In addition to discrimination, the political system is further weakened by poor governance and the repression of freedom of the press and speech (US Library of Congress 2005).

Emigration from Ethiopia is influenced by gender. Women in Ethiopian society face different circumstances from their male counterparts. Within the traditional ethnic groups of the country, societies are often patriarchal in nature and women are allocated domestic work or simple tasks. In some regions such as Amhara, 50 percent of women are married by their 15th birthday and girls are often married to older men living in polygamous families. Men can divorce their wives with relative ease, which leaves women extremely vulnerable (Population Council 2004). In addition to high rates of child marriage and low rates of schooling for female children, women face sexism in the job market and may not be able to find employment as easily as males (de Regt 2010). Many Ethiopian female migrants state that they chose to migrate because they did not score high enough on their exams to be able to advance to university, as is the practice in Ethiopia. Due to the few other economic opportunities available to them, they felt that migration was one of the only ways with which they could improve their lives or the lives of their families (de Regt 2009).

Demand for Migrant Workers in the Middle East

The drivers for Ethiopian emigration are further fueled by new emerging markets for migrant labour in the Middle East. Ethiopian women migrate in large numbers to countries such as Saudi Arabia or the UAE to perform domestic and care-giving work (de Regt 2009; Fransen and Kuschminder 2009). Likewise, Ethiopian men travel to the region, although in much smaller numbers, to perform a variety of tasks including agricultural jobs, construction work or general day labour (Harroff-Tavel and Nasri 2013). Ethiopians travel to the Middle East through three main routes. The first is termed 'public migration', in which Ethiopians are officially registered as migrant workers through the Ethiopian Ministry of Labour and Social Affairs (MOLSA), but are in fact still responsible for arranging their own work contracts. The second route is through the numerous Private Employment Agencies (PEAs) that find and secure contracts abroad for migrant workers. These agencies represent the blurred line between regular and irregular migration in the Ethiopian case, as registered agencies may charge illegal fees or make illegal migration arrangements for workers, with or without the worker knowing about it. Following these channels, workers will often take international flights from Addis Ababa or from neighboring countries directly to the country of destination. Third, Ethiopians may also use illegal brokers and travel by land to Saudi Arabia (Fernandez 2010). This route, however, is mostly used by Ethiopian men, as there is less demand for their services in the Middle East and it is harder for them to arrange working contracts ahead of time.

Working Conditions in the Middle East

Working conditions in the Middle East are notoriously harsh for migrant labourers. Unfavorable employment conditions stem from a variety of sources, including systemic and institutionalized discrimination against migrants within the legal systems of Middle Eastern countries, widespread racism and xenophobia on the societal level and the use of misleading or false information on job placements in the migrants' home countries. While conditions vary greatly, these structural trends work to remove safeguards and checks against situations of exploitation and abuse.

One prominent legal element that can lead to abuse is the "Khafala System" used by many Middle Eastern countries. Through this system, the employer of a migrant worker is also their legal sponsor and the worker's regular status in the country is tied directly to the employer/sponsor. It has become common practice for the employer/sponsor to confiscate the passports and documents of their employees to attain a greater degree of control (Fernandez 2010). Within the IS Academy: Migration and Development Survey sample, 35 of the 38 Ethiopian women working in the Middle East were employed as domestic workers. The Khafala System leaves such workers unable to switch employers and isolates them within their employer's household. Accordingly, they have little recourse if the situation turns abusive or violent. The legal framework for domestic workers in some countries is particularly difficult. In the UAE, domestic workers have to abide by the labour regulations ordered in the Khafala system, but they are not offered even the limited protection granted by the system, as their profession is classed in a special category (Mahdavi 2013). In many countries, workers are technically allowed to bring labour disputes against their employers in court but must take the risk of being deported under the broad charge of 'moral wrongdoing', which employers often use as a threat (Mahdavi 2013). Under the system, migrant workers who break their work contracts by running away immediately become irregular and can be arrested or face time in prison (Kuschminder 2013).

The Khafala system also has negative effects on the working conditions of male migrants within the region. Many male migrant labourers in the Middle East are employed through construction companies where, similar to domestic workers, they live on site and are isolated from the rest of society (Plant 2008). Research initiatives funded by both Amnesty International and the International Labor Organization found that the majority of migrant construction workers did not possess their passports, as the documents were being held forcibly by their employers (Amnesty International 2013; Harroff-Tavel and Nasri 2013). Reports from these organizations also found that the exit visa requirements employed by some Middle Eastern governments further disadvantaged migrants, as the migrants are then dependent upon their employer to first return their passport, then issue them an exit visa and pay sometimes exorbitant fines on expired residence permits that the employer did not renew (Amnesty International 2013; Harroff-Tavel and Nasri 2013). Amnesty International reports that some workers felt that the only way they could leave their country of migration was to actively refuse to work, thereby eliminating the purpose of their employers keeping them in the country.

In addition to institutionalized discrimination, Ethiopian female domestic workers face a unique challenge when they arrive in a Middle Eastern country, as there is often a racial hierarchy in place concerning domestic workers. Employing a migrant domestic worker in the home has come to be understood as a symbol of status and wealth (Fernandez 2010). Asian (predominately Filipina) women are at the top and often employed by upper class families. Next in the hierarchy are Ethiopian women, who make a lower salary and are often employed by high middle or middle class families. They are followed by Somali women, who often enter the region as refugees, are paid the lowest salaries and are deemed the least desirable. De Regt (2008) found that while Asian women are normally assigned tasks such as caring for the children and elderly, African women are often given heavy workloads of cleaning, sometimes for multiple households. Much speculation has taken place as to why this hierarchy exists, with some scholars finding that the hierarchy results from the level of distance from and similarity to the employer (Hansen 1989; Destremau 2002; De Regt 2008). De Regt (2008) argues that Asian women are deemed most desirable in part because they have little in common with their employers in terms of religion or language. Somali women, on the other hand, often practice the same religion and speak similar languages to their Middle Eastern employers, which makes some employers uncomfortable and raises questions about how to treat other Muslims. Ethiopian women fall somewhere in the middle of this imagined hierarchy. Additionally, Ethiopian women often come for temporary periods as opposed to Somali refugees and therefore are more likely to accept hierarchical employment situations and do not attempt to gain citizenship (de Regt 2008). As a result of this hierarchy, Ethiopian women face harmful gender and racial stereotypes on a daily basis both inside and outside of the work environment.

Discriminatory factors mentioned above include a prejudiced residence permit system in many Middle Eastern countries, in addition to discriminatory housing laws, de facto racial hierarchies and widespread societal xenophobia and racism. These factors work in tandem to limit or halt the integration and incorporation mechanisms discussed by Gebrewold in Chapter 1, specifically Esser's 'acculturation, integration and assimilation' and Eisenstad's 'process of absorbtion'. Operating on an institutional, as well as individual level, these factors work to exclude migrants from the social fabric of Middle Eastern societies, thereby eliminating protections against abuse and exploitation.

Despite the factors discussed above, working conditions vary greatly by individual placement. While some workers may find suitable placements with fair working conditions and payment, some find themselves in exploitative and abusive situations. Among domestic workers, nonpayment and underpayment, as well as overwork, are often the most common complaints. Human Rights Watch also reports cases of beatings, burnings, acts of humiliation and food deprivation among domestic workers in the Middle East (Human Rights Watch 2008). Sexual violence is used against women, with migrant workers reporting rape, attempted rape and harassment by their male employers. Employers also sometimes try to prevent the domestic worker from having contact with other Ethiopians as a control mechanism (Human Rights Watch 2008). All of these factors can have a profound negative effect on a person's mental health. From 1999–2005, 129 female Ethiopian bodies were returned from Saudi Arabia, the UAE and Lebanon, with the cause of death ruled exclusively as suicide (Anbesse et al. 2009).

Among male migrant workers in the region, research has shown that salaries are almost always lower than what was promised to the migrant prior to migration. Additionally, many experience delayed payments of salaries or nonpayment for overtime hours (Plant 2008). Other grievances among male migrant workers in the region include failure of the employer to pay for or allow treatment of workplace injuries or to provide proper safety equipment, working excessively long hours, not being supplied with drinking water or air conditioners in dormitories, overcrowded sleeping arrangements and improper sewage management in dormitories (Harroff-Tavel and Nasri 2013; Amnesty International 2013).

The trafficking of migrant workers into the Middle East has received a great deal of attention. While this practice is occurring, it is important to recognize that the term trafficking represents a spectrum in which migrants have more or less opportunity to exercise agency and free will in making their migration decisions. Regarding Ethiopian women, Fransen and Kuschminder (2009) found that they most often make the initial migration decision of their own free will, but that this choice may be informed by misleading or false information. Women are sometimes given false job descriptions and inflated salary indications, perhaps making them more willing to migrate than if they knew what sort of employment was actually available abroad (de Regt 2011). The same deceptive practices are commonly used in bringing male migrant workers into the region (Plant 2008; Harroff-Tavel and Nasri 2013).

Within Ethiopia, researchers have also found a predominant 'myth of migration', whereby migrants do not believe tales of poor working conditions due to the obvious materials gains of these returnees. A similar phenomenon is also reported by Adurshi in Chapter 10 of this volume, in which the warnings of negative living and working conditions in the destination country given by return migrants are not heeded by future potential migrants. In regards to women specifically, it has also been shown that while women are aware of the risks, opportunities for them in Ethiopia are so limited that they may choose to migrate hoping for a pleasant family and moderate workload (de Regt 2008; Kuschminder 2013; Mahdavi 2013). In response to potentially harmful working and living environments, women are sometimes even informed prior to their arrival in some countries, such as Yemen, that they can run away from their initial employer and gain freelance domestic work. Through this type of work, women often receive higher salaries and better work conditions, although they do have to accept being undocumented in the country. These examples illustrate the wide variation in degrees of free will and agency involved in migration decisions. It is clear that information about bad working conditions in destination countries is insufficient to protect the rights of migrants if alternatives are unavailable.

Results/Analysis

This chapter uses data from the IS Academy: Migration and Development Survey, which was conducted in 2011 in Ethiopia. The survey includes information on the returnees' situation prior to migration, their decision to migrate, their experiences in the country of migration, their decision to return and their experiences upon return. Specifically, it examines the migration and return experiences of 96 migrants (43 males and 53 females) who migrated from Ethiopia to the Middle East and returned back. From the data, explicit gendered differences for many variables are apparent. Gendered distinctions were visible not only within the background characteristics of the migrants, but also within variables relating to the migrants' time abroad and their experiences upon return. These differences therefore warrant an examination of the data and results through a comparative lens, contrasting the experiences and perceptions of male and female groups. This section will analyze the migration cycle, with subsections providing information on the profile of respondents, their life before migration, their experiences abroad and their experiences upon returning to Ethiopia.

Profile of Respondents

Employment opportunities in the Middle East are often highly gendered, which can lead to men and women migrating primarily to different countries.

The study found that, within the sample, men migrated predominately to Saudi Arabia (77% of male informants) and to a lesser degree to Yemen (16%). The destinations of women were more diverse, with large numbers migrating to the UAE (39% of female informants), Saudi Arabia (35%) and to a smaller extent Lebanon (16%). Overall, the Mediterranean Middle Eastern countries were more common destinations for Ethiopian women than Ethiopian men.

The survey data also included information on the individuals and parties that were involved in helping migrants migrate. Factors such as who was involved in the decision to migrate, as well as how the migration was financed, can impact the migrants' own perception of their migration experience later on. Over 50% of both genders made their initial migration decisions alone. This can partly be explained by the survey finding that migrants (especially women) would sometimes not include their families or friends in their migration planning because they were afraid their families and friends would try to dissuade them out of fear for their safety and security. However, this trend does not apply to the entire sample. Twenty-six percent of women were influenced in their migration decision by either their mother or father. As only 4.65% of men were similarly guided by their parents; this finding is illustrative of the patriarchy and male dominance that is common in (especially rural) communities and family systems in Ethiopia. In this case, it is evident that parents are more involved in the migration decisions of their female children than their male children and may even make the migration decision for them without their knowing about it (Kuschminder 2013). It was also found that the majority of both men and women undertook their migration journeys alone. However, a larger percentage of women participated in an individual migration (84.91%), than did men (60.47%). This difference was also statistically significant at the .01 level.

Regarding the financing of the migration, it was found that a larger percentage of males (60.47%) used their own personal resources as a primary funding source for their journeys abroad than did females (13.21%). This difference was statistically significant at the .01 level. A large proportion of women, on the other hand, either borrowed resources to pay for their migration (41.51% as compared to only 11.63% of males) or had their expenses paid by a third party (43.40% as compared to 27.92% of males). This finding corresponds with survey results discussed later on which found that many Ethiopian women largely migrated due to unemployment or a low salary, meaning that they would be unlikely to have the resources to fund their own migration. Only 16 of the 96 return migrants indicated a secondary source of funding, illustrating that mixed funding was relatively uncommon. Of the reported secondary funding mechanisms, selling assets and gift giving from family and friends were the most common.

The documentation of the migration differed for males and females. In the sample, 48.84% of men were undocumented, while only 11.32% of women were undocumented. This difference was statistically significant at the .01 level. In contrast, women migrated predominately with work visas (77.36%). These findings correspond with the high demand for female domestic workers within the Middle East and the ease with which women can find formal labour contracts as domestic workers. Formalized employment opportunities are not so numerous for Ethiopian men within the Middle East, thereby possibly pushing them into irregular channels.

Life Before Migration

As was highlighted in the background section, Ethiopian migrants to the Middle East tend to come from socially or economically disadvantaged backgrounds. However, the data revealed that these backgrounds are varied between men and women. It was found that a much higher proportion of women completed at least some secondary education than did men (41.51% versus 16.28%). This result was significant at the .01 level. Men and women also participated in different activities prior to their migration. Approximately 26% of men were subsistence farmers before their migration, while only 1.89% of females shared this profession. Conversely, women were largely either in paid work (24.53%), in education (26.42%) or unemployed and actively searching for a job (20.75%). These findings correspond with wider survey results that some women in Ethiopia migrate as a result of low grades in secondary or preparatory school and a resulting inability to continue to the university level (Kuschminder 2013). Furthermore, women who were employed immediately before their migration may have been receiving salaries that were too low to support themselves or their families. Lastly, women may have also migrated due to the sexism and discrimination that women face in the job market in Ethiopia.

Experiences in the Destination Country

Experiences in the destination country play a critical role in how migrants perceive their migration experience and can also impact upon their return and reintegration into Ethiopia. One important aspect is occupation. The study found that out of the sample of 43 men and 53 women, 29 men and 38 women were working in their destination countries. Both men and women predominantly lived at their work sites within their destination country. Living in employer-provided accommodation, as was discussed in the Background section, can create a problematic environment for the migrant because he or she can become isolated not only from the wider community but also from other migrants, creating possibilities for abuse and vulnerability. In the Middle East, the vulnerability that can stem from living in employer-provided accommodation is even greater due to the Kafala system, in which the employer is also the migrant's sponsor and decides whether or not the migrant can remain legally within the country.

The occupations of male and female groups in their destination countries were drastically different. Ninety two percent of the 38 women who were employed in the destination country worked as domestic workers. Male migrants had a wider range of occupations, but predominantly clustered in agricultural work, daily labor and various trades.

The isolation that can be a result of living at the work site can be theoretically linked to feeling unaccepted or unwelcome in the destination country society (Anbesse et al. 2009). Of those studied, the majority did not feel at all a part of the destination country society (76.74% of men and 62.26% of women). Perceived social isolation can then have negative impacts on a migrant's perception of his or her time spent abroad (Kronfol at al. 2014). The sending of remittances was also discussed with survey participants, as this practice can influence in part a migrant's return experience and their perceptions of the success of their migration. Over 50% of both the male and female groups sent remittances home to family or friends in Ethiopia. Women were more likely to remit however, with 79.25% of women and 58.14% of men participating in remittance sending.

Return Experience

The return experience of a migrant to his or her origin country can be made more successful through labour market access and social integration. Regarding the labour market, the majority of both male and female groups had not found paid employment since their return (90.70% of males and 83.02% of females). This can be linked to other findings within the survey that people who came from a lower socioeconomic background in Ethiopia (such as domestic or agricultural workers) may be barred full access from the labour market or institutions (Kuschminder 2013). Despite limited labour market participation, both groups predominantly felt that they were part of a community in Ethiopia.

Although results were similar for men and women for the two previous variables, data on perceptions of the impact of migration on mental health, economic status, and the position within the household and the community varied greatly between males and females. Overall, men seemed to have better return experiences in their Ethiopian communities, but seemed to have more traumatic or negative perceptions of their experiences abroad than women. Conversely, women seemed to fare worse in their return and reintegration to Ethiopia on a variety of different indicators.

Regarding the actual experience abroad, Table 8.1 shows that women seemed to have more positive perceptions of their trip than did men. Forty one percent of 49 women reported that their migration had improved their mental health, while only 30.25% of men reported the same. Furthermore, 23.26% of men said that their migration had placed them in distress, while 15.09% of women answered similarly. In regards to a violation of their human rights, a larger proportion of men (46.51%) answered this question

Table 8.1 Perceptions of time abroad by gender

Migration improved mental health	Male		Female		Total	
	# obs	%	# obs	%	# obs	%
No or neutral	30	69.75	29	59.18	59	64.13
Yes	13	30.25	20	40.82	33	35.87
Total	43	100	49	100	92	100
Migration placed me in distress						
No or neutral	33	76.74	45	84.91	78	81.25
Yes	10	23.26	8	15.09	18	18.75
Total	43	100	53	100	96	100
Migration violated my human rights***						
No or neutral	23	53.49	43	81.13	66	68.75
Yes	20	46.51	10	18.87	30	31.25
Total	43	100	53	100	96	100
Migration was a mistake						
No or neutral	28	65.12	39	73.58	67	69.79
Yes	15	34.88	14	26.42	29	30.21
Total	43	100	53	100	96	100

Source: IS Academy: Migration and Development Survey, 2011

† Significance based on a T-test of means. *** $p<0.001$ ** $p<0.05$ * $p<0.1$

affirmatively, while 18.87% of women said that their migration had violated their human rights. Lastly, 34.88% of men said that their migration was a mistake, while 26.42% of females said the same. While these results show that a larger proportion of men perceived their migration abroad negatively, the results are still not overwhelmingly positive for females. Significant numbers of women said that their migration placed them in distress, violated their human rights or was a mistake. Accordingly, women's migration experiences abroad cannot be classified as 'positive', only as 'less negative' than men's.

The story differs significantly when considering the return to Ethiopia and the effects of the migration on the everyday lives of the migrant. Men overall experienced more positive outcomes in Ethiopia than women. Table 8.2 illustrates that 46.51% of men reported that their status in their household had improved, while only 31.37% of women said the same. Furthermore, 53.49% of men said that their own living conditions had improved, with 34.62% of 52 women saying the same. Additionally, 58.14% of men, as compared to 39.62% of women, said that their household living conditions had improved. Lastly, 51.16% of men said that their migration gave them more decision-making power within their household, with only 28.30% of women reporting the same. These results illustrate that within their own families and as individuals, men seemed to experience more positive processes of return than did women.

Similar results were found on a wider community level within Ethiopia. Table 8.3 shows that 53.49% of men, as compared to 45.28% of women

Table 8.2 Perceptions of return within the household by gender

Change in household status	Male		Female		Total	
	# obs	%	# obs	%	# obs	%
Decreased	0	0.00	2	3.92	2	2.13
Not changed	23	53.49	33	64.71	56	59.57
Improved	20	46.51	16	31.37	36	38.30
Total	43	100	51	100	94	100
Change in own living conditions						
Much worse	1	2.33	1	1.92	2	2.11
Worse	2	4.65	6	11.54	8	8.42
Stayed the same	16	37.21	23	44.23	39	41.05
Improved	23	53.49	18	34.62	41	43.16
Very much improved	1	2.33	4	7.69	5	5.26
Total	43	100	52	100	95	100
Change in HH living conditions						
Much worse	0	0.00	0	0.00	0	0.00
Worse	2	4.65	10	18.87	12	12.50
Stayed the same	15	34.88	20	37.74	35	36.46
Improved	25	58.14	21	39.62	46	47.92
Very much improved	1	2.33	2	3.77	3	3.13
Total	43	100	53	100	96	100
Migration gave more decision making power in HH**						
No or neutral	21	48.84	38	71.70	59	61.46
Yes	22	51.16	15	28.30	37	38.54
Total	43	100	53	100	96	100

Source: IS Academy: Migration and Development Survey, 2011

Table 8.3 Perceptions of return within the wider community by gender

Migration improved social status in Ethiopia	Male		Female		Total	
	# obs	%	# obs	%	# obs	%
No or neutral	20	46.51	29	54.72	49	51.04
Yes	23	53.49	24	45.28	47	48.96
Total	43	100	53	100	96	100
Migration increased ability to contribute to community						
No or neutral	22	51.16	33	63.46	55	57.89
Yes	21	48.84	19	36.54	40	42.11
Total	43	100	52	100	95	100

Source: IS Academy: Migration and Development Survey, 2011

reported that their migration had improved their social status in Ethiopia. Additionally, 48.84% of men said that their migration increased their ability to contribute to their community, while only 36.54% of 52 women said the same. These results may be largely due to the common and pervasive sexism within Ethiopian society and the limiting and damaging effect it has on women's lives.

Discussion

Migration is a complex and multifaceted phenomenon with many interlinking processes and interactions. Yet the social construction of gender seems to touch many of these facets, with both positive and negative consequences. The results previously discussed provide numerous examples of this. In the Ethiopian context, it is evident that gendered labour demands such as those for domestic workers or construction labourers attract women and men to different migration destinations. The nature of the work contracts offered by different types of employment affect the channels these migrants will travel through to get there, ranging from irregular to regular, with many options in between. Gendered labour demands also influence the final destination of migrants, with women migrating towards countries with the highest demand for domestic workers and men perhaps towards areas with more agricultural or construction work available.

The Ethiopian case represented here showcases the differences that exist not only in the migration itself, but also in events and decisions leading up to the migration. Women in Ethiopia may face more limited opportunities in accessing education or jobs with sufficient pay than do their male counterparts, thereby making them more likely to have to take out loans to finance their migration. Furthermore, the very existence of such barriers and limitations may give women a stronger motivation to travel abroad to seek opportunities and advancement elsewhere.

The results presented in this chapter highlight that the men in the sample in general perceived their actual time abroad more negatively than did women. This could be due to a number of factors, including that a much larger proportion of males were irregular and therefore may have been subject to a greater level of exploitation and abuse during their time overseas. Conversely, women had a less positive perception of their return experience to Ethiopia. This could also be the result of various dynamics. This may include sexism within the job market and limited societal expectations of women to a poor reintegration experience. The restricted opportunities allowed to women in Ethiopia may prevent them from using skills learned or contacts gained abroad, thereby limiting both the personal and professional development that could be leveraged from an international migration.

It is clear that gender is a prevalent factor in the perception of a migration or return experience. Accordingly, migration theories and policies need to take gender constructions into consideration and actively work to negate their negative effects. For example, reintegration support for return migrants from the Middle East is clearly necessary in Ethiopia. Yet this support must not exclusively address the difficulties faced by migrants abroad and upon return, but also the gender constructions that sometimes enable these difficulties to be possible. Psychological support must take into account the different types of abuse that men and women might have experienced abroad. Employment training and placement services must address not only the difficulties migrants experience in reintegration, but also the unique problems that women and men face in Ethiopian society.

Post-Survey Institutional Changes

The study that served as the subject of this chapter, the IS Academy: Migration and Development Survey, took place in 2011. Since the study concluded, much has changed at a governmental level in regards to Ethiopian migrants to the Middle East. Notably, in 2012 and 2013 the Ethiopian government implemented a series of moratoriums and bans on labourers traveling to some Middle Eastern countries. The government stated that the move was intended to stem human trafficking through illegal employment agencies (Aljazeera, 2013; Kannan 2012). While the good intentions of the Ethiopian government are recognized, the effectiveness of this ban is questionable, as irregular migration functions outside of legal boundaries. While there is scarce data on the subject, the ban could also push formally regular domestic workers into irregularity. Ethiopian migrants who travel abroad for employment will now be forced to take different routes and to depart from neighbouring countries, adding extra costs and dangers to their journeys (Kuschminder 2013). Crucially, however, up-to-date data is needed on the decision-making processes of Ethiopian migrants to the Middle East in order to develop a better understanding of implications of the policy changes described and the other changes in the Mediterranean Region upon migration decision-making.

Changes have also taken place outside of Ethiopia in primary destination countries within the Middle East. Most notably, conditions in Syria, one of the destination countries that featured in the IS Academy Study, have changed significantly since the study period, starting with the popular uprisings that began in 2011. Further research is urgently needed to understand the impact of the violent situation that has developed in Syria, particularly upon the Ethiopian female migrants there, and the way in which this is affecting the migration decisions discussed in this chapter.

In 2013 Saudi Arabia conducted a 'crackdown' against irregular immigrants residing in the country. Estimated numbers of forced Ethiopian returnees vary widely, but the IOM reported that by November 2013 it had assisted over 21,000 returnees. The IOM also noted that it only had resources to assist those in the most dire conditions and estimated that another 23,000 Ethiopians might be detained in Saudi detention camps (IOM Ethiopia 2013).

Although these changes will undoubtedly have great impacts on the flow of Ethiopian workers to the Middle East, current data does not exist to determine the extent of these impacts. Future research will be able to more accurately portray the effects of the changing conditions, the moratoriums and travel bans on Ethiopian workers and can then be used to craft more effective policies that work to safeguard the rights of migrants as well as realizing the positive effects of migration.

Conclusion

This chapter has used results from the IS Academy: Migration and Development Survey to illustrate the immense impact that gender constructions can have on the entirety of the migration lifecycle within the context of Ethiopia. It has been shown that gender constructions take many forms and are applied by numerous actors, affecting migrants not only while they are abroad, but also during the migration decision-making process prior to departure and during reintegrating upon return. Most importantly, it has been shown that negative gender stereotypes can act as a damper to the sometimes positive effects of migration. In conjunction with ethnic and socioeconomic stereotypes, migrants face sexism both abroad and in their origin countries. To negate this harmful pattern, it is necessary to develop migration theories and policies with the aim of abolishing harmful gender constructions. Only when migration for development policies take into account the limitations created by gender constructions and actively work against them can migration's full development potential be released. Developing such policies requires information and research. The current lack of information about the decision-making processes of migrants travelling from the Sub-Saharan region impedes good policy-making. Most crucially, a second phase of the IS Academy study is needed, in order to understand how recent changes in the Mediterranean Middle Eastern states have affected the way in which Ethiopians, and in particular Ethiopian women, are thinking about migration.

References

Aljazeera (2013) 'Ethiopian banned from moving abroad for work', *Aljazeera Online*, http://www.aljazeera.com/news/africa/2013/10/ethiopians-banned-from-moving-abroad-work-20131025122214540953.html [22/10/2014].

Amnesty International (2013) 'The Dark side of migration: Spotlight on Qatar's construction sector ahead of the world cup', https://www.amnestyusa.org/sites/default/files/mde220102013eng.pdf [22/10/2014].

Anbesse, Birke, Charlotte Hanlon, Atalay Alem, Samuel Packer and Rob Whitley (2009) 'Migration and Mental health: A Study of low-income Ethiopian women working in Middle Eastern countries', *International Journal of Social Psychiatry* 55 557–68.

Anteneh, Anteneh (2011) *Trafficking in persons overseas for labor purposes: The case of Ethiopian domestic workers* (ILO Report ISBN: 978-92-2-125132-3).

Calavita, Kitty (2006) 'Gender, migration and law: Crossing borders and bridging disciplines', *International Migration Review* 40/1 104–32.

Castles, Stephen and Mark Miller (2009) *The age of migration: International population movements in the modern world*, Palgrave Macmillian, London.

De Regt, Marina (2010) 'Ways to come, ways to leave; Gender, mobility and il/legality among Ethiopian domestic workers in Yemen', *Gender and Society* 24 237–60.

De Regt, Marina (2008) 'High in the hierarchy, rich in diversity', *Critical Asian Studies* 40/4 587–608.

Destremau, Blandine (2002) 'L'Émergence d'un Marché du Travail Domestique au Yémen: Une Étude sur Sana'a', *Revue Tiers Monde* XLIII/170 327–51.

Donato, Katharine, Donna Gabaccia, Jennifer Holdaway, Martin Manalansan and Patricia Pessar (2006) 'A glass half full? Gender in migration studies', *International Migration Review* 40/1 3–26.

Ethiopia Data Series (2014) *UN Data; a world of information*, The United Nations, http://data.un.org/Search.aspx?q=ethiopia [22/10/2014].

Fernandez, Bina (2010) 'Cheap and disposable? The impact of the global economic crisis on the migration of Ethiopian women domestic workers to the Gulf', *Gender and Development* 18/2 249–62.

Fransen, Sonja and Katie Kuschminder (2009) *Migration in Ethiopia: History, current trends and future prospects* (Paper series: Migration and Development Country Profiles), http://mgsog.merit.unu.edu/ISacademie/.../CR_ethiopia.pdf [22/10/2014].

Grieco, Elizabeth and Monica Boyd (1998) 'Women and migration: Incorporating gender into international migration theory', *Center for the Study of Population, Florida State University, Working Paper* 98–139, www.fsu.edu/~popctr/papers/floridastate/1998.html.

Hansen, Karen (1989) *Distant companions: Servants and employers in Zambia, 1900–1985*, Cornell University Press, Ithaca.

Harroff-Tavel, Hélène and Alix Nasri (2013) 'Tricked and trapped: Human trafficking in the Middle East', http://www.ilo.org/wcmsp5/groups/public/—arabstates/—ro-beirut/documents/publication/wcms_211214.pdf [22/10/2014].

Hondagneu-Sotelo, Pierrette (2000) 'Feminism and migration', *Annals of the American Academy of Political and Social Science* 571 107–20.

Hondagneu-Sotelo, Pierrette (1994) *Gendered transitions: Mexican experiences of immigration*, University of California Press, Berkeley.

Human Rights Watch (2008) *As if I am not human; Abuses against Asian domestic workers in Saudi Arabia*. ISBN: 1-56432-351-X.

IOM Ethiopia, (2013, Nov. 26). 'IOM aids over 21,000 Ethiopian returnees from Saudi Arabia', *The International Organization for Migration*. http://www.iom.int/cms/en/sites/iom/home/news-and-views/press-briefing-notes/pbn-2013/pbn-listing/iom-aids-over-21000-ethiopian-re.html [22/10/2014].

Kannan, Preeti (2012) 'Ethiopia bans citizens from jobs in the UAE', *The National UAE*, http://www.thenational.ae/news/uae-news/ethiopia-bans-citizens-from-jobs-in-the-uae [22/10/2014].

Kronfol, Ziad, Marwa Sale hand Maha Al-Ghafry (2014) 'Mental health issues among migrant workers in Gulf Cooperation Council countries: Literature review and case illustrations', *Asian Journal of Psychiatry* 10 109–13.

Kuschminder, Katie and Melissa Siegel (2010) *Understanding Ethiopian diaspora engagement policy* (UNU-MERIT Working Paper Series 2011-040), www.merit.unu.edu/publications/.../wp2011-040.pdf [22/10/2014].

Kuschminder, Katie (2013) *Female return migration and reintegration strategies in Ethiopia* (Doctoral dissertation). Maastricht University, Maastricht.

Kuschminder, Katie (2014) 'Shattered dreams and return of vulnerability: Challenges of Ethiopian female migration to the Middle East' (Policy Brief No. 18), http://migration.merit.unu.edu/publications/briefs/ [22/10/2014].

Mahdavi, Pardis (2013) 'Gender, labour and the law: The nexus of domestic work, human trafficking and the informal economy in the United Arab Emirates' *Global Networks* 13/4 425–40.

Mahler, Sarah and Patricia Pessar (2006) 'Gender matters: Ethnographers bring gender from the periphery toward the core of migration studies', *International Migration Review* 40/1 27–63.

Pessar, Patricia and Sarah Mahler (2003) 'Transnational migration: Bringing gender in', *International Migration Review* 37/3 812–46.

Plant, Roger (2008) 'Temporary contract labour in the Gulf States: Perspectives from two countries of origin', Summary paper of the Gulf Forum on Temporary Contractual Labour, http://www.oit.org/wcmsp5/groups/public/—ed_norm/—declaration/documents/publication/wcms_090662.pdf [22/10/2014].

Population Council (2004) *Child marriage briefing: Ethiopia*, http://www.popcouncil.org/uploads/pdfs/briefingsheets/ETHIOPIA.pdf [22/10/2014].

UNICEF (United Nations Children's Fund) (2013) *Background: Ethiopia*, www.unicef.org/infobycountry/ethiopia_12162.html [22/10/2014].

US Library of Congress (2005) *Country profile: Ethiopia*, http://lcweb2.loc.gov/frd/cs/profiles/Ethiopia.pdf [22/10/2014].

World Bank (2011). *Migration and remittances factbook 2011*, 2nd Edition, http://siteresources.worldbank.org/INTLAC/Resources/Factbook2011-Ebook.pdf?bcsi_scan_14cf79d043f374a1=0&bcsi_scan_filename=Factbook2011-Ebook.pdf [22/10/2014].

World Bank (2013a) *Atlas of global development* 4th Edition, http://www.app.collinsindicate.com/worldbankatlas-global/en-us [22/10/2014].

World Bank (2013b) *Ethiopian economic overview*, http://www.worldbank.org/en/country/ethiopia/overview [22/10/2014].

9 'Living without Possibility'

The Implications of the Closure of an Autonomous Space Created by Undocumented Sub-Saharan Metal Scrap Collectors in Barcelona, Spain

Sophie Ramløv Barclay and Ann Laudati

> 'The hands represent a thought process, and the face is looking into the Horizon, which represents Europe' explains Ibrahim, an artist who used to live in the Nave, as he shows me his artwork. An African face is chipped into the centre of the wooded cupboard door, which he collected from the street. Two hands, palms facing upwards, sit under it, and on either side of them is a tall palm tree. 'We have always looked toward the European Horizon. But now that we are here, living in these conditions and with the uncertainty of the future with the eviction notice up, we realise that the Horizon is Africa'.[1]

Introduction

Since 2012, in the district of Poblenou, east Barcelona, Spain, Ibrahim and 300–600 undocumented immigrants were residing in a block of abandoned industrial warehouses known as the 'Nave', with no electricity or running water. Largely of Sub-Saharan African origin, the residents of the Nave had formed a metal-collecting cooperative, providing local businesses with an informal supply of 'chatarra' (scrap metal in Spanish).[2] The Nave, however, served more than an economic function. It came to represent the unity of migrant struggles and aspirations (to become citizens) and offered a unified space in which to push for the mobilization of their rights. The implications of this geographic alignment among an otherwise diverse migrant community were profound, as it allowed not only the expansion and development of the chatarra trade within which they had become central actors, but it also provided the centralized space to better organize on behalf of Sub-Saharan African migrant claims to their 'right to the city'. Less than two years following the establishment of 'the Nave,' the Barcelona city government ordered the residents out and demolished the old buildings shortly

---

1 Conversation with Ibrahim, 9 June 2013, in the Nave.
2 Chatarra literally means 'scrap metal' but it also can refer to the community of persons that collect it and the activity of the collection. One can 'do chatarra', and one can be part of the chatarra community.

afterwards. Today, the only thing remaining from this recently productive space is a chain-link fence and the iron doors that enclose it, where even the graffiti proclaiming 'we are not animals' has been erased. Residents of the Nave are now scattered throughout the city and work of chatarra continues but has become more precarious and less profitable while the movement to acquire legal status continues albeit in more limited means.

This chapter considers the changing conditions in this specific Mediterranean city, and how these changes can shed light on local factors that may influence migrant decision making of persons from Sub-Saharan Africa moving to and through the Mediterranean. In particular, this chapter argues that the demolition of the Nave was not simply the destruction of a geographic place but a dismantling of a space that stood for the political possibilities for the African migrant community and looks at the potential consequences of this loss on local decision-making processes. The Nave represented the geographic unity of migrant struggles and aspirations (to become citizens) and offered a unified space in which to push for the mobilization of their rights. The demolition of the Nave resulted in the physical displacement and geographic dispersal of the Sub-Saharan African migrant community; it disrupted not only a tangible space made from brick and mortar that connected the African community through socio-economic networks facilitated by the work of the chatarra but, as we argue here, it also dismantled the political powers that were created and were being created at the Nave. Through the acquisition of this space, the inhabitants were able to unite, gain representation on a local level (through local associations) and create a platform to speak out about their concerns. Most importantly, their illegality had not prevented them from gaining legitimacy as participants within what was an organized service economy of scrap collection for the communities in which they lived and worked. In this, they claimed what in theory they ought not to be entitled to as 'illegal' immigrants: work, housing, community membership and a livelihood.

This chapter examines how the losses of these local possibilities are reflective of wider political and economic processes occurring at national, regional Mediterranean and international levels. The first section provides a general background of African migration to Spain, and Barcelona in particular, looking at reasons for the initial journey to the city and the decisions made by migrants for joining the chatarra. It follows with a description of the chatarra network, its business and opportunity structures. The chapter then delves into a brief history of the beginnings of the Nave since early 2012, as a growing centralized space not only for chatarra, but, as we argue here, as a pivotal space for the organization of political power amongst the undocumented Sub-Saharan migrant community. Finally, the chapter discusses the implications of the destruction of the Nave for its former residents, how its short history can only be understood in light of wider political and economic forces, and lastly, how these changes ultimately link to broader discussions of migrant decision-making processes in the Mediterranean region.

Methodology and Literature Review

This study relies on primary and secondary qualitative data gathered both prior to and following the shutdown of the Nave. Beginning in April 2012, in-depth interviews with residents of the Nave and local and religious associations, as well as participant observation were undertaken. This included attending weekly Mouridism mosque ceremonies, observing legal consultations by residents of the Nave every Wednesday with local lawyers from the ACRS (*l'Associació Catalana de Residents Senegalesos,* 'The Catalan Association of Senegalese Residents' in Catalan) over the course of May–June 2013, as well as multiple site visits to the Nave, chatarra collection places and alternative shelters following the closure of the Nave. In addition to primary evidence, this chapter draws from secondary sources including online manifestos, news articles, documentaries and press releases.

This chapter builds on and contributes to two fields of literature, which have been previously examined largely in isolation: migration studies and the informal economy of waste-pickers. Empirical research available on irregular[3] migrants has mostly been studied in the context of Mexico and the United States, while very few studies have examined undocumented migrants from Africa to Europe (Ryan 2008; Mbaye 2013). Of the existing literature on irregular migrants from Africa to Europe, the majority of studies focus on examining the factors related to the actual migration of Africans to the EU, including immigration policy, determinants of illegal migration including the individual decision making of the migrants themselves, the dynamics of border control and the integration of immigrants into the host society upon arrival. Few studies, however, consider the lives of undocumented migrants after having arrived in their host country and in particular how wider forces happening at national and global levels are shaping those experiences in profound ways. Furthermore, this chapter provides insight from an area often overlooked in most studies on waste picking communities, which largely focus on waste-pickers within the developing world. In such contexts waste-pickers are considered emblematic of the high levels of unemployment, which tend to be a permanent feature in the urban areas of the developing countries in which they are found. Such studies have thus largely focused their attention on the poor working conditions and occupational health hazards that waste-pickers face while highlighting their contribution to developing

---

3 Based on similar usage by Ryan (2008), who argues that migrants are placed into a category of irregularity due largely to their lack of necessary documentation, we employ the terms 'undocumented' and 'irregular' migrant interchangeably.

countries' broader waste management systems. While these studies have provided much needed attention to the plight of waste-pickers around the world (notably in Brazil, India, China and several African countries), they do not represent the experiences of waste-pickers in developed world contexts such as Spain, where the majority of waste-pickers are irregular migrants rather than communities that, while marginalized in society, are citizens. Thus what pulls many waste-pickers to the work in Spain is their exclusion from entering into the legal labour market, not a lack of employment opportunities per se. As a result, policies aimed at waste-pickers in developing countries which seek to promote the full productive inclusion of waste-pickers within integrated waste management systems would not work for those in developed world contexts such as Spain who engage in the work as a transitional means of survival which none consider to be a long term career.

African Migration in Spain and Barcelona

In 2013, 107,000 people were detected trying to enter the European Union without papers, up from 75,000 in 2012, according to Frontex, the EU border-control agency. While reliable numbers for irregular entries are difficult to determine, some estimate that undocumented migrants account for only 6 or 7% of documented entrants, and irregular entry from places experiencing political and economic problems is at most a third as common as legal applications for asylum from such places. Others speculate that out of 214 million migrants in the world, around 10–15% or 20 to 30 million are undocumented (IOM 2010). In general, irregular migration into Europe has been in decline since 2008, due to the crisis and stricter border controls, says a report by the Migration Policy Institute (Morehouse and Bloomfield 2011: 5). According to the Organisation for Economic Co-operation and Development, African migration to developed countries is marginal in relation to overall flows (Bossard 2009). Most Sub-Saharan migrants originate from West Africa – Ghana, Nigeria and Senegal, in particular. Half of the 30,000 irregular migrants who arrived in the Canary Islands, a Mediterranean archipelago governed by Spain, in 2006, for example, were Senegalese, while 1,000 of 7,000 African irregular migrants who died during the crossings in the same year were Senegalese. But the Migration Policy Institute believes there are between seven and eight million irregular African immigrants living in the EU – depending on regularisation schemes in the member states (Kohnert 2007). As the closest European country to the African continent, Spain is on the frontline for irregular migration.

Although the choice to migrate is highly correlated with the income opportunities of the destination country (Mayda 2010; see Chapters 1 and 6), immigrant decisions, particularly those of irregular migrants, are based on a host of additional factors, including the presence of migrant networks (Epstein and Gang 2006; Stark and Fan 2011); socio-cultural expectations and obligations; as well as migration costs (Arcand and Mbaye 2013).[4] Among documented skilled African migrants the decision to migrate to a particular destination is highly influenced by ex-colonial relations. But for irregular migrants, historical ties, cultural proximity and language hold less importance in the choice of destination country. Rather, irregular migrants favour destinations with less restrictive immigration policies and where entry is considered less difficult (Pena 2009; Bertoli et al. 2011). In a study conducted by (Mbaye 2013) on potential irregular Senegalese migrants, for example, 41% of individuals surveyed preferred Spain as a destination despite their country's historical and cultural links with France as irregular migrants perceive they will experience fewer immigration sweeps and random searches in Spain than might have greeted them in France. OECD statistics from 2010, which show that the inflow of Senegalese people into Spain and Italy increased between 2006 and 2009 whilst remaining stable in France, reflect such claims.

The growing immigration of Africans from Sub-Saharan countries with no historical or colonial ties to Spain is a fairly recent phenomenon. Spain's present popularity as a destination for Sub-Saharan Africans entering into the European Union is partly due to its geographical proximity to the continent and a porous coastline, but more so, migration to Spain by Sub-Saharan Africans follows wider trends occurring in the country and across the European Union. According to Cornelius (2004), Spain's integration into the European Community in 1986 created the pull factors that drew economic immigrants to Spain for the first time to take advantage of the substantial growth and expansion that its economy was experiencing. Increased labour demands in secondary sectors such as agriculture and construction followed a real estate boom in the country. The decade of 1991–2001 thus marked Spain's transformation from a country of emigration to one of immigration (INE 1998; INE 2003a; 2003b), and the numbers of migrants entering the country confirm this demographic and geographic shift. Between 1996 and 2001, the number of documented Senegalese migrants in Spain more than tripled from 3,575 to 11,532, while the number of Gambians almost doubled from 4,401 to 8,473 (INE 1998; INE 2003a; 2003c). As immigrants tend to concentrate in areas where greater job opportunities in the secondary sector exist, most of Spain's Sub-Saharan migrants settled primarily in the regions of Madrid and Catalonia (King and Rodríguez-Melguizo 1999). Of the total number of documented Africans residing in Spain in the early 2000s, including Moroccans and Equatorial Guineans who both have historical ties to Spain, 36% were living in the region of Catalonia and of that portion, 66% were living in Barcelona, the regional capital (INE 2003d).

---

4 For more on the factors that influence migrants in their decision to make this journey, see Poeze 2013.

Today, the Metropolitan Area of Barcelona (MAB), the second largest urban area of Spain (after Madrid), still attracts a high percentage of migrants, and it is the urban area with the second largest number of non-EU foreigners. Barcelona's attraction, particularly among Senegalese migrants who try to migrate without papers is canonized in the motto, 'Barsa wala Barsakh' which in Wolof means 'Barcelona or Death' – symbolic of the risks that irregular migrants are willing to endure on the treacherous journey. Entry into Spain for most of the Nave's undocumented residents occurred in one of two ways. Some came to Spain via a long and dangerous overland trek through North Africa and then by boat across the Mediterranean Sea, while others initially entered with an official visa and then stayed on once it had expired. Most were young men when they left their homes in Africa, the majority having left to seek out better economic opportunities in Europe and escape the seeming perpetual poverty of Sub-Saharan African countries. Many left families behind with the promise of sending remittances and/or not returning without having achieved a certain level of wealth. But as the journey requires substantial financial resources (see Chapter 10), most migrants arriving from Africa tend to be middle-class urban men between the ages of 18 and 35, some having arrived with valuable trade skills such as sewing, construction or carpentry. Few women make the voyage, but those who do play an integral role, providing African meals through unregulated but income earning pop-up cook houses that accompany many of the chatarra locales. Oftentimes, the decision to choose Spain as a destination is shaped through the direction or counsel of relations who came previously. Ibrahim for example, whose words opened the chapter, followed his elder brother who had become established in the country prior to the time of his entry into the region. Thus, while some of the Nave's residents are recent arrivals to the country, others have been settled in Spain for close to a decade.

Barcelona has seen a more or less steady decline in the number of Sub-Saharan migrants since 2009 (Ajuntament de Barcelona 2014). Sub-Saharan African migration to Barcelona peaked between 2008 and 2009 according to Barcelona City Council statistics. After the collapse of the housing bubble and the economic crisis that followed many migrants living outside of Barcelona lost their jobs in agriculture and construction and came to the city in search of better opportunities. Spain became the most dramatic example of migrant unemployment after foreign unemployment reached 32% in 2011 (OECD 2012). It is estimated that 1.6 million jobs were lost between 2007 and 2009, of which 800,000 were in the construction sector, as reported by the Migration Policy Institute (Collett 2011). Sub-Saharan migrants were one of the most affected immigrant groups in terms of losing employment and housing by the crisis due to their large representation in the construction and agricultural sectors (Domingo and Sabater 2008). The construction opportunities that drew many of Barcelona's previous economic migrants, however, had similarly halted mid-condo and the same people who had had been employed to build the houses turned around and started selling off the parts as scrap, as part of Spain's emerging informal underground economy. Spain's unemployment rate, which reached record numbers following the economic crash, remains a staggering 26.3%. It was during this period when many migrants, who just two years prior had formal if precarious employment, rented homes, and their documents in order while some were even enrolled in universities, lost not only their incomes but their homes as well, and found themselves out on the street. Cuts in public spending and job losses have been particularly hard on the African migrant community in Barcelona, resulting in a rapid decline in social mobility.

Chatarra and the Nave

The birthplace of the Nave, Poblenou, is an area that has deep historical roots with working class labour movements and autonomy struggles. In the beginning of the nineteenth century, the rise of industrialization in the area resulted in a growing textile industry attracting workers from across Spain. The influx of internal migrants in the poor working-class area was met with harsh living conditions: overcrowded shanty houses, little fresh water, poor sanitary conditions, low wages and high mortality rates. It was in these conditions that a strong labour movement arose, setting up cooperatives and associations throughout Poblenou from as early as 1870. It was in this area that, in 1912, the newly established and well-known Anarcho-syndicalist Confederación Nacional del Trabajo (CNT) ('National Anarcho-Syndicalist Confederation of Work' in Spanish) set up their first offices. Its history of autonomous self-organization as a means of overcoming hardship and gaining rights is one that still powerfully resonates today, as economic migrants from Sub-Saharan Africa settle in the area. Faced with many of the same hardships, they created the Nave against this backdrop, a notable example emblematic of wider political and economic processes occurring at both the national and the global stage, yet remaining little known outside the streets of Poblenou.

The 'Nave' was established towards the end of 2011, becoming a home for both the Chatarra business and those involved in the activity. The chatarra revolves around scouring the city's trash bins for raw materials that can be sold onto the world market or salvaged and sent to Africa as part of a booming second-hand economy. This work involves a process of deliberation over what constitutes 'rubbish' – that which has no redeemable value – and what can be recycled from thrown out items and materials. These found items are then collected and transported using abandoned supermarket trolleys that are pushed around Barcelona, until the trolleys become full or too heavily loaded to collect more or the fatigue of the chatarra collection, having pushed their cart around the city often for several kilometres, sets in. Found items were then brought back to the Nave where they were disassembled (in the case of metals and raw materials), divided and organized in different rooms. Metals and raw materials would then be weighed and sold for cash while recycled items such as clothing, handbags, shoes, and electronics would be stored until a container could be organized, filled and sent to relations in Africa for resale or as gifts.

Many would not choose to do this kind of work if they received temporary legal status and had an opportunity to find other employment. Many specified that chatarra was not an occupation but rather a way to survive, not a life but a way to live in a time of economic crisis. Before the crisis, undocumented migrants could gain legal residence through the validation of certain requirements – notably, language acquisition in Spanish and/or Catalan, three years of residence in Spain, and a work contract of at least one year. The importance of acquiring a regular status can be summed up by a metaphor explained by Baye, one of the ACRS members: 'having papers versus not having papers is like some having shoes on in a race and others running it barefoot. We do not need to ask ourselves who will do better in the race'. For example, if someone is a professional electrician and would like to continue to learn within his field with more education, but does not have papers, they would have more trouble acquiring it than someone with papers.

Being undocumented, therefore, has real life consequences, not only on personal development, but also on individual well-being, as it puts one in more vulnerable situations. The economic crisis has only worsened this context, exposing many in the undocumented migrant community in Barcelona to more 'precarious living conditions, exploitative work conditions, low income, lack of health insurance, restrictions on mobility, lack of proper housing, hunger, homelessness, and social stigmatization' (Quesada 2012: 895). The increased difficulties in obtaining documents status has at the same time been accompanied by the decreasing valuation of what a regular status can now afford as such a status no longer guarantees gainful employment. Indeed, many Spanish citizens are suffering similar difficulties due to the crisis. Such a shifting socio-economic context has meant that the possibilities once associated both in the attainment and through the obtainment of gaining documented status has decreased. The Nave therefore highlights how a group of irregular migrants cope with 'living without possibility' as Ed, a Congolese migrant living in the Nave said – to the exigencies of survival after the crisis as an undocumented migrant, where the feeling that nothing is possible is very present.

The 'Nave' in this chapter refers to the largest of the Naves ('warehouses' in Spanish) spread within Besos, an area within Poblenou. And this Nave was far from simply a scrapyard. In addition to large industrial-sized rooms filled with raw materials such as copper wire or aluminum stripped from window blinds, there were bars, restaurants, a cinema, a bike repair shop, a hair salon, a tailor's as well as some shops selling clothing and shoes to service the workers. And the types of work available to its residents were equally diverse. One informant, for example, was paid to collect and deliver water to the various businesses and individuals living in the Nave. The money earned through chatarra (roughly estimated at 10-15€ a day) therefore circulated back into the community, functioning as a micro-economy that created work opportunities for a much wider population beyond simply those directly involved in the chatarra collection. It was therefore a place where one had the possibility to 'survive', as one informant said, a place where people as well as things could be 'organized'. Informants also spoke of the role that the Nave played in reducing the number of Africans involved in petty crimes such as theft – a sentiment that was expressed by Spanish-born residents of Barcelona as well. Several informants, for example, noted that work in chatarra kept young men 'occupied'. For the former residents of the Nave, the Nave therefore fulfilled a number of functions (a place of work, a place to sleep) but also clearly represented a social (a place to meet), an economic (a place to exchange) as well as a political space (a place of revolution, a place of autonomy).

It was, however, also a place of great poverty and difficulty. Absent from the Nave was any reliable or fixed source of electricity (although they had managed to tap into an intermittent supply) or running supply of water. People slept amongst the scrap metal, often in cramped dark rooms, and washed themselves in the local public fountain down the road – a harsh reality compared to the expectations that a migrant's successful crossing into Spain would attain. But it is precisely the struggle for a better life which the Nave represented. This complex semi-structured community helped support what was in fact a diverse group of migrants not only in their attempt to attain a livelihood but also in their struggle for their 'right to the city'.

Although the majority of migrants originated in West Africa, and notably Senegal, a plurality of nationalities – from Eastern European to Latin American – belonged to and benefited from the existence of the Nave. The notion of 'community' in this context however must be used cautiously as it is important not to romanticise the Nave as a unified front, an apolitical collectivity free from power struggles, internal divisions and conflict. There were fights and conflicts between English-speaking and French-speaking inhabitants, and in-depth conversations revealed continuing disagreement over leadership, as well as departing points of allegiance to the collective. Despite these contestations, the collective in general, and the Nave in particular, is credited by many of its residents as having brought people together.

This is most obvious in the formation of networks of support and guidance with local and religious associations and the inhabitants of the Nave, which would not have been so strong had the undocumented migrant community been dispersed across the city. This was most notable in the number of concerned local associations and neighbours who joined the migrants' struggle for their 'right to the city'. The neighbourhood association, Associació de Veïns i Veïnes del Poblenou, became aware of the migrant community's difficulties when a group within the Nave were starving. That was three years before the shutdown. They began to fund-raise for them, and every week volunteers would bring rice and other supplies to them. They also began a microcredit banking system to support those who did not have enough money, for example, to go to the pharmacy, fix glasses or to pay for a train ticket to Madrid to renew passports. They also made campaigns against disease and illness in the area.

Their movement gained momentum over the years, and when the eviction notice came up with the looming threat that all these people would be sleeping on the street, a group of associations joined together to support the inhabitants of the Nave by forming the *Assemblea Solidària Contra els Desallotjaments* (Assembly of Solidarity Against Evictions).[5] The assemblea brought together national and neighbourhood associations, community movements and religious groups by appealing to the Universal Declaration of Human Rights, requesting all to be in solidarity, and to fight for a vision of society which is based on respect and dignity for all. They wrote an online manifesto, which was founded on wider principles of a guarantee of integrity, housing and jobs – that all persons have the same rights and that 'no one is illegal'. It claimed that with the eviction, the City Council of Barcelona was rendering this community invisible as opposed to addressing the real issues at hand,[6] such as broader problems of poverty and national-level issues concerning housing and job shortages, as well as those associated specifically with irregular status. The assemblea, alongside those active undocumented immigrants living in the Nave, tried to bring this large, increasingly invisible community into the public and political sphere. This large group of united associations came to be the main political force behind the immigrants' claims, supplying lawyers for the eviction court cases, writing new articles and organising campaigns. The degree to which the immigrants were involved and incorporated was however contested, and some migrants felt that these associations were pushing their own ideologies and agendas. However, against the City Council, it was a united front.

Another group that supported the Nave inhabitants was the Bayefall, a group within the Sufi-Islamic Mouridism community – a branch of Islam with roots in Senegal, which holds the doctrine of hard work and dignity as one of

---

5 This is made up Xarxa de Suport als Assentaments (composed of Apropem-nos, Associació de Veïns i Veïnes del Poblenou, CEPAIM, Assemblea Social del Poblenou, l'Associació Catalana de Residents Senegalesos [ACRS], la Coordinadora d'Associacions de Senegalesos de Catalunya [CASC], l'Observatori del Sistema Penal i els Drets Humans de la UB), Papeles y Derechos para Todos, Tanquem els CIES, CEPAIM-ASISI, AVV del Poblenou, Assemblea Social del Poblenou, ARRAN del Poblenou and concerned neighbours.

6 Quotation from the Manifesto, with reference to the Nave inhabitants: '(el govern) No volen que siguin un problema, l'Administració els vol fer invisibles.' Which means: 'the government does not want a problem, and so the administration wants to make them invisible'. Accessed online (13/06/2014) (http://assembleacontradesallotjamentsp9.wordpress.com/2013/03/23/manifest-de-lassemblea/).

its core beliefs. They had a space in the Nave filled with sofas, where they met every Thursday to talk and sing. Although there were varying degrees of devotedness in the Nave, their presence was felt throughout the abandoned set of buildings – made particularly visible through the graffiti of Cheikh Ahmadou Bamba, the Muslim Sufi leader and founder of the Mouride Brotherhood who dedicated his life to 'the other' through work and preaching non-violent struggle against French Colonialism. The majority of the young community attended the Bayefall meetings, which frequently included discussions on how to compose and educate oneself and within which the chatarra was promoted as a form of respectable and dignified work.

The Destruction of the Nave

In 2012, the property owner of the Nave, Fincas Riana S.L., began an eviction process that ended in the rapid expulsion of the residents. Originally set for eviction on 18 June, the assemblea appealed to the court but were unsuccessful, and the inhabitants were evicted from the Nave on 24 June 2013, at 5:30 in the morning. The implications of this decision were profound, as it resulted not only in the loss of a roof over their heads, but it also severely disrupted the economic as well as the social lives that were being created. The short timeframe of the eviction and the loss of a collective space to store their found goods resulted in a substantial loss of the materials and metals that they had collected over the years. Likewise, the companies that had come to rely on the Nave and its function within the chatarra community as a centralized collection place of metals and materials lost a reliable and easily accessible source of raw materials. When finally evicted on the 24th of June, the members of the Nave were forced to find other means of shelter quickly. Some sought accommodation with friends, and others moved into temporary housing (hostels) provided by the government or alternative squats. Still others, finding no such opportunities, ended up on the streets. The work began again for many, but the efforts of their work have become scattered and their business decentralized. Many of the chatarra collectors interviewed complained that the shutdown of the Nave further cut their profits, as chatarra collectors are now forced to bring their materials to non-African scrap metal collectors who buy at lower prices.

    The shutdown of the Nave signified not only the dislocation from the physical location that united these immigrants, but also a relational dislocation with local associations. In particular, immigrants relayed a sense of disappointment in those who claimed to support their interests and fight on their behalf. As one respondent relates, 'we left the Nave calmly because of the promises made by the assemblea, which have still to be fulfilled one year later'.[7] These promises made to the immigrants by the assemblea

---

7 Interview with Ed, Gracia Barcelona, 15 July 2014.

solidaria contra els desallojaments came about after having brokered a verbal deal with the City Council before the eviction. In the verbal deal, the City Council had assured the inhabitants of the Nave that no one would be left on the street and that it would provide assistance in the form of housing, job training programs, and even regularization for those evicted.

The reality however has been far different. The promise of housing turned out to be six square meter rooms, which sometimes housed up to 7 or 8 people with no cooking facilities and one shared bathroom for an entire floor. Despite the cramped and poor conditions of the rooms, those immigrants who were lucky enough to receive shelter still spoke favorably about having a reliable source of clean water and access to sanitary facilities that had not been available at the Nave. Even these substandard shelters were only temporary, however, and four months after speaking with the immigrants on their hostel beds, we found that they had been once again displaced to other areas of the city. Today many are still sleeping on the street and others are in churches that have given them refuge. Shelters have a curfew, no cooking facilities and little space to store the material collected after a day's work by the chatarra. As a result of the dispersed effort to find adequate housing and the limitations of the housing options themselves, families and couples have been separated and put in different housing sometimes 30 km away from each other. As time passes, immigrants are being moved to housing further and further out of the city.

Of central concern for the former inhabitants of the Nave is the official recognition of their rights – through the obtainment of legal status. However such recognition is a hopeful aspiration at best, as the regularization process occurs at the national level. The regional government has said it will speed up the process of arraigo social,[8] a process which normally takes a month to be considered, to be fast tracked to occur within a 24 to 48 hour period and that they will hand it over to the national government quickly. This has had little effect on most of the immigrants because they cannot even be considered for the application process without a work contract, which is something that they do not have. The arraigo social was implemented in 2006 as a law that allowed continuous regularization on an individual level (Franch Auladell et al. 2011). As one Catalan media source reports, just one year in, of the individuals evicted from the Nave, 87 people were processed for work and residence permits. Of the 87, a paltry seven people have received them, while over half (47) have been rejected by the state, and the remaining applications are still pending. According to Spanish law, the arraigo social, gaining temporary legal status in other words, can be granted after three years of living undocumented in Spain, if three conditions are met: proof of residence in the country for three

---

8 Arraigo Social is a temporary legal permit acquired on the basis of having social roots, or being socailly embedded in a country (usually proved through time spent in the country, language proficiency and a work contract).

years (usually through registration with the municipalities), evidence of effort towards becoming part of the community (usually through language proficiency) and a work contract. As most immigrants speak Catalan if not both Catalan and Spanish, either self-taught or by having enrolled in formal language courses (which the government sponsors and pays for), and all immigrants (regardless of legal status) are registered upon entrance into Spain, the only effective means used to deny immigrants temporary legal status falls on the (in) ability of immigrants to gain a work contract. Acquiring an 'arraigo social', in other words, has become de facto determined by one's ability to acquire a work contract. What constitutes work, therefore, and how the Spanish government defines work remains particularly significant for those working in chatarra, let alone any immigrant involved in the informal urban economy.

Recently, the government appeared to be attending to the plight of those removed from the Nave, and in July 2014, a training program to legalize the work of the chatarra based on the experiences of South and Central American waste-pickers was initiated and will be piloted for a one year term – and promises of regularization have been widely announced. Many, however, are suspicious of the program's ability to provide adequate benefits to the hundreds of residents of the Nave, let alone the wider chatarra community which numbers in the thousands, as the pilot includes only 12 members, and it is unclear if they are former members of the Nave or even how many are irregular African migrants. The failed promises made by the assemblea to the inhabitants of the Nave which were later negotiated with the City Council, have helped divide the community politically and socially. Distrust between immigrants and local associations have widened, the Bayefall lost their meeting spot, and internal leadership splits between the immigrants has resulted in the weakening of the political mobilization and a reduction in income for the chatarra workers.

Contextualizing the Destruction of the Nave

The weakening of social and political networks within the Sub-Saharan migrant group in Barcelona must be understood within the wider social, political and economic contexts that were occurring at the national level. The pressures being put onto the migrants by city and municipal officials, of which the closure of the Nave is one example, is firstly a result of a change in the political administration of the country. Secondly, it is a result of the economic crisis which placed a greater number of Spanish citizens out of work and in search of alternative ways to survive, of which chatarra provided one such opportunity. Thirdly, it is a reflection of Barcelona's ambition to become a model of modern urban planning. Many of the buildings that were razed, or from which people were evicted, adjoined refurbished or soon to be refurbished areas. The visual contrast between the empty lots where the Nave once was and poster displays of a modern and clean

Barcelona that colour the sides of these adjoining buildings, is striking and deserves critical introspection into the questions of what as well as who is considered necessary to dispose of in order to realize such visions.

Aside from the wider economic context of the financial crisis affecting Barcelona's migrants, which has been previously explained, a shifting political climate has further shaped a more restrictive regulatory process for the city's migrant community. Barcelona has been previously credited with having an 'intercultural and inclusive approach' to immigration, asserting not multiculturalism nor assimilation but rather promoting a focus on language acquisition, education, and identity affiliation with the territory of Catalonia (Conversi 2000; Generalitat de Catalunya 2005; Hepburn 2011). In 2011, the conservative government was elected, after eight years of having been dominated by socialist leadership. This change radically altered policies related to social welfare, including the current law which excludes undocumented migrants from public healthcare. However despite Spain's economic and social difficulties since the crisis, it has not seen the ascendance of a far-right party that has been witnessed in other EU countries such as Greece (Chapter 6). However, results from ACCEPT PLURALISM, an EU funded project on cultural diversity and tolerance in Europe, demonstrate an increasing shift in Catalan political discourse towards less tolerance of immigrants and immigration – themes which have become a rallying platform of several mainstream party representatives' electoral agendas. One example of this rise in anti-immigrant rhetoric is the growth of the Plataforma per Catalunya – a young anti-immigrant party that has recently been gaining seats in regional rural elections in Catalonia. While such change has yet to manifest into new anti-immigrant legislation, as Zapata-Barrero et al. (2012) argue, the increasing popularity of such anti-immigrant discourse is testing the limits of intolerance in Catalan politics. 'Even if there has not been much change in the policies (towards migrants) since the economic crisis, the cordon sanitaire against racist political discourses has been weakened in Catalonia' (Zapata-Barrero and Burchianti 2013: 5).

According to Delgado (2005), Barcelona's urban model is one that has always prioritized the flow of capital rather than 'urban policies promoting and facilitating residential functions, social relationships and citizen welfare' (cited in Parés et al. 2014: 4). Its focus on macro-projects and mega-events, such as the Olympics of 1994, exemplifies such an urban development model (Parés et al. 2014). In 2000, Barcelona shifted its focus away from macro-level projects and is currently investing money into a plan known as @22 in order to transform the old industrial area into a knowledge-intensive and technologically innovative urban space. This plan depends on dividing and selling off large sections of Poblenou to local and international corporations to boost the economy – the Nave buildings being one such deal. Its importance to the government and its link to the shutdown of the Nave is so significant that it was mentioned as one of the factors for the judge's ruling on the eviction: 'Dicha finca se encuentra afectada por el plan urbanístico 22@, que no permite su rehabilitación y esta previsto su derribo' ('This property is affected by the @22 urban plan, which does not permit the building to be rehabilitated and which is scheduled to be demolished').[9] Many local and social associations have been critical of the @22 plan and the wider 'Barcelona model of urban planning', however, referring to it as a reflection of global neoliberalism, which has served as a catalyst for the growing social inequalities in the city (Parés et al. 2014) particularly in the context of the economic crisis. The city's urban model, set against the backdrop of healthcare budget cuts and reduced welfare planning where the money for integration is drawn from, has, by drawing funds away from these programs, been viewed by many in the area as indirectly contributing to the social regression of many of the already economically and socially vulnerable residents, including the irregular migrants of the Nave.

Conclusion

Since its ingression in the EU, Spain has had six regularization campaigns (1985, 1991, 1996, 2000, 2001, and 2005) in which undocumented immigrants already residing in Spain could apply for residence permits (Levinson 2005). Each of these campaigns has received more applications than the previous one, and while the actual numbers of permits issued has increased, the rate of approval has steadily decreased. As Huntoon (1998) notes, because of their rigid application requirements, the actual effect of these regularization campaigns has been minimal, and the majority of immigrants that it was intended to reach were in fact ineligible and thus have been forced to maintain their undocumented status. Irregular migrants from Sub-Saharan Africa were further underserved by these campaigns, which disproportionately benefitted individuals of Ecuadorian, Colombian, Moroccan, and Romanian origins (Levinson 2005). Such actions could be seen as a deliberate strategy to help fill gaps in the domestic labour market without openly embracing immigration (e.g. Calavita 2002). Sabater and Domingo (2012) support such claims, citing that 'despite some restrictive policies . . . Spanish authorities openly admit the necessity of immigrants to fulfil labour market demands.' Thus irregular immigrants find themselves in what Calavita calls a 'legal limbo', an ambiguous status that perfectly reflects the contradictions of their role in the political economy (quoted in Ryan 2008: 4).

This condition is clearly expressed in the contradictory treatment of Barcelona's chatarra collectors, who are consistently expelled from the

---

[9] Tribunal Report, accessed online (15/06/2014) http://rereguardaenmoviment.org/wp-content/uploads/2013/06/sentencia_son300.pdf.

temporary squats they inhabit in abandoned buildings around the city but who pass city police on a daily basis with their shopping carts filled with illegally collected scrap metal that will eventually be sold to Catalan-owned companies for below-market rates. While further research is needed to clarify the extent to which Barcelona officials deliberately designed the shutdown of the Nave as a strategy to maintain this group of irregular migrants in a constant state of detection and expulsion in order to continue to benefit from their position as easily exploitable workers, the closure of the Nave arguably did just this. Already forced to the margins of society by their irregular status (Moreno 2005), former residents of the Nave have found themselves geographically dispersed throughout the marginal folds of the city, literally scattering what was potentially a new form of multi-ethnic and multi-national migrant cosmopolitanism (Mbembe 2001) and reinstating their position in Catalan society as what Ifekwunigwe (2014) calls '(in)visible strangers'. The erasure of the graffiti written on the buildings in the Nave – testimonials of the marginalization felt by migrants –could be said to represent the silencing of a movement that had been enabled to collectively assemble in the shared space that was the Nave.

The Nave, although a unique space that successfully if not seamlessly combined the wider interests and struggles of a group of Sub-Saharan migrants and which helped facilitate the migrants' ability to organize for reform, to reinvent themselves, and to gain credibility and a living through their work as chatarra collectors, was not without problems. Drug use, conflicts over leadership and desperate poverty confronted its inhabitants. Yet these were not reasons given for the shutdown of the Nave. This chapter provided a 'focusing event' (Ryan 2008: 2) of the closure of the Nave to understand how wider political and economic processes are shaping irregular migrant experiences at the local level. By doing so we hope to further understand the integration and segregation of migrant space in current Catalan society and to encourage dialogue that considers the importance of a place for migrant struggles to survive and to be heard.

In particular, the destruction of a space that created political and economic possibilities for the Sub-Saharan undocumented population in Barcelona has subsequently weakened the network ties and collective opportunities for these migrants, in an already difficult climate of limited possibilities following the economic crisis – a context that holds implications not simply at the level of this particular case study. As a local exploration into Barcelona's migrant population, it allows us to understand the general view among the city's Sub-Saharan irregular immigrants that they are 'living without possibilities' while connecting the changing conditions of Barcelona's migrants to wider socio-economic processes, allows us to better understand the broader dynamics of migrant experiences and the changing map of migrant movements in the Mediterranean region. In particular, this chapter highlights the emerging contexts in which migrant decision-making is increasingly linked to struggles for and over urban space, which have become a global feature of the modern era.

References

Ajuntament de Barcelona (2014) *INFORMES ESTADÍSTICS: La població estrangera a Barcelona*, http://www.bcn.cat/estadistica/catala/dades/inf/pobest/pobest14/pobest14.pdf [20/09/2014].

Arcand, Jean-Louis and Lingure Mously Mbaye (2013) *Braving the Waves: The Role of Time and Risk Preferences in Illegal Migration from Senegal.* IZA Discussion Papers 7517. Institute for the Study of Labor (IZA), July.

Bertoli, S, J Fernández-Huertas Moraga and F Ortega (2011) *Crossing the border: Self-selection, earnings and individual migration decisions*, Discussion paper series, Forschungsinstitut zur Zukunft der Arbeit, No. 4957.

Bossard, L (2009) *The Future of International Migration to OECD Countries.* Regional Note West Africa, OECD, Paris, http://www.oecd.org/dataoecd/3/42/43484256.pdf.

Calavita, Kitty (2002) 'Un 'ejército de reserva de delincuentes': la criminalización y el castigo económico de los inmigrantes en España', *Revista Española de Investigación Criminológica* 2.

Collet, Elizabeth (2011) *Immigration Integration in Europe in a Time of Austerity*, Migration Policy Institute, Washington, DC.

Conversi, Daniele (2000) *The Basques, the Catalans and Spain: Alternative Routes to Nationalist Mobilisation*, University of Nevada Press, Reno.

Cornelius, Wayne A (2004) 'Spain: The Uneasy Transition from Labor Exporter to Labor Importer', in Wayne A Cornelius, Takeyuki Tsuda, Philip L Martin and James F Hollifield (eds) (2004) *Controlling Immigration: A Global Perspective*, 2nd edition, Stanford University Press, Stanford, 387–429.

De Hass, Hein (2007) 'The myth of invasion: Irregular migration from West Africa to the Maghreb and the European Union', *International Migration Institute Research Report*, University of Oxford, Oxford.

Delgado, Manuel (2005) *Elogi del Vianant. Del 'Model Barcelona' a la Barcelona Real*, Edicions de 1984, Barcelona.

Domingo, Andreu and Albert Sabater (2008) 'Segregació, enclavaments i discursos institucionals al voltant de la població subsahariana a Catalunya', Chapter Two in *Col·lecció Ciutadania i Immigració, núm. 8 Recerca i immigració IV Convocatòria ARAFI-2008*, Generalitat de Catalunya. Departament de Benestar Social i Família.

Epstein, Gil S and Ira N Gang (2006) 'The Influence of Others on Migration Plans', *Review of Development Economics* 10/4 652–65.

Franch, Xavier, Andreu Domingo i Valls and Albert Sabater i Coll (2011) 'Perspectiva municipal del arraigo en la provincia de Barcelona, 2006–2009', *Documents d'anàlisi geogràfica* 57/3 517–47.

Generalitat de Catalunya (2005) 'Pla de Ciutadania i Immigracio´ 2005–2008' (Plan of Citizenship and Immigration 2005–2008), Catalan Ministry of Social Welfare and Family, Immigration secretary, www.gencat.net/benestar/societat/convivencia/immigracio/pla/introduccio/index.htm [07/09/2014].

Hepburn, Eve (2011) ''Citizens of the Region': Party conceptions of regional citizenship and immigrant integration', *European Journal of Political Research* 50 504–29.

Huntoon, Laura (1998) 'Immigration to Spain: Implications for a Unified European Union Immigration Policy', *International Migration Review* 32/2 423–50.

Ifekwunigwe, Jayne O (2014) 'Reframing Senegalese Youth and Clandestine Migration to a Utopian Europe', ITPCM International Commentary ISSN. 2239–7949.

IMO (2010) *World Development Report: The Future of Migration: Building Capacities for Change*. International Organization for Migration, Geneva.

Instituto Nacional de Estadística (INE) (1998) *Anuario Estadístico 1997*, Instituto Nacional de Estadística, Madrid.

Instituto Nacional de Estadística (INE) (2003a) *Foreigners Currently Resident in Spain Classified by Country of Nationality, 1991–2000*, http://www.ine.es/inebase [06/03/2003].

Instituto Nacional de Estadística (INE) (2003b) *Efectivo de extranjeros residentes en Espana clasificados por ccaa de residencia 1992–2001*, http://www.ine.es/inebase/ [06/03/2003].

Instituto Nacional de Estadística (INE) (2003c) *Extranjeros residentes en Espana 2001. Extranjeros residents en España por nacionalidad y grupos de edad*, http://www.ine.es/inebase/ [06/03/2003].

Instituto Nacional de Estadística (INE) (2003d) *Extranjeros residentes en Espana 2001. Extranjeros residents en España por CCAA/prov. de residencia y nacionalidad*, http://www.ine.es/inebase/ [13/02/2003].

King, Russell and Isabel Rodríguez-Melguizo (1999) 'Recent Immigration to Spain: The Case of Moroccans in Catalonia', in Floya Anthias and Gabriella Lazaridis (eds) (1999) *Into the Margins: Migration and Exclusion in Southern Europe*, Ashgate, Brookfield 55–82.

Kohnert, Dirk (2007) 'African Migration to Europe: Obscured Responsibilities and Common Misconceptions', GIGA Working Paper No. 49, http://www.giga-hamburg.de/content/publikationen/pdf/wp49_kohnert.pdf.

Levinson, Amanda (2005) *The Regularisation of Unauthorized Migrants: Literature Survey and Country Case Studies*, Centre on Migration, Policy and Society, University of Oxford, Oxford.

Mayda, Anna (2010) 'International migration: a panel data analysis of the determinants of bilateral flows', *Journal of Population Economics* 23/4 1249–74.

Mbaye, Linguère Mously (2013) ''Barcelona or Die': Understanding Illegal Migration from Senegal', *IZA Discussion Papers* 7728, Institute for the Study of Labor (IZA).

Mbembe, Achille (2001) 'Ways of Seeing: Beyond the New Nativism: Introduction', *African Studies Review* 44/2 1–14.

Morehouse, Christal and Michael Blomfield (2011) *Irregular Migration in Europe*, Migration Policy Institute, Washington, DC.

Moreno Fuentes, Francisco Javier (2005) 'The evolution of Spanish immigration policies and their impact on North African migration to Spain', *Studies in Culture, Polity and Identities* 6/1 109–35.

OECD (2012) 'Country Notes: Recent Changes in Migration Movements and Polices', http://www.oecd.org/els/mig/SPAIN.pdf [02/10/2014].

Parés, Marc, Rubén Martínez and Ismael Blanco (2014) *Collaborative governance under austerity in Barcelona: a comparison between evictions and empty urban space management*, City Futures International Conference, Special Session: Collaborative Governance Under Austerity, 18–20 June 2014, Paris.

Pena, Alves (2009) 'Locational Choices of the Legal and Illegal: The Case of Mexican Agricultural Workers in the U.S.', *International Migration Review* 43/4 850–80.

Poeze, Miranda (2013) 'High-Risk Migration: From Senegal to the Canary Islands by Sea', in Alessandro Triulzi and Robert McKenzie (eds) (2013) *Long Journeys. African Migrants on the Road*, Brill, 45–66.

Ryan, A (2008) *Learning From the Cayuqueros: What the African "boat people" are teaching Spain – and Europe – about immigration policy*, International Catholic Migration Commission, Geneva.

Sabater, Albert and Andreu Domingo (2012) 'A New Immigration Regularization Policy: The Settlement Program in Spain', *International Migration Review* 46/1 191–220.

Stark, Oded and C Simon Fan (2011) 'Migration for degrading work as an escape from humiliation', *Journal of Economic Behavior and Organization* 77/3 241–7.

Zapata-Barrero, Ricard, Flora Burchianti and Blanca Garcés-Mascareñas (2012) 'Tolerance and Cultural Diversity Concepts and Practices in Spain', ACCEPT-PLURALISM 2012/32; 5. Country Synthesis Reports, European University Institute.

Zapata-Barrero, Ricard and Flora Burchianti (2013) *New Knowledge in Spain*, http://cadmus.eui.eu/bitstream/handle/1814/27478/ACCEPT_2013_17_New_Knowledge_Spain.pdf?sequence=1 [19/09/2014].

10 'You make a decision and you start your journey'

Reflections of a Ghanaian Economic Migrant and Founder of the NGO, CEHDA

Iddrisu Wari[1]

Introduction

Potential migrants in Sub-Saharan countries often do not know much about the situation in Europe. For them, they cannot imagine that things will be difficult here. That is how I thought before I left, and it is still the way the people I meet are thinking. I arrived in Barcelona in 2001 after travelling from my village in Ghana by road, passing through Niger, Algeria, Libya and Morocco. As soon as I could, I set up my organization, CEHDA. To begin with, we worked to support Africans living in Barcelona. Then, I started by travelling back to Ghana and talking to people about what things are like in Spain. Then I extended my work to include migrants in North Africa. If you ask me whether the problems in Europe and in North Africa affect the people's decisions to move, I will tell you 'no, not really'. When they are making decisions, people are not thinking that there may be problems in Spain, and they do not know about the problems in North Africa. They are thinking about their own situation and how to make it better. And they have an idea of Europe. They are making very dangerous journeys to get here. Sometimes I meet people from Ghana in North Africa, even those who have already made unsuccessful boat crossings, preparing to cross again. They can't even think to go back. Some of them decide to stay in North Africa. The problems we encounter along the way and also in Europe change our perception about Europe and affect us physically and mentally. In this chapter, I want to emphasize the situation for the people that do not arrive in Europe due to difficulties or are deported, and to examine the support given to them by organisations. I also want to show how African people, after many years in Europe, are unemployed and without

---

1 This chapter is based on a series of conversations between Iddrisu Wari (popularly known as Rashid) and Tendayi Bloom. The conversations were recorded and then faithfully transcribed and edited down into chapter form, with further collaborative effort. For videos about the author's projects, in Gonja, Catalan and Castilian Spanish, please visit: www.cehdaghana.org/als-mitjans [31/07/2014)]

resources and may be looking for new possibilities to survive or looking to return to our countries.

Reflecting on My Own Migration Decisions

The Decision to Migrate

I grew up in the countryside, but I went to boarding school for my secondary studies. There, you meet people from the city. They used to talk about Europe. One said he had a friend living in Italy making four hundred dollars every hour. We believed these stories. Three of us decided if we are spending all these hours to study and to find a job, why don't we migrate to work? Either we have to travel to South Africa, or we have to go to Libya, and from there to Europe. Every vacation, we took a map and were looking at where to move. We didn't even know that a passport existed, but we wanted to travel. After 1995, we'd completed our studies at that school, and everyone went their separate ways.

In Ghana we have the private schools and then we have the other schools. I wanted to go to a particular school. I had good results but I could not pay extra money to the director. If I had gone to that school, I'm sure I would have continued with my studies. One of my school friends was very keen to go abroad. I also had a friend who went to the south and came back and told me we really should think about going to Libya because if you stand in Libya and if you throw a stone you can reach Italy. If you look on the map, it looks very close. My family didn't want me to travel. My sister wouldn't allow it. She had travelled before to Côte d'Ivoire. She was telling me it's not easy to travel. I fought with her, but I agreed to stay.

Then my friend left, and after six months, he sent me a cassette with pictures. He'd made a picture with a taxi and said that this was his car. So I thought that this guy had left less than six months ago and he already had a car and was working and was doing well for himself. He gave a telephone number and said that if I call, I could catch him on Fridays. I didn't have an idea of anything. I fought my sister and I took my bag, even though I had another mission to go to study in a technical school in Bolgatanga, which is very close to Burkina Faso.

In March 1998 I took the money that I had to pay for the school fees. I took my bag and left my home. I went to Bolgatanga and then to Burkina Faso. From Burkina Faso I went to Niger, and it was in Niger that I became stranded. And I called my friend, I was calling and calling but no one was answering.

But still, nothing could stop me, because I had it in my head that I would be able to make four hundred dollars an hour. I didn't mind what happened, because I knew that I had to get to this destination. When this gets into your brain, you can never change it. Even if someone is dying on the way, you see it, but you say, yeah, that is his destination. My destiny doesn't match with his destiny. The decision is how to get to where you want to be. I was crying when I was there. I was thinking about my friend who hadn't come to help me out. I only realized it was a lie he gave me when I got to Libya. Before, I thought maybe he was working, maybe he was busy.

From there I had to make my way by car and by foot. This included many dangerous situations. When I finally met with the friend who had gone before me, he said he'd never have believed I would have made it to Libya. I reminded him of the cassette he'd given me, the photos. I told him they'd influenced me and made me stop my studies. He denied that he had sent anything. From then, he was trying to be so good. He collected me and took me to Tripoli. From there, I started to work.

The Decision to Cross the Sea

What happened in Tripoli is that there were no documents, no passport, it was just a question of finding a way to survive by yourself. My friend was working in construction, so I was learning from him. He said that as he had come first, he should go to Europe first. While working in construction, I fell from two flights and I had problems with my knee. But as soon as I started walking again, we thought of travelling. I started to explain to him the route I had taken. We had taken different routes, but he had heard of some of the places I had seen.

And I told him that I had found an address from Ghana. You find along the way that people write their own stories on a stone. It's like, you open that pen and take a stick and write a story and put a telephone number. Someone had put a message to call that number and say that he was dead and he had been here and he was dead because of this issue. So he asked 'Please send a letter to my family or call this number and tell my family I am no more'. He had done that before he passed away. I think they must have buried him and put this stone on his grave. You find a lot of that along the way. When I saw that I was moved. I started to think of my family, how I was with my father. My father was sick. I was thinking about my brothers and sister. I was thinking how a lot of things happen. But I lost that number.

In Libya I could make money. So in Libya I was sending money and buying books, things for my sister to study. I had decided before I left I wanted to send her to a good school. I was making good money in Libya, but in Libya, you could imagine that the police could come to your house and ask for your documents. But you don't think that would happen in Europe. When you get here, you realize that you have a dream about something that doesn't exist in real life.

What we knew about Europe was that when you get here they give you everything free. From Libya we could even see what happened – and on the television – they take them, they give them clothes. We thought it was a very good treatment. That's not what you meet when you get here. But you will never know until you get here. Even if I was told about it, it'd be very difficult to believe what they would tell you. Because if a European man is telling me if you go to Europe you will sleep in the streets, I would believe he just doesn't want me to go to his country. But if an African person would tell me that they are telling me, as an African person, because they've been through it: *if you go there, you are going to suffer more than you are in your country*, then I would start to listen to that person. And make decisions.

In Tripoli, I was working, and I agreed to help my friend to go to Italy. We had money. He went and paid one thousand eight hundred dollars. There were seventy-five people and the money disappeared. An Algerian man took the money and we didn't see any boats or any money or any travelling. It was finished. So he tried six times, and all the money was lost each time. It was different amounts, but always a lot of money. So I said to my friend that he had tried six times and I should also try, so perhaps I could try and I could help him, but he wanted to get there first. So then we started to each save our own money. In Libya I also made a passport. Actually, I didn't know the year I was born because that information is not available where I am from. But I put some age. You have to send your passport to a friend in Europe and not take it in the boat.

Then one Friday (Friday was a holiday, so no one works on a Friday) he went out and he told me he'd seen a boat that was leaving. He said we should try and get on it. We paid one thousand or one thousand and five for the boat. I wrote to my sister and I said this date I take the boat. If you don't hear from me in three months then something happened.

For three days, we were on the boat, and then we had a breakdown and we were for three days on the sea. We were waiting for a ship to appear and try to help us. We weren't having luck. A ship coming from Napoli to Tunis found us. They asked where we were going. We said we were going to Italy. They said we were very close to Italy, but still in no-man's water. So they stood for four hours. They gave us food. They arranged the boat. But they had already communicated with the Italian navy. They told us there were two poles with light on them. If we got to the poles, we would be in their waters and they could take us. But if not, they couldn't.

We could see far away there were two navy boats waiting that we should get to before they would collect us. But the wind was blowing us backwards. Then the boat that had helped us said that they had to go. They had called Italy who said they couldn't come. They had called Malta. Malta said they could come, but we didn't want to go to Malta because they will just take us to our country. We wanted to get to Italy.

They said they had to go and they couldn't leave us, so they had to take us with them. But we preferred to be where we were. We were twenty people so they couldn't put us in their ship but they could pull us. So they brought a very long rope and they attached it to the front part of our boat and it was pulling us, but there was a lot of water coming against our boat and the top of the boat was up, but the back was going down bit by bit. We were inside.

Then we could see the water coming in and before we realized, the bottom part was already under the water. Everyone was trying to get to the hull.

The captain of the ship was told, and they were trying to arrange for those small boats to be taken down to the water. None of us knew how to swim. They were pulling the ropes as fast as they could and after ten minutes, they were able to take everyone into the big ship. They cut the rope and we watched our boat go.

When we entered the ship, the cook of the ship was a black guy from Tunis. He asked why we wanted to go to Italy. He said that if you go to Italy, you will sleep on the street. He said that Africa is very good but we thought it was a lie.

We got to Tunis and the police put us in the cells to make interviews with us. And so we pretended that we didn't speak any of their languages. No Arabic, no English, only African languages. And there was only one person. We said this is the only person who can speak Arabic. He was made the person to communicate with us and with them. But we could understand everything that was being said in Arabic, English or French.

When they asked where we were from we told them we were from Sierra Leone. They said that was impossible. We said that we'd just got in a boat and ended up here. They didn't believe it. They insulted us in Arabic, but we could understand. When we'd got on the boat in Libya, we'd been told by the captain to change our watches, if we had them, to West Coast time. So we all changed the time. They were looking for everything to say we weren't coming from Sierra Leone. They looked at the time, which was from West Africa. They looked at the clothes we were wearing, but the clothes can be bought anywhere. They asked if we had any money of our country. We said we didn't because it's not useful everywhere, so we had changed it to dollars before travelling. They were sure we were lying but they couldn't prove it.

They said that United Nations law says that if someone says they are a refugee and they're not, they have to be jailed for five years. That is the law of UN.[2] So people started to think that after spending five years in Libya, they didn't want to spend another five years here. They wanted to tell the truth. But others said that they should first give us someone from the United Nations and we would speak to that person. And they said no. Then finally, we said ok, we are from Sierra Leone, but we took the boat from Libya. So they took us four people by car into the desert. They stopped and they said just go straight. If you go either direction you will find police. So we just walked. We walked for several hours before we saw a village.

The Decision to Try Again to Cross the Sea

I kept on to Algeria. From Algeria I went to the border of Algeria with Morocco. We had the town. We call it Maghnia. And Maghnia it is where

---

2   There is no such provision from the United Nations.

you have the ghetto and that ghetto is full of stranded people that try to go to Europe through Morocco.³ They get caught and they have to remain there. So they have a lot of tents and there are people that control this place. People that are moving from like Ghana and Nigeria directly to this place, those controllers know they have money already, so they pay a ghetto fee. My fee was like a hundred dollars. You pay and then if you are ten people, ok it is a thousand dollars, they give it to someone that was already stranded. Then he guides you to Morocco then he uses the money to pay for his travel to Europe. It was well organized. In this way you pay and you have your accommodation and your food. And we went to Morocco and so I paid eight hundred dollars and they took us to El Aaiún⁴ and from El Aaiún we took the boat.

We got to Fuerteventura. That's the island in the Canarias. So those who brought us, their boat, it is drugs they are carrying. And we were like fifteen people, each and every one of us paid eight hundred dollars. And some pay a thousand, some pay a thousand and two. You pay what you have. But they would never tell you that. They would tell you it's a thousand and two but then you have to see the connection man personally and say my money is like this. When we got to Fuerteventura, there were two Moroccan guys that brought us to the island. One went to the town. He called the police and said that he'd found some people and he left and in just like two seconds, the police arrived and picked us up and took us to the deportation camp.

I found people I already knew from Libya there. I was asking them, how long are you here. You have to be there for forty days for them to interview you and know your route and take you back. But always we give names that they can never identify and always you give a country where there is a problem, so we said Sierra Leone, and everyone was from Sierra Leone. I was there for thirty-eight days. They took me to Las Palmas and they freed us to go. But they didn't tell us 'you are free'. They just take you out in one street and they say to you, 'straight on!'.

Then we were walking. There were fifteen of us. We walked to the street end then we came back to the police and we asked where do we have to go. And the same policeman that was speaking English to us before, now he doesn't speak English any more. We asked 'where do we have to go?' and he started speaking Spanish to us and we didn't understand anything. One said, 'yeah, we are free, we can just start moving'. So we started looking for black people to ask them questions. And we just saw one guy and we just called him and he said 'go to this place'. So we got to the plaça and I saw a lot of people and asked them 'where do we have to sleep today?' and they just said 'anywhere you find'. The first night, I passed in the street. The next day I bought a ticket with money I still had with me. Actually my friend had

---

3 These difficulties are detailed in Gnes 2013.
4 Also sometimes written Laayoum.

managed to bring it with him. I asked him 'how did you manage this?'. He told me it was in the World Bank. You know what that means where he put it. They sold me the ticket and I took the flight to Barcelona. I used the paper the police had given me. I didn't have the passport because I had already sent it to someone in Europe. I get to Barcelona. I don't know where to go. Luckily when I came out I found two Nigerian guys. I asked where do we have to go?' and he said I should take a bus to Plaça Catalunya.[5] I asked if it is expensive and they just said 'take this money'. I took the bus.

When we got to the end of the bus, everybody was out and I was still there. The driver asked me 'where are you going?'. I said that I am going to the final destination. He said 'this is it'. So I came out and I was walking around in Plaça Catalunya and I found thousands of black people in the square. They were sleeping there. So I got to the place and I found people that I knew from Libya as well. It is like you keep meeting all these people that you met somewhere on the journey or you met in one town. You will meet the person again. I just met one guy and I said 'where do you sleep?'. And he said 'here'. I asked how and he took me to Las Ramblas, to Carrefour market.[6] We took some packing cases we came and we just opened it and this is the bed. We found a stone and put it to make the pillow and we started sleeping there.

Activism

Obtaining Documents (April–May 2001)

So we were there and some organisations started coming to make interviews, asking how did you arrive, when did you come? One girl asked me, 'do you want to learn Spanish?' I said 'why not?'. She started giving us classes. Life was a struggle against the law. They just like documents. They ask for papers papers until we asked somebody 'what is a paper?'. You find a job and they just say you need a paper to work. We don't really understand what paper means. So we asked one of the people, 'what is a paper?', because we go to a restaurant to ask for job and they say paper. They laughed. Paper is the documents. He showed his ID card and he said 'this is the paper'. Then I started to organize people coming to the church to have the classes. One day we are just meeting, planning, deciding what to do. And they said that this place you are living, nobody knows your situation. The only thing to call attention to the situation is to demonstrate and one of the best ways to demonstrate is to make a hunger strike.

I convinced three people and we started the hunger strike. Then the person that gave us a place to stay for the classes just called the media that

---

5 Central square in downtown Barcelona with a major airport bus terminus.
6 Las Ramblas is a street leading off from Plaça Catalunya on which is a large Carrefour supermarket.

the African people are making a hunger strike here. Immediately it was all over the news[7] and everybody was arriving to us. It also became covered by the Pakistanis and everyone. Then they came out with the flags saying 'Papeles Para Todos'.[8] They said they were going to give documents to the African people but not all the immigrants here. And Papeles Para Todos said, papers for everyone.

The strike took one month. In two days, they said they would give us our documents so we should stop the strike. But we had a lawyer from Papeles Para Todos. They wrote a letter. The government said yes, we will get documents, we should stop the strike. But without any confirmation we shouldn't leave the strike. So they sent a letter back to Madrid and they signed. So then we stopped the strike and all the people got documents except for me. And we didn't know what was happening, so the lawyer tried to find out. And finally, they gave the documents to me. And I started to work.

Setting up CEHDA Ghana: Helping People Make Informed Decisions (2001–2007)

So I sat one day, just thinking, about when I was making a decision to travel to make money and go back. What I am seeing now, it's not true. And it is the same story for many of the people here. But most of the people would never want the family to know they are suffering and they would never make their friends to understand that they are suffering. So they keep on encouraging them. Of course, if your friend asks you for twenty euros, you send twenty euros. He sees money, so you have money. But you don't explain how you are getting through it.

We decided to form an organization to explain the reality. We decided on different kinds of names. Then we thought, let's use CEHDA, which is Cultural Environmental and Human Development Association. We use the culture to call the attention of the people, and when the people come we explain to them the journey. So we started with the African drums. Then when the people come, we give the message to them, and we see how it develops. We were thinking to do this back home in Ghana. There are a lot of people who are still travelling, but they don't really know the consequences of the journey.

I can say from my village there were five people that left and I was the only one that got here. One is still in Morocco, the guy that wrote me the letter. He left Ghana in 1996 and he is still in Morocco.[9] He cannot go

---

7 The protests in Barcelona were discussed in El País at the time (Cia 2001). This was in a period of a generalized movement of hunger strikes of migrants without papers in some parts of Spain (Laubenthal 2005: 159).
8 Literally 'Papers for Everyone', the Barcelona group has had a blog spot since 2009: https://www.blogger.com/profile/04504568303925060656.
9 As of July 2014.

back, he wants to get to Europe. Two were dead, taking a boat from Libya. There were seventy people and their boat sank. Nine survived and sixty-one didn't. These two guys were among them. My cousin also came and he was trying to cross the barbed wire from Morocco and Moroccan police shot him. They say they are rubber bullets, but we don't believe that. So the number we see what is happening on the way is more than those we meet here in Barcelona.

There are many difficult stories. One man told me he had seen someone buried alive for five hundred dollars in the camps in the area in Maghnia. In that area they have a square where they take you and they tie you and ask you to bring a number, they call your family and tell your family to put money into this account or else your life is finished. They asked him to pay five hundred dollars, but he said if I call my parents, they also have no money. So they just tied him and they made the hole and threw him inside and were covering him. You don't have any information from what is happening there.

Many things are happening that are not coming out until you get there to see it. So we sat down to think about how to prevent this. Prevention is to get this information to the people who don't have this information. Mostly they are the African people. We formed the organization and were deciding on a logo. We selected the footstep, because we thought that they see the same foot that made this way, they see the same foot that has to go back and explain what it's all about along the way. In 2007, we went with five Catalan people. I took them to my hometown.

Ghanaian Perceptions of Destination Europe: Evidence from the Village of Sawla

Initial Interviews (2007)

Those Catalan people started making interviews in the schools, asking everybody what they would like to do after their studies. Everybody said

Figure 10.1 Logo of the organization, CEHDA

they would like to go to Europe. When asked why, they said to earn more money. 'How do you know you can earn more money working there?' 'Of course there is money'. 'Do you know that when you get to Europe, you need papers to work?' They said 'what papers?' 'How do you want to go to Europe?' They say 'if I go to Morocco I go to Europe'.

So we started making a presentational video showing how the sea is and how the people struggle to get there. The people lived in the interior part of the country. When they saw the sea, I said 'this is the water you have to cross'. We also took about twenty people to the south, to Accra. We saw that this is the sea, and this is what you have to take a boat and cross to get to Europe. They had been thinking of the sea like a river you can just cross. The people started changing their mind. They asked 'what if the boat breaks?', and I said, 'yes, if the boat breaks, you will remain there'.

After showing the practical aspects of the project, we went back to the village and we met the Chief and the Elders. The Catalan people said 'we know your community and we would like to collaborate. What would you like us to do here?' The Chief said he would like them to work with the children because they are the people you can educate. Those who have already grown up, it is very difficult to change their perceptions. So then we started a project with the Chief.

Figure 10.2 Classes in Sawla with CEHDA's first teacher (photo: CEHDA)

The Young People that Think about Moving

The first project was with children that have lost their parents. Those orphans are the responsibility of the Chief. And every market day there is a collection of food and this food goes to these children. We've had this thing since the world has existed. I could see this was useful, and I was playing my part with them, but I could see that this was not the real thing that we had to do.[10]

I decided to do something else as well. We took some of the children. Fifteen out of them. What we are doing is we have a centre for young people who are relying on their extended family with extra classes.[11] We register them at the normal schools. They go to public schools but when they close, we have a teacher that gives them an extra class again. Because what happens as we have an extended family, it's like every person has five or six children, so when the parents died, the uncle and the others have to take care of the child. So if the uncle already has five children, he will have to take care of another five children, and the level of living reduces.

So what the people do is put the children that don't belong to them directly to work on the farm and his children go to school but the child will never be in the street or be empty. You have a place to sleep. You have at least something to eat, but you do not have the right to go to school because it's expensive and the person cannot leave his own child and let you go to school.

So because of that, we take the responsibility of that child. You don't take any costs of this child, but you leave the child free to go to school. We pay the school fees. But he doesn't loose the child. I am doing that because I know that most of them are those that are always travelling because they feel like they are treated like the second child. So the person will move from the village, go to the city, struggle there, and after try to find his way. I learnt this also from my experiences.

Considering Options

There were young people who used to sit under the tree from six to six. I was with them for three days sitting and talking. And all the conversation is about what you can do if you go to Japan or US or other places. They dream of something they never see. I sat there for three days but I didn't see what came of it. They told me 'there are no jobs for us to do'. I said that there are jobs, because the land is there. You can start doing farming. They laughed at me and asked me if, when I was here, I ever wanted to do farming. I said

---

10 The Children's Project: http://www.cehdaghana.org/projectes-africa/cehda-childrens-project/ (accessed 4 July 2014).
11 Els Joves de Sawla: http://www.cehdaghana.org/projectes-africa/els-joves-de-sawla/ (accessed 4 July 2014).

Figure 10.3 Adults of Sawla involved in cultural and literacy activities organized by CEHDA (photo: CEHDA)

that when I was here, I didn't realize farming was a good thing, but after travelling, I realized that it is a good thing. They said that they needed machines and tractors. I said 'do what your strength can give you then you take what you can. It's like a challenge.'

I wanted to form a youth organization in the town. Everybody was thinking that by being part of the youth organization they could go to Europe. Everybody was writing names and one day I had forty-two people. And I said 'that is enough, and anyway today it is forty-two, but I'm sure some of you will run away'. I was there with one volunteer from Barcelona. She was taking everything down. We had meetings and I asked everybody to write something about themselves, their experience, their level of education, so that we could see how many of them had a common experience, to see how I could put them together for a project. But each of them were saying 'I need money for business, to sell'.

They would go to the capital, buy things, bring them back to sell. I could see that nobody was talking about the farm. I asked them what they would buy, how much it would cost, how much it would cost to get there, how much you would have to pay to bring the goods out, and what company to buy from. I couldn't find anyone who was able to define exactly what they wanted to do. Most of them were after secondary school, but they couldn't continue because from secondary school, you need money to continue. And most of them didn't have enough education.

The CEHDA Farm in Sawla

I decided we would start up a farm and see what happens.[12] My organization would finance the land. We would rent a tractor to clean it, we would buy the seeds to grow, you would have to take care of it, and we would see what happens. We spoke to the Chief, who gave us six acres for the project and we started. Out of the forty-two, they went one by one and then there remained only one person who was taking care of it.

Then they called a meeting again and they said that they thought that we were going to help them because all the White people that come try to help the people. I said that they don't help you. We are having a daycare centre, a day nursery. All of us attended that nursery. When the missionaries left you can look at what is happening to it, it's no more existing. If we look at the agri sector, there were German people that came and were training our animals and how to farm with them. When they left it is no more existing. Why isn't it existing? It's because of mismanagement, because you don't know the origin of it. They brought it and they put it and when they leave, it cannot continue. So why my organization is poor, because we want you to understand how to make an organization. Don't think that an organization will come and pay you money to do business. It's impossible.

But what we can do is give an orientation for you to realize that what you have around you is very important and how to make use of it. So if you expect someone to come from Spain to find money for you to do business, it will never work. CEHDA won't give money. CEHDA can give an idea based on what I saw, as a citizen from here, and knowledge of Europe. I can tell you what you have to do. This is what we can transmit to you. So they started changing.

One asked why I don't talk about Europe. I said that if I tell you my personal experience you will cry. I asked 'where are the people from this village? Dead. Just to get to Europe'. I said 'do you want to die on the way? If you want to go, you are welcome, but if you are in the desert and you contact me and say you need money, I will not give it to you because I will not have money to send you?' They believed I was telling the truth. I said that you are welcome to go, but be sure that you will suffer more than what you think you are suffering here. Here you are not suffering. If you go there then you will suffer.

I grew up with them, I travelled, and I came back. If I was another person, they would never have listened to me. We have someone there now taking care of the farm. When they see volunteers coming from Europe, going to the farm to work, they get surprised and go to help them. The volunteers say that if they had land like this in Europe, you are the richest person. If you buy trousers today, tomorrow you won't buy it. If you put that kind of business here in this town, it will never work. But if you sell food,

---

12 Camp de conreu ecològic: http://www.cehdaghana.org/projectes-africa/ecologycal-farm/ (accessed 4 July 2014).

if you buy food today, tomorrow you will also buy food. If you work on the farm you will make money.

They started to get our point. They said that we would need fertilizer to get the product. I said let's start an ecological farm and see what we can get, because then we don't lose anything. You don't buy chemicals, then you don't spend much. You will put your effort to work on the farm. We did the first one in 2008 and the product didn't come up in the way we expected. So they said that we need fertilisers. But we started farming without putting in fertilisers because of the experience with fertilisers and cotton in my region. We are making it step by step.

If a person is really convinced, he would never take the risk of that journey. But the person really needs to understand what is going on. If you just say don't go to Europe because it is difficult, that person will never understand it, because most of the organisations that came to help the people are from Europe or America. They give support to the people but they don't educate the people to live by themselves, and when they leave, the project fails.

Every day is like that. People are thinking to migrate and this is very difficult to work out. The information we have on the African TV show it's football and parties everything here. It should be showing what the people are going through here. Then they would see the real thing. The people are not travelling because they are dying of hunger or because of poverty.

Figure 10.4 Iddrisu Wari with Catalan volunteers and dedicated farm manager at CEHDA farm in Sawla (Photo: CEHDA)

Figures 10.5–10.8 Community engagement in CEHDA farm project in Sawla (photos: CEHDA)

But it's like a disease that is injected in their minds that they don't know how to solve it.

The Perceptions of Those Left Behind[13] (June 2013)

Last year, I invited my mum to come and visit[14] and I took my mum to the squat houses. We went to them before they closed this space. We shared food there and she was like an old woman. She stood and said, 'why are they here?' I said 'they are here because they are jobless and they have no homes'. Then

13 CEHDA also installed latrines with running water in the village (http://www.cehdaghana. org/projectes-africa/letrina-compostera/ accessed 4 July 2014) and built a multi-purpose space for activities of the organisation in the village (http://www.cehdaghana.org/ projectes-africa/nou-espai-polivalent/ accessed 4 July 2014).
14 It was necessary to hire a Barcelona lawyer to fight for the visa, which took more than a year to secure.

she was realizing that maybe their parents will be saying that they have their son in Europe, but they don't know what their son is experiencing.

She came and she spent about three months. I guess I wanted my mum to experience it really. Since I was born, I'd never had time to sit with my mother for one hour. It's like I was always running and moving somewhere. Then I went to Europe. Then whenever I go back, there's no time. So I decided that I had to bring my mum here so that we could sit here and we can talk. So being with my mum I could realize that she felt something in her because then I could say she was crying. She said sorry that sometimes when I asked for money, I was blaming you when you didn't send money. She said that now she could see the reality, if you can't send money it's because you didn't have money to give.

Then when she went back, she never asked me for money again. I didn't want to tell her that I couldn't send it to her because I don't want to shout at my mum. But now she feels it and she realized how difficult it is. So she asked me if I had passed through all the difficult conditions that she could

Figure 10.9 Iddrisu Wari described this as his former 'Teraza' (photo: Copyright 2013 by the United Nations University. Reproduced with the permission of the United Nations University. Author: Samuel Aranda)

Note: This image was hanging on the wall in the coffee area at the office of UNU-GCM in Barcelona, where some of the work on this chapter took place. When he saw it, Wari did a double take. He referred to this very area as having been his `teraza' during a period when he was living rough in Barcelona.

see people suffering, and I said yes, I had passed through all the conditions before I got here. She said 'but home is better'. I agreed with her that home is better. But I feel that now I am here. I will go when it is time for me to go. I want the project to be developed there before I go. Then she saw that this is why I work with orphans because maybe not everybody has an opportunity to arrive here, so if I arrive and I don't spread the message, it is like I am doing nothing.

Ghanaian Perceptions of Destination Europe: Evidence from the City of Barcelona

Looking Back

Sometimes you ask yourself, 'why do I travel, why?' It's a question that would never come to you before you start your journey, but once you are here you face a lot of challenges. So you just say 'really why am I here?' I have examples of three people that wanted to go back. When I was working in an organization[15] we had a project called 'Voluntary Return'.[16] And I helped three people that went back, one from Nigeria and two from Ghana.

The one from Nigeria didn't pass through this experience. He came to our office and said he had never experienced this life. He had never slept in the streets, but here he has to. He said he didn't come by boat, but he came for a meeting because his company sent him there for seminars and meetings so I decided to run from Greece to here and live in Europe because life would be better. But he had made a big mistake. He said that if he could go back he would. It took about six months to help him to go back. We started the process. We went to Red Cross, asking for support. He said that his father is a big politician. There was a street constructed in the region of his father. And his father's name is put on the name of the street. It is one of the famous streets there. And here, he has to go to social housing, sleep on the street, and make a queue to go for food. When we gave the ticket to this guy, he was very happy. And once he arrived in Nigeria, he called back, very happy. He had thought he could work better in Europe than what he had there, but he couldn't.

The other two guys from Ghana said that they had to go back. One guy said that in two years in Europe, he hadn't seen twenty euros with his own eyes. He had never been able to work, had never been paid twenty euros. He said that he was a dressmaker, with a machine, and land that he could work with his family. He said that if he isn't there, it doesn't work. He'd thought that if he came to Europe, he could earn money and pay for

---

15 An organisation originally set up to help emigrants, then helping immigrants (now closed in Catalonia). Iddrisu Wari worked in their Day Centre for three years.

16 Voluntary return projects have been the subject of criticism when the return is not really voluntary. This is also critiqued by Iddrisu Wari later in the chapter.

people to do this farm work for him, and produce a lot of cocoa. But his wife cannot take care of it. He had come to Europe by boat. He wanted to go back but he couldn't see how. So I said we could find a solution. We applied for passports and for everything. When he had the ticket, he went back. When he was coming on the way here, there was nothing that could stop him. When he suffered, he thought that he would win more than that, but when he got here, he could see that what he left was better than what it is for him here.

The ones who realize and then cannot go back are the ones for whom the families hold property for him to travel. If he doesn't cover this property he cannot go back from shame because the family would blame him that they had spent the property for him. It would be insulting. But once you are here the people have a mental problem because of all the problems and too much thinking.

Perceptions of Ghanaians and Ghanaian Perceptions of Barcelona

I used to give lectures. Sometimes the police invited me. They didn't know how to work with the African people and I could give an explanation to them. They wanted to know the function of the police in my country. They asked me a question, in Vic,[17] they have a lot of African people who are driving without licenses. But I asked the police, is it a problem if the person knows how to drive and he drives well? I said the license is just a paper. But the license doesn't drive. The person drives. So if the person knows how to drive, what is the problem? They said, yes but here you need documents in order to drive. I said yes, here you always need documents. And they said that in your country, could somebody drive without a license. I said of course. The police wouldn't take you and stop you and ask you for a license because that doesn't make sense. And they looked at me as if I was attacking the police, like what they are doing is not the right thing. They said that here you need documents because it is the law that you need it.

They asked me if in my country it is allowed for people to sell anything anywhere. I said that this is how the people survive. If you are the policeman and someone is selling drugs or someone is selling bags on the street,[18] which one do you prefer? Of course, the one selling the bags on the street. Does the immigrant get a salary for not working? They don't have food. Imagine you go to somebody's country and they say you need papers and with papers you need three years to put that in the country. What do you do with these three years? Can you sit down for three years without eating? If you don't give them the right to work and you don't give them any salary

---

17 Vic is a small town just under seventy kilometres from Barcelona.
18 Another key income-source for Sub-Saharan migrants in Barcelona is the selling of copies of brand-name bags and sunglasses on the street.

for being unemployed in this country, then tell me what the person has to do. Then he goes to sell the bags and you chase the person not to sell the bags. He goes to sell drugs, he's told not to sell drugs. Anything he does, it is a crime. Then how do you want that person to survive? The people need to survive. You have to know that. If the only thing he can do is take some bags to sell in the street, what's the crime in that? It's the human rights. The law is the crime, not the person. If there's a law that says you can't earn anything or eat anything, you have to wait three years, then of course, this is not a law.

We miss a lot of things when we get here. You are here alone and you cannot be with people. You walk in the street, everybody looks at you like a criminal person, but there are people here who have their studies. They came here for studies, and when they remain here, when they walk in the street, you look at them like they're a thief. So you think: I know what I am. I know I am not a thief. I'm not a bad person. I can say I am traditionally educated as we have the traditional education and we have the occidental education that they brought to us so like the police say that most of the African people are not educated. But if you say that you make a big mistake, because we know that we have two types of education, we have the traditional education and we have this occidental that they brought in the school.

Those you see on the streets selling these things, they don't want to do it. If they had jobs they would do that. There is no alternative. But if that person comes to your police office, and says 'take me to my country because I am tired' you would say, that person doesn't cause a crime and you will never do it. I have a case of someone who came and said to me that he wants me to take him home, but the voluntary return programme was finished, so he went to Plaça d'Espanya and to the police and said this is my passport, I want you to take me back to Ghana. The police said that you didn't cause any crime. If you want to go, bring your ticket and we will facilitate it for you to go. But what he wanted was for them to buy him a ticket.

But also, you could get someone who didn't cause a crime and you could decide to take that person away from this country and another person comes and says I want you to take me back to my country, this is my passport, and you tell him that he didn't cause a crime.[19] You should bring your ticket and your passport. You ask why you don't go back if you are coming. But of course, how could people know they are going to face these problems here? You don't know. Unless you get here. And when you get here, the government says you have no documents until a number of years, then, the police will be following and monitoring your life. What do you want me to do? To die? This is not right.

---

19 This refers to the involuntary return of irregular migrants.

Survival Options for Ghanaians in Barcelona

Metal Collecting ('chatarra')

The chatarra[20] came because we are finding things from the street when they throw out televisions, radio cassettes, they find it, they take it, and there is a teef market. Then you go there, and you try to sell it. There are people, with anything that you have in your hand, there is somebody that needs it. It wasn't like chatarra. People sent containers with used materials to Africa to sell. It wasn't only metal. I find a television set in the street. I need to have thousands of them if I have a container. But somebody is already doing it, so you sell to that person, that person takes everything. He has documents he goes, he sells them, and he comes back. So it was a kind of self-employment. There are centres where you go or maybe they go to a place and you go there and they buy from you.

Then from there, the chatarra came. It's like, that kind of teef market, people come to buy metals and when they come, you don't know what its use is for the person. Finally what happened is some African people found that there are companies that do the recycling, but these companies don't move around to take the things from the street. So they formed squat houses and they try to put the materials there. That has become a real business for them.

Chatarra is the only job now I can say that put the people away from drugs and away from selling these bags on the street and the police chasing them. If the people focus on chatarra, this is where they live, this is where they do their life, they only go look for the things, they come back to the centre, they are no more being seen in the street. So what happened? They tried to close it. Everything you do you have to pay tax, and they can't tax somebody who has no documents who is making chatarra, so the only thing you do is stop the person making the business. This is why the police are very concerned about these squat houses.

The CEHDA Farm (2010, 2013)

Most of the people arriving here already have knowledge about farming. So instead of them doing a course, an electrician course, or in construction, which they can never work because there are no jobs, why don't you focus on farming because they have the experience. We found an organization[21] that would support us to give three months theory of ecological farming processes in 2010, and now, with the experience they had, we found an abandoned land, and they are working there. The person that gave the land bought these

---

20 As detailed in Chapter 9 of this book, 'chatarra' is the word used in Spanish for scrap metal.
21 Fundació Roca i Pi (http://www.rocaipi.cat, accessed 4 July 2014).

kind of wood houses. So they live there, they work, and this product is going to come and we'll have money. This is in Maçanet de la Selva, so I go there three times a week to visit them.[22] This centre is not in the town, but the people are very happy because they have something growing there. The police will never go there and say why are you working in the farm.

So first of all, what you want to do is to know what the person needs. They give you money to rent. But money to rent is not a solution for the person. The person needs another thing. So if you don't really understand what the person needs, you cannot have a solution for that person. You can have a temporary solution, but if the person cannot work, that person will come back to the same situation. It will never finish. We looked to see if someone had abandoned land to give us, and we started the project there. You live by yourself and you work there. You are contributing. You are going to sell the food. You have some income for yourself and you take it to yourself. We found that most African people have farm experience, but in the city they can't use it, so we looked to see how they can do it. So now we have the land, and we have the seed. It's better to live like that than to be chased by the police in the street. At first it was very difficult for them to go and live there but now when you ask them to come back to the town, they say 'no, we are ok here'.

The Adjuntament[23] of Barcelona gave an award to organisations for work with immigrants and they gave a special mention to CEHDA for this farming project. So there is a video about the project on the website.[24]

22 De peus a terra (http://www.cehdaghana.org/projectes-a-catalunya/de-peus-a-terra/ accessed 4 July 2014).
23 City Hall.
24 This refers to the 2013 5è premi Consell Municipal D'Immigració de Barcelona, which awarded CEHDA a Special Mention. More information about the award can be found: http://www.bcn.cat/novaciutadania/arees/es/consell_municipal/Premi_Municipal_Immigracio_de_Barcelona.html (accessed 4 July 2014). The video about the CEHDA Project is available from the CEHDA website: http://www.cehdaghana.org/als-mitjans (accessed 4 July 2014).

Figures 10.10–10.12 CEHDA farm project in Catalonia, from building latrines, to ploughing the land, to celebrating successful crops (photo: CEHDA)

Farming in Catalonia vs. Farming in Ghana

It's like a full circle. Being a farmer in Ghana you have no respect. You have the land, but you want to spend the time in the town. But what the people need here is jobs, it doesn't matter what kind of jobs. But that same job, he has it in his country, but he doesn't respect it. He doesn't want it. This is why we try to make the person there realize that what he has is very important. And to forget going to Europe to work. He can go to Europe, but it's only the lucky one that can survive here.

I know what the person has, because I had it in my country and I didn't respect it. Then you arrive here and what you didn't want to do, you do here for somebody to pay you. Ok, so imagine you have the land and you work by yourself and you sell the food by yourself. Which one do you want? Of course, I'd want to work by myself. So we have the land. The people have to live there and work and in three years, you have to make benefit there and you let another person enter. We are already making contacts to sell the product. It is an ecological product. They make the product, they check the balance, they make the prices that they want. We found people. I also sell it to people I know. We can see how they organize themselves now to work like a team.

One of them was working chatarra and now he is working with us. I asked him 'how much can you gain a day with the chatarra?' He explained that you can have nothing because you didn't find any good metal to sell. And sometimes you can maybe have fifty euros. Fifty euros in a day can often happen, but between the chatarra and the farm, I asked him which is better. He said that at first it was hard for him. But now, he says that he feels more relaxed. Because he could walk like half of Barcelona and not get anything and have to walk back home because you cannot take metro looking for chatarra or bus. You have to walk. Then you spend most of the day walking walking walking walking and maybe you don't get anything. Or maybe you get something. Or maybe you get some of the material and then how you get the material to where you have to take it is another problem. This is what you have to think, to create something by yourself, not just let me go find some chatarra. You can't make your life with it. Because the chatarra, you need to eat, you need to make calls, how much can you save and give to your parents when they're asking? This is what you have to think.

Conclusions and Recommendations

By encouraging people not to migrate are you encouraging an unjust law?

If the law of migration changes, what we are seeing, we would never see. Why cannot I take my passport, take a visa, and travel, why? And anyway, the policy doesn't stop the people. So you should change the people moving in the dangerous ways. It is the policy that makes it so they have to do that. People need to know what it is, the decision that they are making. I think that the policy is wrong, but I can't do anything about that, and I believe those who put in the policy know it's wrong. They know, but they have interests in it. The better way is to do the right thing for those who want to travel. But the migration system can never stop.

We never understand why they don't allow people to travel. It is an unfair way of acting. Why you can move, and why I cannot move? We say that these persons have no human feelings towards people, that's why this is happening. You think if an African person goes to the embassy and takes the visa, he will travel passing through that way [by land and sea]? No. That way is also more expensive than travelling by the flight because you have to take two, three, four, five boats, and every one you pay a thousand, plus.

So it's time we said ok, we know their country is bad, it's why they don't want us to travel by visa. But if you come and you see it is bad, you'll go back, because you can travel freely. You can just say, well, Europe is very bad. But because they make you want to understand that Europe is very good, so it is very difficult to get to Europe. They put the conditions that a rich person has to come, not any other person. But I'm sure if they want to they can change it. They can just tell the embassy that if someone wants to travel, allow him. Then he'll see the conditions. If he doesn't like it, he'll go back. If you cannot come in, you come in an illegal way, but then there's no way to go back the same way you came. You come and that is all. Of course, it would be nice if it changes, then there would be no problems any more.

What would you say to the policy-makers?

The question is what did the policy-maker think for making this policy. I would ask them what do you want for putting this law? What do you get out of it? If there is something that can be negotiated, we can put it out. I think it's good for Africa leaders to see what is happening and then they can sit with the leaders here, or the embassies here and they can ask why do you make things difficult for the African people? Why can't people go to England? Why? If you know what the policy-maker wants from this, we can see if it can be negotiated. Then the person has the right to go, to see with their eyes what is happening. Then if he cannot survive, he will come back. It would be finished.

Of course, if they want to put a wall to the sky, they can put a wall and nobody can cross it. If they really want to make it that nobody comes, they can do it, but it's like, ok, they make it like open, they don't close it. It's open. They see you can do it. Then they put another person to watch you and then they put the newsperson to take the image. To tell people what is happening there. We don't know really what the policy wants. And actually, of course, in Germany, when there was a wall there was a wall. So if they want to put a wall they can put a wall.

How would you advise others (who do not work for governments) who want to help the situation for Sub-Saharans thinking about crossing the Mediterranean?

I can tell you that my organization, we work with people that arrive here. But what happens is I've been in a similar situation like them, going to Red Cross, they give me sometimes food, give a place for three months, then after, I come back to the same situation because they cannot take care of you for life. And I have worked as a social worker and people that came to our centre when I was working for one NGO, you meet people, and after three or four years, you meet the people in the same situation in the street again.

So when I formed this organization, I was like, let's work for the situation of people, but not the policy makers asking you to work with the person.

What the others are doing is they try to move out the person from that situation, but they don't create another way for you. Make a person to understand and maybe you can find the possibilities together. They have their ability of thinking and understanding things. But don't say don't do this. It's the same, if you say don't come like this, they'll find another way. And of course, the visa is easy to be given out. If the visa was very easy, nobody would take that route [via land and sea].

It's like, of course, I can see my country's things here. Bananas from my country, cocoa and pineapples from my country, things from my country. I am not allowed to be here, but the things from my country are allowed to be here.

References

Cia, Blanca (2001) 'Decenas de miles de personas exigen en Barcelona "papeles para todos" los inmigrantes', in *El País* newspaper Monday 5 February 2001, http://elpais.com/diario/2001/02/05/espana/981327604_850215.html [04/06/2014].

Cross, Hannah (2013) Migrants, Borders and Global Capitalism: West African Labour Mobility and EU Borders.

Gnes, Davide (2013) *Maghnia: Crossing the Uncrossable Border*, Mission report on the vulnerability of Sub-Saharan migrants and refugees at the Algerian-Moroccan border, Euro-Mediterranean Human Rights Network, Copenhagen.

Laubenthal, Barbara (2005) 'La Emergencia de las Protestas de Inmigrantes sin Papeles en España: El Caso de la Región de Murcia', in Manuel Hernández Pedreño and Andrés Pedreño Cánovas (eds) (2005) *La condición inmigrante: exploraciones e investigaciones desde la Región de Murcia*, Universidad de Murcia, 159–73.

Conclusions and Recommendations

Belachew Gebrewold and Tendayi Bloom

> *'People need to know what it is, the decision that they are making. I think that the policy is wrong, but I can't do anything about that, and I believe those who put in the policy know it's wrong. They know, but they have interests in it. The better way is to do the right thing for those who want to travel. But the migration system can never stop.'*
> (Chapter 10, this volume)

This book is based upon three minimal observations/commitments. First, it assumes that avoidable substantial loss of human well-being and life should be avoided and is not an acceptable outcome of migration policy. As such, the current context of significant loss of the well-being and lives of many of those travelling to and through the Mediterranean Region indicates that there is something amiss in the existing policy framework in that area.

Second, generally and broadly understood, migration is part of the human experience. While most people do not migrate, travelling is common among people and much more likely when conditions (economic, security, etc.) are considered to be more comfortable in one place than another. The EU free movement policies and the increasing prevalence of visa waiver and easy visa schemes demonstrate an acknowledgement that people want to migrate and that migration is also useful for their home and host states. Moreover, it is to be expected that persons in a situation of extreme threat to their personal security will seek to leave that situation by moving physically.

The third basic observation is that migrants need to be seen as individuals, each with his or her own reasons for travel, perhaps as part of a household strategy, perhaps to fulfil personal aims, perhaps to escape untenable conditions. People travel as agents, making decisions even when the range of options available is extremely constrained. Even the decision between fleeing and being killed is a decision, and the people moving are, therefore, decision-makers and actors in a global system that, largely, tries to constrain their movement without examining the decisions they are taking.

The context of decision-making presented in this book is complicated. People are moving for different reasons and in different ways. The experiences of migration presented are various and the factors impacting on how decisions are made to migrate, to migrate onwards, to stay or to return, may depend on an individual's personal situation before, during and after migration. Some migrants are significantly and directly affected in the way they make decisions by what they know about changing conditions in the Northern and Southern Mediterranean. However, others are affected only indirectly. For most, changing conditions in the Mediterranean only affect the decision of how to migrate or where to migrate, but not whether to embark on the journey at all, though Mediterranean conditions may impact upon the home country context, indirectly affecting decision-making.. Still others are largely unaffected by the recent events in the Mediterranean region, with conditions in their home countries, transit countries, and professional aspirations driving decisions about migration. All of these aspects of Sub-Saharan migration decision-making to and through the Mediterranean are important for understanding this complex and changing migration context and highlight the risks of a policy approach based on single theories or overview formulas.

An interdisciplinary volume with a diverse range of perspectives is vital, but it can make it difficult to follow the themes and threads. Based upon these three observations, this concluding section brings together the ideas that run throughout the book, to present four key talking points for policy. These help to show how the conclusions reached here can contribute to a better policy framework relating to the migration processes under discussion. Primarily, though, it advocates more work and more thinking in this area, based around the themes presented. The focus in this book is largely on persons moving *in extremis*, with the exception of Silja Weyel's analysis in Chapter 7 of Morocco's call centre sector. This focus can obscure the fact that much migration from Sub-Saharan Africa to and through the Mediterranean is highly skilled and there is a long history of Sub-Saharan workers moving to fulfil skills shortages and contribute expertise. This history is an important part of the picture and should not be lost in the urgency of the currently emerging situation for those unable to participate in such schemes.

Talking Point 1: Migrants as Individuals and Migration as a Process

Discourse relating to the migration of persons to and through the Mediterranean Region sometimes characterises migrants merely as part of a phenomenon, a theory or a system. This makes it easy to miss the human facts of their migration stories. Each person that makes a journey is an individual with his or her own set of drivers, desires and beliefs. This is not to say that persons must then be acting individualistically. As Belachew Gebrewold's examination of migration decisions in the Horn of Africa in Chapter 1 shows, it is often the case that decisions are made on a household basis, not by an individual acting alone. Indeed, the relationship of an individual within a family or community structure may affect whether and how to migrate. This is shown also in Chapter 4, in Delf Rothe and

Mariam Salehi's research among Sub-Saharan migrants who have moved from Libya to Germany. Family and social structures can themselves affect who migrates and their experience of that migration, as is discussed in Julie Snorek's discussion, in Chapter 3, of migration decisions of pastoralists and former pastoralists in Niger. In Chapter 8, Sarah Langley draws particular attention to the constraints of gender roles in countries of emigration, immigration and through-migration within this, for example. There is, then, a complex interplay of subjective and structural factors (to use the phrasing of Rothe and Salehi in Chapter 4) which will affect whether a person decides to migrate and how he or she decides to migrate. Individual migrants are also part of a larger migrant phenomenon affecting decision-making, so that individual migration projects and processes feed into and draw upon the resources in a larger movement of persons.

It is a mistake, however, to see migration decision-making as a one-off act. The contributors to this volume present the migration from Sub-Saharan Africa to and through the Mediterranean Region as a process, in which decisions are made and re-made en route, evolving based upon a range of factors that is as complex as that involved in the initial decision to leave home. An individual may not set out with the desire to end up in Germany, for example, as Rothe and Salehi show in Chapter 4. For some, the decision is initially only one to move from the countryside to the city, or into an adjoining country, as discussed by Snorek in Chapter 3. For others, larger overall plans may be made from the beginning, though they may change en route, as shown particularly clearly by Iddrisu Wari in Chapter 10. As such, as Marieke Wissink and Orçun Ulusoy show in the case of the Eastern Mediterranean in Chapter 6, migration should not be seen as a mere act of moving from one country to another. Instead, it is a process, and individuals who have undertaken a migration process made up of many decisive acts may alter one step or another, without abandoning the migration project itself.

The authors in this volume have observed a proliferation of policies of deterrence in the Mediterranean Region, directed at stopping persons travelling from Sub-Saharan Africa and as we write, increasingly also towards others moving from the Middle East. If reducing migration is an aim and migration is seen as a process in this way, this book suggests that blocking moments of migration may be inappropriate in achieving this aim. This is because such policies will only block certain options, pushing those already committed to the migration process to seek alternative, perhaps more risky, strategies. In Chapter 10, Wari observes that deterrence policies can even be counter-productive, making those moving for economic betterment wonder why there would be such policies if life were not wonderful on the other side of them. Moreover, as Pedro Marcelino, Maria Ferreira and Natalia Lippmann Mazzaglia note in Chapter 2, those moving to flee violence and persecution, for example, will still need to flee, irrespective of deterrence structures put in place.

Some authors also note that seeing migrants as individual agents problematises policies that remove agency from those individual decision-makers. In Chapter 2, Marcelino, Ferreira and Lippmann Mazzaglia describe how policy towards Sub-Saharan African migrants in the Mediterranean Region has largely involved the creation of regulations and rules about which the primarily affected individuals have no say, making them 'receivers of normative dispositions'. This is problematic within a liberal discourse of individualism and individual autonomy and, given the power dynamic weighted in European favour in the region, this can have implications for the legitimacy of 'European Values' of human dignity, individual freedom, and for the notion of consent within the liberal democratic system. In their research among the scrap metal collecting community in Barcelona, Sophie Barclay and Ann Laudati show in Chapter Nine how local Spanish citizens have found it useful to trade with the new businesses that had arisen as a result of Sub-Saharan migration into Barcelona. Barclay and Laudati also present the development of localised solidarity movements with migrants, against police evictions and other official actions. That is, the analyses in this book show up the inequality of power between State (including liberal democratic States) and individual (noncitizens, but also citizens) across this region.

To conclude: Seeing migrants as individuals (though making decisions as part of household strategies and complex systems of need and desire) and seeing their migration itself as an evolving process means that policies that seek to stop or reduce migration through single-act interruptions will be inappropriate. If the migration process is interrupted, it is likely that migrants will seek alternative routes. As those routes are interrupted, they will be forced to take increasingly difficult and dangerous decisions. This therefore potentially increases individual vulnerability and decreases agency without reducing movement.

Talking Point 2: It is Necessary to Examine the Structures that Shape the Mediterranean Migration Landscape

States do not construct the policy in the Mediterranean alone. While European states have tried to assert control over migration policies in the Mediterranean (discussed particularly usefully by Marcelino, Ferreira and Lippmann Mazzaglia in Chapter 2), this fails to take into account the interests and constructive powers of others. Of primary interest in this book, and presented above, are the individual migrants themselves. Talking Point 1 also touched upon the role of citizens and non-migrants. However, there are other powerful entities that alter the way in which this can be enacted. In this book, three particular types of entity were highlighted. The first and second are the media and inter-state groupings like the European Union, which were mentioned throughout the book and appear across our talking points. The third is the private sector, and given the emphasis given to trafficking in the debate, it is worth dealing specifically here with trafficking. Lack of space meant that there was not scope to discuss in detail international organisations, NGOs and labour movements, though these are important to consider. Migrant networks are also important, and while those who have arrived in North African or European refugee centres look forward to life outside the centres, many others are and will be dreaming of what the former have achieved. And, as Wari presents in Chapter 10, the 'successful' persons who have reached a desired point on their migration journey may not tell the would-be movers about their sufferings on their way and upon their arrival. If they do tell of their situation, the listeners may not believe that it is so dramatic, or that life in Europe could be worse than theirs at home.

The construction of migration as a threat comes from a number of quarters, including states, their media outlets and also the private sector actors that will be discussed below. There are fears of importation of disease, terrorism and criminality. However, this makes it difficult to address the real difficulties that may be experienced as a result of migration. It also hides the solidarity that many in Northern states may have with migrants, even in unlikely quarters, as common opponents to the threats which may have driven people to move. This is particularly the case for those moving to escape terrorism and violence (e.g. see Gebrewold in Chapter 1 and Marcelino, Ferreira and Lippmann Mazzaglia in Chapter 2), but also for those seeking economic betterment and an escape from under-development, and for those seeking access to political systems which, they may feel, better represent their own world-view. Constructing migration and migrants as threatening, even as an existential threat, impedes engagement with genuine concerns about economic incorporation of individuals, ensuring that they do not interrupt existing welfare service provisions, and so forth. Indeed, these worries are issues of internal public policy, rather than of migration at the regional level – especially given the absence of collaborative regional programmes of migration assistance and incorporation.

Traffickers and smugglers are often presented as the demons in the Mediterranean migration debate (this is discussed particularly by Bloom in Chapter 5). They are blamed for the risks taken with individuals' lives, for example, for putting people into unseaworthy vessels, charging high fees and adopting troubling measures to recoup these funds (see Wari's description in Chapter 10). However, two main distinctions need to be made. First, trafficking and smuggling are not the same thing. Human smuggling is when a person is helped to cross a border that he or she would not have been able to cross using regular channels. In situations where individuals need urgently to move and there is no regular route, human smuggling can be seen as a heroic enterprise. That people pay for the services of smugglers shows that it is a viable business enterprise. The condemnation for smugglers' use of unseaworthy boats needs to be examined. The criticisms that smugglers use unseaworthy boats or that they extract sums that are too high from their customers seem to be arguments as much for providing safe legal migration routes or turning a blind eye to circumventing borders as for increased border controls. Smugglers would be simply unable to claim such large sums if there were other viable options. The smugglers could be put out of business quickly by making migration easier and/or less urgent. In the meantime, they may provide the only means for many individuals to escape persecution, violence and extreme poverty.

A trafficker not only facilitates an individual's movement, but also puts him or her into a situation of servitude. Traffickers may physically keep a person prisoner, requiring him or her to perform work or services. They may also remove travel documents or other means to escape or access rights. Trafficking networks also manage camps like the notorious one mentioned by Wari in Chapter 10, the stories from which describe unimaginably inhumane treatment of individual migrants. Trafficking is very different from smuggling, as it plays upon the vulnerability and weakness of individuals in order to exploit them further. While the line may sometimes be difficult to draw between trafficking and smuggling, it is clear that there is a big difference between: overcharging someone and not taking enough care of safety in transit; and intentionally depriving a person of his or her liberty, forcing him or her into prostitution, unpaid or underpaid work, and removing his or her identity.

However, the conditions that make smuggling viable also make trafficking viable. This is for two reasons. First, while a person may think that he or she is paying a smuggler, he or she may instead be putting him or herself into the hands of traffickers. Second, a person who is very desperate, desperate enough to sell everything he or she has in order to travel, may also be willing to indenture him or herself. Either way, while trafficking is appropriately considered a crime, it is not traffickers, nor smugglers, that create the conditions in which their businesses can thrive. As was presented in Talking Point 1 above, migrants are individual agents. They make decisions throughout their migration processes based on the options available and their assessment of risks. The fact that they are making the decisions to contract smugglers and traffickers can be seen as a further indicator that the conditions in which they are making decisions are problematic.

It is also important to acknowledge, with Bloom in Chapter 5, the wider involvement of private entities in Mediterranean migration. While smugglers and traffickers can make fortunes facilitating people to circumvent migration controls, other private sector entities are involved in the lucrative business of creating, enforcing and developing migration controls. Indeed, such entities have interests in supporting the rhetoric of security discussed by Marcelino, Ferreira and Lippmann Mazzaglia in Chapter 2 and above and in encouraging the increasing sense of fear and threat in order to ensure that states continue to use their services. As has been written elsewhere (see Thomas Gammeltoft-Hansen and Ninna Nyberg Sorensen's edited book on this subject), the migration facilitation and control industries are mutually beneficial. As migration controls become increasingly sophisticated, individuals will increasingly need the help of experts in order to move. However, as migration facilitation techniques become more advanced, states increasingly require the services of outside private sector experts in order to prevent movement. As well as being a lucrative private sector industry, this cycle lowers both State and migrant autonomy in migration decision-making.

To conclude: States and migrants are not the only ones involved in migration decision-making. Indeed, this book's authors draw attention to those that propagate the rhetoric of fear, threat, and the need for security. They also observe the increased movement of migration powers away from migrants and States, in both facilitation and control, potentially removing decision-making away from both States and migrants.

Talking Point 3: Changing Conditions in the Mediterranean

This book finds that today's changing conditions in the Mediterranean do have some impact upon decision-making, though this may be overshadowed by other factors and be experienced indirectly. It is also highlighted (e.g. by Marcelino, Ferreira and Lippmann Mazzaglia in Chapter 2 and Snorek in Chapter 3) that longer-range changes and histories in the region need to be acknowledged, including, for example, historical connections across the Mediterranean Region developed through colonial networks and trade. Recent years have seen conditions in the Mediterranean change through a number of different dimensions, and contributions to this volume look in particular detail at changing economic, environmental and security conditions. Importantly, they also emphasise that none of these factors can be understood as being experienced in isolation, so that no one of these factors can successfully be used to characterise a person's decision-making process.

In Chapter 6, Wissink and Ulusoy provide a particularly useful analysis in this regard. They present how, while trends and changing circumstances may shape the migration context in various ways, they do not *determine* how migrants navigate them. Drawing back to Talking Point 1, that is, migrants act *as* agents, but dealing with constraints. As such, several chapters in this volume demonstrate that the key question when looking at possible impacts of changing conditions in the Mediterranean Region upon how people decide about migration is not 'why' or 'whether' people move from one place to another, but about what mechanisms and under what strategies they decide and re-decide upon routes. Indeed, as is shown by Gebrewold in Chapter 1, migrants cannot be seen as following one strategy alone, or exemplifying one or another theory in their mode of migration. Instead, persons make migration decisions based upon overlapping and conflicting sets of interests and drivers. Indeed, he shows that, even in cases of emergency migration, driven by war or persecution or other immediate threats, external circumstances may help to shape how individuals decide upon the best route to take and whether to move onwards or to stay put.

The Mediterranean Region has seen a period of much change in terms of economic conditions on all sides of the sea. This is presented in more detail in the Introduction to this volume. However, some chapters show that these changes have to be understood in terms of even more complex changing dynamics on a sub-regional level. For example, if we look at the analysis of Turkey and Greece developed by Wissink and Ulusoy in Chapter 6, it is clear that a climate of change in the Aegean region has driven a dynamic context of migration in which individuals may make decisions based upon a range of factors, such as business opportunities and networks, relative economic conditions, social networks, and their experience of xenophobia and receptiveness. These may also be affected by and affect individuals' considerations regarding onward movement or return. As well as the important analysis of the Aegean, Wissink and Ulusoy demonstrate the complexity of the migration dynamics examined in this book more generally, which, if we are trying to understand individual decision-making, will not be well understood within a single theory and can be best reflected as a process.

In Chapter 1, Gebrewold focusses on the security aspects of individual migration decision-making, both in countries in the Sub-Saharan Region and in the Mediterranean. While, as discussed above, physical threat to personal security has been a decisive factor for many in initiating a migration process, compromised personal security for those from Sub-Saharan Africa once in the Mediterranean Region has led people to alter migration plans. As discussed in the Introduction to this volume, Northern African countries were destinations for many Sub-Saharans until the political situations started to change around 2011. Changing contexts in North Africa have led to the interplay of factors such as racism, physical threats, lack of economic prospects and the unwillingness to become involved in civil war. These factors have ultimately led many to decide to migrate out of the Southern Mediterranean countries. A key route for these individuals has been northwards across the sea or westwards around the coastal zone.

While the changing security and economic conditions have been discussed above and are commonly addressed, environmental factors are also important to consider. Snorek's discussion of movement within and out of Niger in Chapter 3 is particularly indicative of the complex interaction of factors. It presents a situation in which climate change has meant that the land of the Sahel is less and less productive. However, individual pastoralists have also become less and less resilient to climatic change. This change in resilience, Snorek argues, derives from a history of increased rural to urban migration and migration overseas. However, the lessened productivity of the land is also a driving factor in migration decisions, so that migration from the rural areas becomes increasingly urgent and, as there is insufficient work in the urban areas of Niger, migration out of Niger becomes necessary for some individuals. There are two important lessons that can be taken from this in terms of the project in this book as a whole.

First, there is discussion in a number of chapters about the devaluing of rural labour and rural knowledge (e.g. Snorek in Chapter 3, Wari in Chapter 10). Where policies, both of local governments and within trade networks, mean that it is difficult for agricultural work to be sufficiently financially rewarding, there is heightened incentive to leave rural areas, and so to embark upon migration processes. This is problematic in a number of ways. The migration is not really a choice, individuals who leave the land for urban or overseas contexts in which they are not able to make a better living than they could in the rural areas are being short-changed by a lack of available information about current realities. Crucially, it also drives a further devaluing of rural labour and resources and lack of development in rural areas, driving further movement away from those areas, hampering the ability for a country to support its own food production. It is also worth mentioning that those that move internally, to urban areas, may experience the difficult conditions of swelling slums in big cities and lack of work opportunities. Chapters in this book mention that if this is to change, it will need input from a variety of actors, including governments in the Sub-Saharan Region providing support for rural development, and from Northern governments, ensuring fair trade arrangements for agricultural produce.

Second, Snorek notes in Chapter 3 that those who have not moved increasingly rely upon remittances which are themselves dependent on stability in the Mediterranean Region. This brings together two themes already discussed in this Concluding section. On the one hand, it reinforces the notion of migration as a household project (where individuals are seen as members of households). On the other hand, migration is seen as a process, such that the migration project is an ongoing and evolving one. It may involve individual decisions about migration onwards, staying or returning; but it also might involve decisions about migration for other individuals tied into the process.

To conclude: Changing conditions in the Mediterranean Region can sometimes affect migration decision-making of those travelling from Sub-Saharan Africa. For the most part, contributors to this volume do not find that such changing conditions directly alter the initial decision to engage in the migration process, but they do find that changing conditions change the *way in which* people migrate. Conditions in Sub-Saharan Africa, however, are more important for initial migration decision-making and improved trade opportunities and development, including rural development, it was argued, would be important in avoiding a situation in which people feel that they have no choice other than to migrate.

Talking Point 4: Uncomfortable Truths

In considering migration and policy in the Mediterranean Region, particularly in recent years, all contributors in this book reflected upon some uncomfortable truths – some truths which it is hoped that the construction of migrants as interlocutors and individual decision-makers can combat in some small way. In Chapter 2, Marcelino, Ferreira and Lippmann Mazzaglia draw attention to an underlying racism in response to Mediterranean migration and several chapters discuss openly xenophobic movements in the countries all sides of the Mediterranean, and to the North of the region. However, this xenophobia is not only presented as extending to the way in which people are or are not integrated into host societies; it is part of the construction of the illegality of the movement of certain human bodies and their constructed dehumanisation. Marcelino, Ferreira and Lippmann Mazzaglia argue that this is made possible by a structural unbelonging of some persons moving from Sub-Saharan Africa, not only from specific states, but from systems of human rights protection. That is, this is not only an unbelonging to one or another state of the Mediterranean or its intersecting regions. It is an unbelonging to the community of individuals that, it is presumed, ought to be protected by existing structures, focused on the Mediterranean. Certain types of people are constructed to be primarily a security threat, even if those people are actually themselves fleeing the same threats that are of concern to the states involved (e.g. see Gebrewold in Chapter 1). Individual claims to humanitarian protection are dependent on persons' membership of certain state citizenries which exclude them; or on arrival to the territory of certain states that make entry as difficult as possible, including entry into internal state systems, and construct justification based on the language of citizenship.

What comes across in chapters throughout this book is that unfair access to the world's resources makes migration, for some, less of a desirable option and more of a necessity, and it is precisely those persons that are located in countries without existing access to the power and development structures that are prevented from access to them through safe migration routes. As is presented in the introductory section to this book, the countries of Sub-Saharan Africa overwhelmingly include those most struggling with poverty and economic under-development. Almost all countries in the region have also experienced colonisation from those countries to the North and have thereby contributed significant wealth northwards. As Wari argues in Chapter 10, the northward movement across the Mediterranean is carefully constructed and controlled, not so much to avoid movement of people and goods, but to select among people and goods. That is, while the Mediterranean migration landscape can sometimes seem to be one of control and exclusion, this ignores both the broad freedoms for those with favoured passports or skills that are in demand and the movement of goods and services.

Another truth that is often lost in these discussions, and which is evident from the figures presented in this book's Introduction, is that most people in the world do not move – and that includes those in Sub-Saharan Africa. Moreover, in Sub-Saharan Africa as everywhere else, much movement is within states, and transnational migrants overridingly tend to move into adjoining states, staying within their global region. As such, the huge infrastructures built around controlling Mediterranean migration can seem farcical. The huge death toll of migrants in the Mediterranean in the period under discussion is not huge because the numbers moving across that sea are huge. The death toll is high because the *rate of death* is high – because, even before the increasing migration movements of 2014 and 2015, in the world's most surveilled stretch of water, more of those embarking on crossing the sea were perishing than anywhere else in the world (UNHCR and IOM regularly release figures on this, but one useful volume is IOM's book, *Fatal Journeys*, edited by Tara Brian and Frank Laczko).

To conclude: It is necessary to acknowledge uncomfortable truths about the migration policies in the Mediterranean. The apparent implicit racist undertone to Mediterranean migrant policy and the fact that little of the world's migration actually happens through the Mediterranean, make it even more urgent to examine carefully the rationale behind policies that allow/enable the particularly high incidence of death and trauma of migrants in the Mediterranean Region.

Final Thoughts and Recommendations

This book is not putting forward a new theoretical approach. Instead, it is demanding that policy debate in the area of Sub-Saharan-Mediterranean migration takes into account migrants as individuals, moving for a wide range of reasons. Many move for work, for personal reasons, to see the world, and to do business. These are the same reasons that people move the world over. And much of this movement is via visas, visa waivers, and study exchanges, for example. People also move for other reasons. These may include extreme economic need, or dissatisfaction, and experiences of war, persecution and other forms of violence and instability. That is, factors that compromise an individual's or that person's household's security. For individuals in the first category, the lack of available visa options may be frustrating. However, for the people in the second category, the lack of available legal options, safe routes for travel and the increasing securitisation of the Mediterranean threaten basic personal security.

The absence of safe and legal migration routes is not only problematic for humanitarian and policy-effectiveness reasons. When individuals lack the possibility of safe and productive labour, their human capabilities and resources become wasted. Those willing to leave their homes and able to navigate very difficult conditions are likely to be those with the creativity, drive and stamina most useful for development. This is counter to the interests of individuals, receiving and sending states, and regional development.

This book draws only tentative conclusions, intended to be a stepping off point for debate and for further work. We now offer some specific thoughts to certain categories of readers.

To Governments:

This book councils inter-regional cooperation and collaboration to protect both the rights of migrants and the interests of states. While it recognises that theories describing trends and correlations in migration patterns may be useful once policy goals have been determined, and in predicting where there will be needs in the future, it argues that such theories cannot claim to be saying anything about the decision-making processes of individuals. As such, it argues that policy discussions need to be rooted in an understanding of how and why individuals make migration decisions. It recommends a self-examination of the reasons for policies as they currently are. It advocates the development of new legal migration routes for those seeking to contribute in interesting job opportunities, to those looking to develop new skills, and those interested in cultural and intellectual exchange. It also advocates safe and protected routes for those seeking protection, this might include in-country determination procedures and facilitated relocation schemes, but must also involve a reduction to the securitisation of borders. This book also advocates a step back from the high-security and privatised migration control infrastructure that makes it extremely difficult and dangerous for those without other means to migrate. It strongly advises against policies that are based around the logic of a one-off cessation of movement. Instead, it promotes development – including rural development – in ways that make it easier for people to meet their basic needs and life-goals *in situ*. In this way, migration can become an option – and a genuine option - but not a necessity.

To International Organisations:

This book recognises that the international community has a key role, not only in supporting States to develop humanitarian approaches to migration governance, but also to ensure that international debate is grounded in a recognition of migrants as individual decision-makers within a complex context of injustice. It invites public criticism of policies that are conducive to severe human suffering and loss of life and recommends ensuring that humanitarian response initiatives are also based in an understanding of individual need, desire, and decision-making. Crucially, it calls for an examination of policy, including international policy, to ensure that it does not build upon or affirm underlying prejudices. Part of this could involve increased access for Sub-Saharans to positions of influence in this area.

To Migrants:

This book asks that you continue to seek the very best for you and for your family and community, and to pursue your rights and entitlements when they are denied. Be aware that there is a huge amount of inaccuracy and mis-reporting about migration routes and destinations, both in the media and by word of mouth and that we all play a role in this. More than anything, though, know that you are not in the wrong for migrating. All of us involved in producing this book have ourselves also migrated at some time, whether regularly or otherwise and for different lengths of time. Many of the world's heads of industry, intellectuals, international policy-makers, themselves migrate, whether temporarily or permanently. All of us, along with our friends and families that have stayed behind, are part of the globalised world that is so often celebrated as emblematic of modernity.

To all Readers:

This book encourages critical thought about the rationale behind policies that currently lead to much brutality and death, predominantly affecting those already on the wrong side of global inequalities of power, economic development and decision-making.

Index

Abalak, Niger 67, 69
Aboubacrine, Saoudata 75
absorption, process of 19
ACCEPT PLURALISM project 188
accommodation, of migrants 166, 186
acculturation 19
ACRS (l'Associació Catalana de Residents Senegalesos) 177
Active Endeavour, NATO 100
activism 200–2
adaptation: migration as 83–4, 86–92; self-sufficiency through 72–4
Adepoju, Aderanti 114
Adi Harush refugee camp 28
Aegean, African migration in the 122–3
African migrants, drownings of 30, 31, 37, 38, 51, 84, 110
African migration: in the Aegean 122–3; to Spain/Barcelona 178–81
Agamben, Giorgio 48–9, 51
agency, of migrants 96, 219, 224
age, of migrants 22
Ahmadou Bamba Mbacké 185
Al Qaeda of the Islamic Maghreb (AQIM) 61
Al-Shabaab 27, 30, 31
AMCI (Agence Marocaine de Coopération Internationale) 141
AMISOM (African Union Mission in Somalia) 26, 27
Amnesty International 162
Anderson, Bridget 151
Annual Risk Analysis 40–1
anticipatory knowledge 39
anti-immigration rhetoric 188

anti-migration discourse 47
AoM approach 82
Arab Spring: and asylum seekers 80; and migration 3, 31, 81, 92, 95; Morocco 147–8, 153
Area of Freedom, Security and Justice (AFSJ) 128
Arens, M. 41
arms embargo, Libya 111
arraigo social, Spain 186–7
Articles on the Responsibility of States for Internationally Wrongful Acts 2001 114
Aspida operation 132
Assemblea Solidària Contra els Desallotjaments (Assembly of Solidarity Against Evictions) 184, 185–6
assimilation 19, 44
Associació de Veïns i Veïnes del Poblenou 183
Association for Solidarity with Refugees (Multeci-Der) 121
assumptions, about refugees/asylum seekers 50
asylum applications, and GDP 22
asylum law, Turkey 131
asylum seekers: and Arab Spring 80; Eritrean/Somalian 21, 28, 31–2; and European Union 21; and migrants 25; motivations of 6
@22 plan, Barcelona 188–9
Augusta Westland 112
austerity measures, Greece 126
autonomy, of migrants 82–3, 87, 90, 92–3, 94, 96

Balkan states, leaving Greece through 125–6, 134
Bangladeshi immigrants, in the UK 21
Barcelona, African migration to 180–1
Barcelona Process 111
Barclay, Sophie 222
bare life, mainstreaming of 45–9, 51
barriers, to migration 114, 116
Bayefall 184–5
Bedouin kidnappers 29
benefit maximisation 22
Berlin Conference 1884–1885 61
Berlusconi, Silvio 41–2
Besher, J.M. 22
Beyene, Winnie 29
bilateral agreements/cooperation, migration management 112
Blair, Tony 20
boat tragedy October 2013 84 *see also* drownings; sea crossings
border controls: EU 84; external 111, 128; extraterritorialization of 111; and smuggling/trafficking 115; Turkey/Greece 133
Border Policies and Sovereignty. Human rights and the right to life of irregular migrants, research project 121
Bosnia and Herzegovina, Immigration and Asylum Law 2008 103, 113
Bossi, Humberto 44
Bubbico, Filippo 31
Butler, Judith 51

Calavita, Kitty 189
call centre work 4, 139, 142–6, 149–52
Canada, as new migration destination 124
capitalism, and migration 23
Carrera at al. 95
carrier companies, private 109
carrier sanctions 109–10, 114, 116
categories of migrants 10–11
Catholic Church 41–2
causality, migration 83, 94–5, 96
CEHDA (Cultural Environmental and Human Development Association) 194, 201–12; farm projects 206–8, 213–15

CETIs (Centros de Estancia Temporal de Inmigrantes), Spain 107
Ceuta, Spain 3
chatarra trade, Barcelona 175–6, 181–5, 187, 189–90, 213, 216
China, as new migration destination 124
Chouchan camp, Tunisia 3
civil society sanction 103
civil war, Libya 38, 61, 80, 88–9
climate change: Ethiopia 159; and migration decisions 63–4, 74, 226; Niger 75; and pastoralism 71, 75
climate hazards 60
coercion, from traffickers 115
cognitive assimilation 19
Cohen, Robin 52
colonial relations 21
Colonial West Africa 61
colonisation: Mali/Niger 61–3; and migration 179; and pastoralism 74
community engagement, CEHDA farm project 206–8
complexity 83, 94
Confederación Nacional del Trabajo (CNT) 181
conflict system, in Horn of Africa 18, 26–8, 32
consumer goods, taste for 24
Convention Concerning the Exchange of Greek and Turkish Populations 1923 129
Cornelius, Wayne A 179
corporate social responsibility 113
cost-benefit-analysis, and migration decisions 23
costs, migration 23, 165
counter-terrorism, as justification for violence 27
Crépeau, François 110
criminality, and migration 128
cultural heteronomy 25
culture, and tourism 24
culture of migration 24
cumulative causation theory 24

danger, in Mediterranean Region 99 *see also* risks
deaths, of migrants 99, 229 *see also* drownings

decision theory of migration 22
dehumanising of migrants 38, 45–9, 51, 228
delegation: of detention facilities 107; of migration management 101–2, 111–12, 116; to third states 116
Delgado, Manuel 188
de Lucas, J. 45, 46
Delville, Lavinge 65
demand, for migrant labour 24, 158, 160–1, 170
Denmark, Somalian migrants 21
deprivation 24
De Regt, Marina 162
de-socialisation 19
detention centres 20, 39, 47, 50, 107
detention, of migrants 107, 108
deterrence factors 20
deterrence policies 221
development policies 74, 230
Dillafata, Niger 67, 72
direct/indirect privatisation 100
Dirkou, Niger 59
discourses: anti-migration 47; political/media 49–51, 52
discrimination: ethnic in Ethiopia 160; gender 157–8; institutionalized in Middle East 162; and migrant decisions 166; migrants in the Middle East 161; racial and migration decisions 89; against Sub-Saharan African migrants 189
displacements: due to natural hazards 60; of migrants 92
distance, and migration 24
Djibouti, conflict system in 27
documents, obtaining 200–1, 211
domestic workers 158, 160, 161, 162, 163
Domingo, Andreu 189
Doxianis, Aristos 126–7
driving factors, to migration 18 *see also* push and pull factors
droughts: adaptation to 61; Ethiopia 159; and migration decisions 59–60; in the Sahel 63, 65, 69, 74
drownings, of African migrants 30, 31, 37, 38, 51, 84, 110
dual labour markets theory 22–3

Dubai, as new migration destination 124
Dublin Regulation 132

Eastern Africa 12
Eastern Mediterranean 11, 133–4
ecological change, and social decision-making 65–6
ecological narrative 43–5
ecological resilience 76
ecological tipping points 60
economic approaches, to migration theories 22–3
economic crisis: global 95; Greece 3, 126–7; Italy 91–2; Spain 180, 182, 187, 189
economic development, reverse in the Aegean 126–7
economic downturn 2, 3
economic factors, and migration decisions 6, 21
economic growth, Turkey 126–7, 133
economic migrants 6, 25, 68, 69
economics, labour 22–3
economic theories of migration 5, 23, 32
economy, Morocco 142–3
education, African 205, 212
educational levels: Ethiopia 159–60; and migration 24; of women in Ethiopia 166
educational opportunities, Morocco 140–1, 147
Egypt, and refugees 29
Eisenstadt, Samuel N. 18–19
emergent causality 83
employment: call centre workers 4, 142–5, 149–52, 153; chatarra trade 175–6, 181–5, 187, 189–90, 213, 216; conditions in the Middle East 161–4; demand for migrant labour 158, 160–1, 170; and gender 164–5; immigrants jobs 24; labour conditions of migrants in Greece 126; labour market dualism 22–3; Libya 196; of migrants 4, 61, 87–8, 91; Turkey 127; waste-pickers 177–8
enduring human insecurity 60
enforcement measures 40, 41

entrepreneurs *see also* chatarra trade, Barcelona: human trafficking 33; immigration black market 23; migrant 120, 123–4, 133
environmental change: in the Sahel 65, 74
environmental displacees 64, 68, 69
environmental migrants 60, 64, 68, 69, 82–3 *see also* climate change; droughts
Eritrea: conflict system in 26, 27; migrants/refugees from 21, 28, 30, 31–2, 156, 159–60; military conscription 30; political repression 17, 18
Eritrean independence war 21, 26
Eritrean Islamic Jihad (EIJ) 27
Esser, Hartmut 19
Ethiopia: conflict system in 26, 27; drought 159; educational levels 159–60, 166; Eritrean refugees 28; and migration to the Middle East 171; patriarchy 165; refugees from 30; returnees to 167–71
Ethiopian Administration for Refugee and Returnee Affairs (ARRA) 28
Eubam Libya project 101, 112
Eulen Seguridad S.A. 107–8
Europe: perceptions of migrants about 202–12; political divide in 38; as transit zone 120
European Council Directive 2004/82/EC 109
European Court of Human Rights 132
European Internal Security Strategy 2010 106
Europeanisation 41
European Neighbourhood Policy (ENP) 95, 111
European Organization for Security (EOS), High-level Security Roundtables 106, 107
European public policies 39, 41, 43, 122
European Research and Innovation Forum (ESRIF) 106
European Security Research Advisory Board (ESRAB) 106
European Union (EU): and asylum seekers 21; free movement policies 219; free travel system 42; migration policies 130, 222; migration system 94–6; and political/refugee crisis 40; refugee policies 95; securitisation of migration 128–9; system of border control 84, 111
European Union (EU) Border Assistance Mission *see* Eubam Libya
European Union (EU) border management agency, Frontex *see* Frontex
European Union (EU)-Libyan cooperation 111
EUROSUR 128, 130
Eurozone: and Greece 3; Mediterranean migration 3
exception: relationship of 48–9; state of 38, 51, 52
exit visa requirements, Middle East 162
explicit privatisation 100, 105–8
extraterritorialization, of EU border control 111

families, as decision makers 157, 227 *see also* households
Farage, Nigel 44
Farmakonisi incident 131
farming, in Catalonia/Ghana 215–16
Fatal Journeys 3
fear, freedom from 25
fear-mongering, as a discursive practice 44
Feller, Erika 109
Ferreira, Maria 221–2
financing, of migration 165 *see also* costs
Fincas Riana S.L. 185
Fiss, Owen 53
foreign policy, Morocco 141
Forum Tunisien pour les Droits Economiques et Sociaux 4
Foucault, Michael 46–7
France: call centres in Morocco 142–6; French Front Nationale 44, 47; migration to 179; and securitarian narrative 42–3
Francis, Pope 48
Fransen, Sonja and Kuschminder, Katie 163
Frattini, Franco 42

freedom, from fear/want 25
Frelick, Bill 40
French Front Nationale 44, 47
friendship pact, Italy/Libya 111–12
Frontex 40–1, 42, 100, 101, 106, 108, 128, 130, 132, 178
Fulani pastoralists 68–9

GardaWorld 101
GDP, and asylum applications 22
Gebrewold, Belachew 220, 225, 226
gender: discrimination 157–8; and employment opportunities 164–5; and labour demand 170; in migration 157–9, 160; and migration experience 168–9, 172; and networks 157; and policies 158; and returnee experience 167
Geneva Convention on the international protection of refugees 1951 131
Germany, migrants in 84–5, 93
Al-Ghaddafi, Muammar 20, 63, 74, 89, 95, 111
Global Detention Project 107
global displacement patterns, new trends in 60
global economic crisis 95 *see also* economic crisis
globalisation 60
Golden Dawn 126–7
governance, privatised migration 115–16
grants, for the ENP 111
Greece: economic crisis 3, 126–7; fence on its border with Turkey 41; irregular migration 132; laws on immigration 103, 129, 131, 132; leaving through the Balkans 125–6, 134; migration to 122; political unrest 3; privatised management of migration 106; racism in 120, 125, 126–7; returnees to Turkey 125, 134; securitisation of migration 129–33; xenophobia 121, 133–4
Gueant, Claude 43
Guiding Principles on Business and Human Rights (2011) 113
Gulf States, influx of migrants and refugees to 30

gunboat surveillance 41, 46, 48
Guterres, António 60

Haradh 30
hard and soft factors 6, 19
HERA operation 100
HERMES operation 106
historical ties and networks 20–1
homeless shelters 85
Homo Sacer 48
Horn of Africa 17, 18, 26–8, 28–32
households, and migration decisions 5, 32, 227 *see also* families
Human Development Report 2013 65
human dignity, devaluation of 51
humanist narrative 48
humanitarian/compassion perspective 46
humanitarian crises 48, 129
humanitarian organizations, voluntary 23
humanitarian passage 109
human rights: of migrants 168, 184, 212; and national security 129–30; state responsibility for 113; violations 47
Human Rights Watch (HRW) 40, 127, 163
human security, of the Mediterranean Region 60
human trafficking *see* trafficking
hunger strike 200–1
Huntoon, Laura 189

İçduygu, Ahmet 130
identificative assimilation 19
identity-building 93
Ifekwunigwe, Jayne O 190
illegal immigrants *see* irregular immigrants
immigrants jobs *see* employment
Immigration Act 1970, Malta 101–2
Immigration and Asylum Law 2008, Bosnia and Herzegovina 103, 113
immigration black market, entrepreneurs 23
immigration law, semi-compliance 151
imperceptible politics 82
implicit privatisation 100, 109–10

income maximisation, and migration 6
inequalities, and neoliberalism 189
informal labour market, Turkey 127
information: and the media 22, 24–5; for migrants 202
insecurity, enduring human 60
institutional issues, Niger 75–6
institutionalized discrimination, Middle East 162
institutional theory of migration 23
instrumental perspective 46
Integrated Border Management (IBM) 131
integration 19
International Code of Conduct for Private Security Providers (ICOC-PSP) 113
International Convention on the Protection of the Rights of All Migrant Workers and Members of their Families 113
International Labor Organization 162
International Organization for Migration (IOM) 3, 51, 122
international relations, complexity of 94
irregular migration: from Africa to Europe 177–8; difficulties facing migrants 109, 182; Greece 132; to Israel 28–9; sanctions on 101, 103; and Saudi Arabia 171; term 11; through external sea borders 108; Turkey 131
IS Academy: Migration and Development Survey 156, 161, 164, 172
Islamic fundamentalism 32
Islamic radicalism, Somalia 26, 27, 30
Islamisation, Morocco 140
isolation, of migrants 166
Israel: irregular African migrants in 28–9; and refugees 31
Italy: economic crisis 91–2; influx of migrants and refugees to 31–2, 91, 95; Lampedusa 48, 50, 84, 91, 106; and securitarian narrative 41–2; Somalian/Eritrean immigrants 21; as a transit country 21

JEMED (Jeunesse en Mission Entraide et Developpement) 67n.3

Kayiki network 121–2
Kel Tamashek (Tuareg) groups 61 *see also* Tuareg people
Kenya, conflict system in 27
Khafala System 161–2, 166
kidnappings, of refugees 29
Knightley, Phillip 50
knowledge: anticipatory 39; devaluing of rural 227; and power 47; and racism 52
Krätli, Saverio 75
Krippendorf, J. 24
Kritzman-Amir, Tally 109
Kubal, Agnieszka 151
Kurds, fleeing Iraq 129

labour conditions, migrants in Greece 126
labour demand, and gender 170
labour economics 22–3
labour market dualism 23
labour migration 142
labour movement, Spain 181
Lahav, Gallya 101, 105
Laitinen, Ilkka 40, 100–1
Lampedusa 48, 50, 84, 91, 106
Lampedusa in Hamburg group 85–6, 87, 93
Langley, Sarah 221
Laudati, Ann 222
laws on immigration, Greece/Turkey 103, 129, 131
Lazarescu, Daria 126
Lee, E.S. 6, 19
legal status, of migrants 92, 95
Lega Nord (Northern League) 44–5
legislative framework, Greece 132
Lemberg-Pedersen, Martin 111
Léonard, Sarah 128
Le Pen, Jean Marie 47
Le Pen, Marine 44, 47
LIATEC (Libyan Italian Advanced Technology Company) 112
liberalness factor 20
Libya: arms embargo 111; civil war 38, 61, 80, 88–9; detention centres 107;

employment 196; migration from 61, 80, 88–90; migration to 63, 87, 196; and refugees 31; role in curtailing Sub-Saharan migration 111–12; and Sub-Saharan migrants 3, 60; as Trans-Saharan migrant route 37–8; Tuareg migrants 74; uprising 49–50
lifestyles 24
Loftsdottir, Kristín 69
London bombings 128
Long, Katy 129

Macedonia 126
Maghreb, Sub-Saharan African migration to 141–2
Mai-Aini refugee camp 28
Mali: colonisation 61–3; migrants from 94; pastoralists 63
Malmström, Cecilia 106, 112
Malta: Eritrean/Somalian asylum seekers 21; Immigration Act 1970 101–2; Safi Barracks detention centre 50
management, privatised of migration 99–104, 105–10, 116
Marcelino et al. 128, 228
Marcelino, Pedro 221–2
marginalisation: of immigrants 190; of pastoralists 73–4
maritime borders: Mediterranean 37; surveillance at 128, 130
maritime carrier sanctions 109
Maritime Situational Awareness 100
Maroni, Roberto 42
Matsaganis, Manos 126–7
Mazzagali, Natalia 221–2
McNevin, Anne 82
media: and migration decisions 22, 24–5, 222; responsibility of 230
media discourse, and political discourse/public opinion 49–51, 52
Mediterranean Region: *see also* individual countries; 11–12; changing conditions in 28–32, 225–7; as dangerous for migrants 99; human security of the 60; migration to 30–2, 75, 220; origins of migrants in 12–14; of the securitisation 229; security company activity in 108; societal trends in Eastern Mediterranean 133–4; xenophobia 228
Mediterranean Sea *see also* drownings; sea crossings: migrants crossing from Libya 60; shipping in 100
Melilla, Spain 3
mental health, and migration 167–8
mercenaries, Libya 89
Middle East: demand for migrant labour 160–1; Ethiopian migration to 171; working conditions in 161–4
migrants: and asylum seekers 25; categories of 10–11; difficulties facing 196, 202, 209–12, 223 *see also* risks; as individuals 220–2; mistreatment of 162–4; origins of 12–13; as political actors 84, 85; as political agents 82; as threat 39, 43–4, 51, 223, 228; typology of 68–9; who are they? 10–14
migrant workers *see* employment
migration: as adaptation 83–4, 86–92; as a business 116; decision theory of 22; defined 5, 18, 19; desire for 219; economic theories of 5, 23, 32; phases of 19; as a process 220–2; theories 18–26, 81–4; as transformation 84, 88, 94, 96
migration controls 106, 224–5
migration crisis 38, 39–45, 81
migration flows, as causers of chaos 48
migration industry, grey- and black-market 114
migration management: bilateral agreements/cooperation 112; delegated 101–2, 111–12, 116; explicit privatisation 100, 105–8; implicit privatisation 100, 109–10; privatisation methods 104; reactive 129–30
migration patterns, diversification of 123–6, 134
Migration Policy Institute 126, 178, 180
migration trends, contemporary/pre-colonial 60–3
militant groups, in the Sahel 61
military conscription, Eritrea 30
Ministry of Labour and Social Affairs (MOLSA), Ethiopia 160

mode of orientation 22
Morocco: Arab Spring 147–8, 153; call centre industry 4, 139, 142–6, 149–52; educational opportunities 140–1, 147; foreign policy 141; Islamisation 140; migrant motivations 143–4, 152; as new migration destination 124, 139; student migration 140–1, 152; Sub-Saharan African migration to 139–42; as transit zone 199
Morsi, Mohammed 29
Mouride Brotherhood 185
Movement for Unity and Jihad in West Africa (MUJAO) 61
Movement National pour la Liberation de l'Azawak (MNLA) 61
Mubarak, President 29
Muslim brotherhoods 140
myth of migration 164

narratives: ecological 43–5; right-wing political 48; securitarian 39–43, 48
nationalism, xenophobic 127
nationalist ideology 49
nationalities, of migrants 11–14
national security: and human rights 129–30; and migration 130 *see also* threat
nation-building, Greece/Turkey 129
NATO: Active Endeavour 100; intervention in Libya 94; no-fly zone 90
natural hazards, displacements due to 60
Nave, the 175, 180, 181–9, 190
Nazi execution camps 49
neoclassical macroeconomic theory of migration 23
neoliberalism, global 189
Netherlands, Somalian migrants 21
networks: and gender 157; historical 20–1; migrant 20–1, 146, 187, 190, 223; and migration 24; transnational criminal 38
Network Theory 157
New Economics of Labour Migration (NELM) 157
new economic theory of migration 5, 23, 32

'New Response to a Changing Neighbourhood, A' 95
Niamey, Niger 66–7, 70, 74
Nicholson, S. E. 65
Niger: Abalak 67, 69; colonisation 61–3; Dillafata 67, 72; Dirkou 59; map of modern-day 62; Niamey 66–7, 70, 74; pastoralists 63, 68; population growth rates 65, 71; poverty 65; research sites 66–7; returnees to 60–1; rural-urban migration 59, 69–70, 74–6, 226–7; the Sahel 59, 63, 65, 69, 74; Tahoua region 61, 65–8
9/11 128
no-fly zone, Libya 90
nomadic groups, sedentarization of 64
nomadic life, unsustainability of 69
non-citizens 45
non-migrants 64, 70, 75
non-refoulement principle 131
Northern Mediterranean 11
Norway, Eritrean/Somalian migrants 21
numbers, migrants in Mediterranean countries 30, 31

objectification, of migrants 81
offshoring sector, Morocco 143
OHCHR Special Rapporteur 110
Omar, Samia Yusuf 30
ONLF (Ogaden National Liberation Front) 26, 27
opportunities, for migrant workers 4
Organisation for Economic Co-operation and Development 178
organization, of migrants 93, 176, 181, 200–2
Others, migrants/refugees as 38, 43, 45, 47, 52

Pakistani immigrants, in the UK 21
Palestine, humanitarian crises 48
Parsons, Talcott 18
pastoralism: and climate change 71, 75; degradation of 74–5
pastoralists: marginalisation of 73–4; Niger/Mali 61, 63; rural-urban migration of 74, 76; sedentarization of 66; WoDaaBe 68–9, 70, 72
pastoral zone, Niger 59

patriarchy, Ethiopia 165
Paulo, I. M. 65
perceptions of migrants, about Europe 202–12
Plataforma per Catalunya 188
Poblenou, Spain 181, 188
policies: deterrence 221; development 74, 230; EU migration 130, 222; EU refugee 95; European public policies 39, 41, 43, 122; and gender 158; governing migration 1, 52; and migrants 10; need to examine existing 229–30; preventing travel 216–17; regional migration 3; restrictive migration 134; securitised migration 51, 114, 121, 128; social welfare in Spain 188; Turkey/Greece 130
policy-making, and security companies 105
political actors, migrants as 84, 85
political agents, migrants as 82
political discourse: European 38, 39–45; and media discourse/public opinion 49–51, 52; on migration 42; racist 188
political disorder and instability 81
political divide, in Europe 38
political mobilization, of migrants 187
political narratives, right-wing 48
political organization, of migrants 93 *see also* organization
political power, of migrants 94
political repression, Eritrea 17, 18
political subjectivity, *Lampedusa in Hamburg/Berlin* 93
political will, lack of 95
politics: far-right 126–7; imperceptible politics 82; race 47; right-wing 44, 48, 188
population exchange, between Turkey and Greece 129
population growth rates, Niger 65, 71
Poseidon operation 130
poverty 2, 22, 60, 64, 65
power: and knowledge 47; political of migrants 94
prediction, of migration 22
private carrier companies 109
Private Employment Agencies (PEAs) 160

private security lobby 106
private security sector 48
privatised management of migration 99–104, 105–10, 116
probability for migration 22
process of absorption 19
profit maximization, and migration decisions 22
protests, Middle East 2011 *see* Arab Spring
public opinion, and political/media discourse 49–51, 52
public policies 39, 41, 43, 122
purposive-rational orientation 22
push and pull factors 5–6, 19–20, 21, 25, 32, 63, 81
'pushback' agreements 112, 131

RABIT operation 130
race politics 47
racial discrimination, and migration decisions 89
racial hierarchy, domestic workers 162
racial violence 61
racism: defined 46; discursive practices of 45, 47; in Greece 120, 125, 126–7; and Mediterranean migration 228, 229; Middle East 162–3; and the Other 52; political discourse 188
radicalisation, of political discourse on migration 42
rapid border intervention teams (RABIT) 130
Rashaida 29
reactive solidarity 20
readmission protocols 131
reception centers 20
Red Cross 217
refugee camps 3, 28, 29, 91
Refugee Convention 1951 95, 101, 109
refugee crisis 40
refugee policies, EU 95
refugees: and Israel 31; kidnappings of 29; and Libya 31; and Sudan 29; torture of 29
refugee status 48, 92
regular status: acquisition of 182; Spain 189
regulation, and privatised management of migration 112–14

relational autonomy 92, 94, 96
relationship of exception 48–9
religious migration 140
removal centres, Turkey 107
repatriation operations 40
research, migration 5–6
residence permits, Turkey 132
residence permit systems, Middle East 162–3
resilience, social and ecological 76
resistance, of migrants 93
re-socialization 19
resource management, lack of 71–2
resources, solidarity as 20
returnees: to Ethiopia 167–71; to Niger 60–1; to Turkey 125, 134
rights, of migrants 230
  see also human rights
right-wing anti-immigrant views 51
right-wing politics 44, 48, 188
risks: management of 5; migrants as 39, 43, 44; of migration 41, 52–3, 71, 128, 164; minimisation of 6, 20, 22
Rothe, Delf 220–1
Roundtables, EOS 106–7
Ruhs, Martin 151
rural development policies 230
rural labour/knowledge, devaluing of 227
rural-urban migration: Niger 59, 69–70, 74–6, 226–7; of pastoralists 74, 76; push and pull factors 63

Sabater, Albert 189
Safi Barracks detention centre, Malta 50
Sahel: drought in the 63, 65, 69, 74; environmental change in 65, 74; militant groups in 61
Sahelo-Saharan zone 60
Salehi, Mariam 221
Salt, John 116
sanctions: on carriers 109–10, 114, 116; on irregular migration 101, 103
Sarkozy, Nicolas 42–3
Saudi Arabia, and irregular immigrants 171
Saunders, H W 18
scale of living 6, 18

scapegoat theory 46, 47
Scheel, Stephan 82
Schengen free movement system 42
Schengen visa 92
scrap metal trade, Barcelona 175–6, 181–5, 187, 189–90, 213, 216
sea crossings: danger of 202; education regarding 203; by migrants/refugees 31–2, 37, 38, 197–200; nationalities of migrants 108; in unsafe boats 110
securitarian narrative 39–43, 48
securitarian perspective 46
securitisation: of the Mediterranean Region 229; of migration 121, 128–33, 224–5; of migration policies 51, 114, 121, 128
security companies, explicit privatisation 105–8
security, decreased state 116
security issues, and migration 105–6
security, personal of migrants 229
sedentarization, of nomadic groups/pastoralists 64, 66, 68
Seeberg, Peter 80, 95
self-organization 181 *see also* organization
self-sufficiency, through adaptation 72–4
semi-compliance, immigration law 151
Senegal, and Morocco 140
Senegalese migrants, to Morocco 142, 145–6
Serramar Vigilancia y Seguridad S.L. 108
sexual violence, and domestic workers 163
Shagarab refugee camp 29
Shimelba refugee camp 28
short-run hedonistic orientation 22
Sinai Peninsula 29
slums, and rural-urban migration 63
smuggling 114–16, 223–4
Snorek, Julie 221, 226, 227
social assimilation 19
social decision-making, and ecological change 65–6
social isolation, of migrants 167
social resilience 76

242 Index

social responsibility, international corporate 113
social status, and migration 169
social tipping points 60
social welfare policies, Spain 188
societal trends, in the Eastern Mediterranean 133–4
Sokoto Caliphate 61
solidarity, reactive 20
Somalia: civil war 21, 26–7; destinations of migrants from 21; Islamic radicalism 26, 27, 30; migrants/refugees from 21, 27–8, 30, 31, 32; state collapse of 17, 18
Southern Africa 12
Southern Mediterranean 11
Spain: African migration in 178–81; arraigo social 186–7; CETIs (Centros de Estancia Temporal de Inmigrantes) 107; Ceuta and Melilla 3; economic crisis 180, 182, 187, 189; labour movement 181; Poblenou 181, 188; regular status 189; social welfare policies 188; unemployment 2, 180–1
Spijkerboer, Thomas 121
standard of living 6, 18
state of exception 38, 51, 52
stay permits 91, 92
stepwise migration 142
stereotypes: gender 172; of migrants 47; racial 162
structural assimilation 19
structural demand for immigrants 24
structural forces 86–92, 96
struggles, of migrants 183–4
student migration, Morocco 140–1, 152
sub-regions 11
Sub-Saharan African migrants: as 'Al Ghaddafi's mercenaries' 61; desperation of 60; detainees 108; discrimination against 189; and Libya 3, 60; to Morocco 139–42; numbers/origins of 12–15
Sub-Saharan Africa, region 11–12
Sudan 28, 29, 48
surveillance 41, 46, 48, 95, 128, 130
Suter, Brigitte 123
Sweden, Eritrean/Somalian migrants 21

Switzerland, Eritrean migrants 21
Syria: humanitarian crises 48; migrants/refugees from 31–2; unrest in 3

Tahoua region, Niger 61, 65–8
Tampa (ship) 110
Taylor, J.E. 20–1
technology: and migrant networks 20–1; and migration decisions 25
terrorism: fears of 3; and migration 128
theories, migration 18–26
Thielemann, E. 20, 21
third-state delegation, of migration management 111–12
threat, migrants as 39, 43–4, 51, 223, 228
Tijaniyya brotherhood 140
Tillia, Niger 67–8
tipping points, social and ecological 60
torture, of refugees 29
tourism, impact of 24
traditional orientation 22
trafficking 28, 29, 32, 33, 39, 114–16, 163, 197–8, 222–4
transformation, migration as 84, 88, 94, 96
transit countries 21, 30
transit processing centers 20
transit zones 120, 122–3, 199
transnational criminal networks 38
trapped populations 64
Treaty of Lausanne 129
Triandafyllidou, Anna 126
triggering events 81
Tsitselikis, Konstantinos 132
Tuareg people 61, 63, 68–9, 74
Tunisia, Chouchan camp 3
Turkey: economic growth 126–7, 133; employment in 127; laws on immigration 103, 129, 131; migration to 122–4; political unrest/economic downturn 3; removal centres 107; returnees to 134; securitisation of migration 129–33
Turkey-EU Twinning project on Integrated Border Management (IBM) 131

UAE, domestic workers in 161
UK Independence Party (UKIP) 44
Ulusoy, Orçun 121, 221, 225, 226
undocumented immigrants
    see irregular immigrants
UNDP, Human Development
    Report 2013 65
unemployment 2; Ethiopia 159; Greece
    126; migrant in Spain 180–1; rates
    and asylum applications 22
UNHCR 20, 28, 30, 109, 110,
    120, 125, 131–2
unified migration systems theory 24
UNIFIED PROTECTOR
    operation 90n.23
Union for the Mediterranean
    (UfM) 111
United Kingdom: London bombings
    128; Pakistani/Bangladeshi
    immigrants 21; UKIP 44
United Nations Global Compact 113
United Nations High Commissioner for
    Refugees 60
United Nations Migrant Workers
    Convention 92
United Nations Permanent Forum for
    Indigenous Peoples 75
United Nations University Institute on
    Globalization, Culture and Mobility
    (UNU-GCM) 14
Universal Declaration of Human Rights
    184
UNODC 110
urban growth, Niger 65
urbanisation, and rural-urban
    migration 65
urban planning, Barcelona 188–9

violence: avoidance of 10; counter-
    terrorism as justification for 27;
    Horn of Africa 26; racial 61; sexual of
    domestic workers 163; state 47, 127;
    xenophobic 133–4
Voluntary Return project 210
vulnerabilities: Tahoua region, Niger
    65–8; of trapped populations 64

want, freedom from 25
Wari, Iddrisu 221, 223, 228
waste-pickers 177–8
well-being, loss of 219
West African trade routes, pre-colonial 62
Western Africa 12
Wieviorka, M. 46, 52
Wissink, Marieke 121, 221, 225, 226
WoDaaBe pastoralists 68–9, 70, 72
women: Ethiopian 166, 170; migration
    decisions of 165; non-migrants 70;
    vulnerability of when men migrate 67
workforce, immigrant 22–3 *see also*
    employment
world systems theory 23

Xenios Zeus operation 132
xenophobia: in the Aegean 126–7;
    Greece 121, 133–4; Mediterranean
    Region 228; Middle East 163; and
    racism 46, 47

Yemen, as transit point 30
young people in Africa, education
    regarding migration 203–7

zabitha 124
Zapata-Barrero et al. 188

eBooks
from Taylor & Francis
Helping you to choose the right eBooks for your Library

Add to your library's digital collection today with Taylor & Francis eBooks. We have over 50,000 eBooks in the Humanities, Social Sciences, Behavioural Sciences, Built Environment and Law, from leading imprints, including Routledge, Focal Press and Psychology Press.

Choose from a range of subject packages or create your own!

Benefits for you
- Free MARC records
- COUNTER-compliant usage statistics
- Flexible purchase and pricing options
- All titles DRM-free.

Benefits for your user
- Off-site, anytime access via Athens or referring URL
- Print or copy pages or chapters
- Full content search
- Bookmark, highlight and annotate text
- Access to thousands of pages of quality research at the click of a button.

Free Trials Available
We offer free trials to qualifying academic, corporate and government customers.

eCollections
Choose from over 30 subject eCollections, including:

Archaeology	Language Learning
Architecture	Law
Asian Studies	Literature
Business & Management	Media & Communication
Classical Studies	Middle East Studies
Construction	Music
Creative & Media Arts	Philosophy
Criminology & Criminal Justice	Planning
Economics	Politics
Education	Psychology & Mental Health
Energy	Religion
Engineering	Security
English Language & Linguistics	Social Work
Environment & Sustainability	Sociology
Geography	Sport
Health Studies	Theatre & Performance
History	Tourism, Hospitality & Events

For more information, pricing enquiries or to order a free trial, please contact your local sales team:
www.tandfebooks.com/page/sales

www.tandfebooks.com